IT IS
WHAT IT IS

IT IS
WHAT IT IS

The Autobiography

DAVID COULTHARD

WITH MARTIN ROACH

First published in Great Britain in 2007 by
Orion Books
an imprint of the Orion Publishing Group Ltd
Orion House, 5 Upper St Martin's Lane,
London WC2H 9EA
An Hachette Livre UK Company

1 3 5 7 9 10 8 6 4 2

A CIP catalogue record for this book is
available from the British Library.

ISBN: 978 0 7528 7492 0 (hardback)
ISBN: 978 0 7528 9086 9 (export paperback)

Typeset by Input Data Services Ltd,
Frome

Printed in Great Britain at Mackays of Chatham plc,
Chatham, Kent

The Orion Publishing Group's policy is to use papers
that are natural, renewable and recyclable and made
from wood grown in sustainable forests. The logging and
manufacturing processes are expected to conform to the
environmental regulations of the country of origin.

Every effort has been made to fulfil requirements with regard to
reproducing copyright material. The author and publisher will be
glad to rectify any omissions at the earliest opportunity.

www.orionbooks.co.uk

CONTENTS

I have absolutely no doubt that my love of motorsport grew through being exposed to karting at an early age. That led to the start of my own karting career aged eleven – the journey through the various formulae was managed by the passion and the vision of my father, aided along the way by his ever supportive wife who, in turn, was my slightly nervous mother.

So, it is to my mother and father that I dedicate this book.

Your loving son,
David

Well, clearly there are a number of people whose efforts have helped my career and in making this book a reality. At the risk of leaving any individual out, I would prefer to say a global 'Thank You' to everyone who I have encountered though this amazing journey from karting in Scotland to racing Formula 1 in all corners of the world.

To my ghost writer, Martin Roach, I just wanted you to know that wearing the white sheet took it further than expected, what do you look like? I really enjoyed our various conversations over the last year and sincerely hope that choosing to work with me doesn't affect your 'bestseller' status.

My nearest and dearest continue to guide my wonderful life.

RUNNING OUT OF DARKNESS

Ask most boys what they want to be when they grow up, and they'll say 'a spaceman'. I tried that once and it was fun, but it wasn't really my cup of tea.

I went to Star City, near Moscow, in 1999 as a guest of the Russian space agency and underwent various astronautical tests including a weightless flight in a cargo plane that, quite frankly, looked like it might not even take off. It did take off and, along with my West McLaren-Mercedes MP4-12 Formula 1 car, I experienced weightlessness. I was also subjected to numerous G-force tests in a specially designed pod called a centrifuge and even saw the insides of a replica MIR Space Station. The capsule was so tiny and, worst of all, near to the solitary window in the corner was a little curtain that curled around a toilet. A space toilet. It would be a bugger to keep the place clean. Plus, you'll probably want a decent meal, like mince and tatties, but all you'll have is some freeze-dried space food. You'll be up there, looking down at earth, it feels dangerous and it *is* dangerous, you're lonely, vulnerable and floating around. So, no, I didn't want to be a spaceman when I was a kid.

Not for a career anyway.

I thought I'd try something much safer, like motor-racing.

The Coulthard family home is in the village of Twynholm, Dumfries and Galloway. This very small village, nestled in south-west Scotland, has a population of only about 750, so it's really more of a hamlet. In among the narrow roads and steep slopes are a school, shop, post office and two pubs. My father – Duncan Coulthard, also known as DC to some locals – was born into a family who owned a well-known local transport business, Hayton Coulthard, one of the oldest haulage firms in the country. The large garage and offices are at the bottom of the small hill in the middle of the village, so it is physically and literally at the heart of Twynholm. It might seem strange to situate a big firm like this in such a tiny village, but in fact the location was ideal – the company's own lifeblood is the A75, the main thoroughfare for trucks and haulage traffic to the port of Stranraer. The local ports were renowned for their scallop catches and, oddly, nearby Kirkcudbright is one of Europe's biggest producers of UHT milk, but most of the local economy is driven by farming. It is a pretty rural and parochial part of the country, a very long way from Formula 1.

Hayton Coulthard was set up by my great-grandfather in 1916 and so by the time my father was a child, the success of the business through several generations meant the family enjoyed a comfortable life by most standards. His father – my grandfather – was a racer himself. He ran at the Tulip Rally in an old Austin Sheerline, similar to a Rolls-Royce, and even competed in the Monte Carlo Rally. He was still obsessed with motor-sport when his own racing career had finished, and this remained a central part of Coulthard family life.

My father was right in the thick of all this. Grandfather was wealthy enough to own race horses and often hired small local aircraft to take the family to nearby motor-sport events. My father talks fondly of going to races in Turnberry, watching Stirling Moss and two-time world champion Alberto Ascari, Fangio's great rival. My father loved it and you can see when he talks about those days that being brought up with motor-racing still fires this passion in him.

Inevitably, perhaps, my father used to race from an early age and was very, very good, becoming the Scottish karting champion. He was a great kart driver and was even offered a test for a Lotus team. Sadly, that fledgling racing career came to a halt after my grandfather died, aged just forty-four. Unfortunately, a terrible accident from the past had caught up with him – his first-born son, my father's older brother, had been run over and killed by a truck passing through the village, aged just four.

The stories I have been told suggest my grandfather had never touched a drop of alcohol before that dreadful incident; within fourteen years he had died, unfortunately from cirrhosis of the liver. The ramifications for the family were obviously awful; the specific implications for my father's racing career were uncompromising – although he would continue karting for a few years, eventually, at the age of seventeen, he had to take a job driving the local parcel lorry.

The difficult circumstances did not subdue my father as a teenager; apparently he was a bit of a showman in his youth: he played in a band and to this day loves his guitars – he's got a beautiful collection, some signed by people such as Jim Corr.

Both he and his sister Morag were lucky enough to have a good mother. Grandmother Coulthard (known as 'Nana Coulthard') was a strong woman who liked her jewellery, a real character.

My dad suffered from a skin disorder as a child and spent a lot of time having this vile medical tar applied to his rough skin. He was in hospital quite a lot and, to make things more difficult for him, he was also dyslexic. I get the impression he was a bit of a loner at school. He got quite heavily into music and that became his outlet. He went to a boarding school but didn't like it – at that point his dyslexia wasn't diagnosed, so he told me one story where the headmaster would always say at the end of every term, 'All those who are going to get the belt, get in the queue behind Coulthard . . .' He wasn't academically bright and his writing was atrocious so, without a diagnosis, he was really struggling. Since he was academically trapped, if you like, he threw himself into other areas and even won a medal for the best all-round sportsman in school.

Being only a teenager, my father was obviously not in a position to run the family business, so a family friend took the reins, as I understand, until my dad was twenty-one, when my grandfather's will stipulated that his son should take over. He became an apprentice mechanic, then drove the trucks and eventually ran the business. When he took over, the firm was struggling rather badly, so he was faced with quite a challenge at such a relatively young age.

The story goes that one afternoon he opened the cupboard and there was one can of beans in there, so the first thing he did that day was to phone the distribution director of Heinz. He got the man in charge on the phone and said, 'I've heard you've been having a few problems with your distribution and I'd like to discuss that with you.' He secured a meeting, won the contract and subsequently had an account with Heinz for years and years.

My mother and father met at a local indoor bowling night and started dating shortly after. Mum's family was very different to my dad's. Her father was a train driver, her mother a nurse. My grandparents on that side still live in the same house, a pretty typical semi-detached ex-council house in Stranraer. My mother was very close to her family and we would go up there quite a lot when I was growing up. Although it was about an hour's drive away, we used to see my Granny Marshall more than Grandmother Coulthard, who literally only lived down the road from us. Granny Marshall is a tough woman – you certainly know when she's not very happy – but she had to be strong because she had eight kids (my mother undoubtedly gets her strength of character from Granny). Her husband, my mother's father, is larger than life, a big man who loves a wee sing and a social; he'll sing and romance you all night. The man of the house used to enjoy pigeon-fancying and still likes a whisky, doesn't like wearing his false teeth and says 'Puck' instead of 'fuck', because he doesn't actually like to swear. As a couple, they used to go to the railway club and have a dance and a wee whisky. Add to that all my aunts and uncles and you had a pretty hectic home! I have fond memories of childhood visits to Granny's house, all the good-natured shouting and screaming and the chaos of family life.

Within that large extended family, there are some real characters, too. I know some aunts and uncles better than others.

A couple have spent periods in jail. My Uncle Richard, a joiner by trade, would allegedly crash every car that was given to him, so he was always having to do joinery work, building something at my mum and dad's house to repay some damage he'd done somewhere else! Unfortunately, my mother's family had its share of tragedy, too. As an eleven-year-old, my aunty Anne accidentally dropped her baby sister Rose. Terribly, this left Rose mentally disabled with learning disabilities, which was an awful event for everyone. Growing up, I actually spent quite a bit of time with Rose – as a kid you don't understand the complications and issues of something like that. I just thought it was great that I had this big person to play together with; she was an adult who liked toys, literally a 'big kid'.

My grandparents always kept Rose at home, even when she got bigger – as an adult she is a big, strong woman and with all the things that go with being mentally handicapped meant it was quite difficult for them at times. Even so, they kept her at home as long as they could; now they are older and no longer physically able to look after her, she's in a home. Rose is in her forties now and, as a result of being around circumstances as unfortunate as that, I have done quite a lot of fundraisers for kids with similar difficulties. My first-hand experience really gave me an understanding of what the problems are.

I don't know if being the one who dropped Rose caused this, but my Aunty Anne ended up becoming really quite religious. I remember going there as a little boy and we'd have to observe the whole Grace at the table, which wasn't something we did at our house, so I knew things were different. It's funny how as a young child you don't see the complications within families. As I have grown up, and with certain situations in the media, I have become more aware of family situations – but we'll come to that.

So my mother and father are a slightly unlikely couple. On the one hand, you had this extremely conventional, working-class family on a council estate; on the other, you had my father's family, considered to be better off, business-oriented and financially very comfortable.

Apparently, my Grandmother Coulthard wasn't entirely happy when my parents started getting serious, because she felt slightly more well-to-do. It mattered not, because they were in love and got married quite young: my dad was only twenty-two, my mum just twenty. Even so, certain members of his family gave my mother quite a hard time; they basically thought she wasn't a good choice for a wife. Even when she was living in the same village, at times Nana Coulthard would only visit the house once a year, at Christmas, which seems a shame. I get the impression she never quite accepted my mother until much later on in life, when she finally saw that here was a fantastic mother for her grandchildren and a fabulous partner for her son.

My older brother, Duncan Junior, was the first child to be born, in 1968. I arrived on 27 March 1971, the same birthday as Henry Royce, one half of the Rolls-Royce name. My mother tells me that even my arrival into the world was fast. She and Dad were watching a late-night movie when my mother went into labour at almost exactly midnight. They hurtled off to Cresswell Maternity hospital where they put my mother on to a trolley, ready to be wheeled into the delivery room. Apparently, I was in too much of a rush to wait any longer, so I was actually born on the trolley itself, only forty-five minutes after they'd left the house – my very first experience of the world was on four wheels! You see, I always was a very fast starter ...

My family home was a bungalow that my grandfather actually built himself back in 1949, naming it Dunmhor after Duncan and Morag, my dad and his sister. Originally, when I was very young, there were only three bedrooms, but my father used one of those as a home office, so myself and my older brother Duncan had bunk beds, to fit us all in. My younger sister, Lyndsay, arrived six years after me, and she had her own room, of course. My very earliest recollections are hazy, like most people's. I recall a Jack And Jill swing with a light on it in our room, which we'd inherited from my father, a nice family heirloom so to speak.

The bungalow was on a hill, so as you approached Twynholm you turned left off the main road and there was our house. The A75 continued on its way and cut around behind the bungalow, so I always remember seeing the lights of cars and lorries hurtling by onwards to the ports for Ireland. The traffic noise and shadows of trees on my bedroom wall, looming large in the light of lorries' headlamps, is a very clear memory I have of that time. When I got to the age of eleven, my father built a swimming pool on the side of the house with the window that overlooked the main road, so I lost sight of the main road after that. It's been suggested to me that some of my earliest sounds and sights were, therefore, of fast-moving cars and that this might have had some impact on my future choice of career. Who knows if that might be true? It is what it is.

I was always a little bit scared of the dark. Winters in Scotland are pretty harsh and it was always dark at four o'clock. I recall vividly going to school in the dark and coming back home in the dark. Sometimes I'd go to badminton or the boys' clubs, but whenever I returned home it always seemed to be in the pitch black. The street lights at the time stopped over one hundred metres before our house and I would have this recurring dream about someone chasing me and actually 'getting me' in the doorway. Mother must have wondered why she'd open the door every day to find me breathing heavily, heart racing and with a huge look of relief on my face. That went on for years. To be fair, I'm a little more comfortable in the dark now! Besides, they've since put a street light at our end of the village.

My father used to tell me pearls of wisdom about business and one thing he used to say to me was, 'Make sure you take care of the wives. If the wife is happy, the husband will follow.' He has always been expert at including the wives and families of people he does business with and in so doing we have made some great family friends. He makes sure the wives have their own separate identity within the entertaining circle rather than just inviting the men on a business trip somewhere.

And of all the wives, my mother was the most involved, in absolutely *everything*. They were both so hardworking. Father would tell stories of getting in the MG with my mother, their first baby – my older brother Duncan Junior – and a nappy bucket, going out looking for new business. When they were in London, they would stay in Holloway, where the nightwatchman's bed was just £2 a night, as against a double room upstairs for £5. They couldn't afford that, so they would sleep in the cheaper room and have to be up by 7 a.m. to let the nightwatchman get back to bed. They'd get up, sort the baby out, do the business meetings that day and head home. They

9

were always such a team and went everywhere together; there was always that sense of being a strong family unit. Looking back, they travelled so much. They had to – the core of the business was going out and meeting customers, but that was a hell of a lot of hard work for parents with a young family.

She's a wee Scottish housewife, but not wee as in 'small', though. She's not fat, she's not thin, she's not tall, she's not small. I think my mother is an attractive lady, and she definitely has some very strong opinions. When I was younger, even if you could prove that a piece of paper was white, if she decided it was black there was no questioning her, that was that. That is perhaps one of her very, very few negative traits, her stubbornness, she wouldn't see reason on certain things, in my opinion. Once she made her mind up, that's it . . . which can be quite annoying when you can quite clearly prove that the white piece of paper is bloody white! Looking back, though, I think a lot of that was to do with them running a business and a busy family home and so she had to be very disciplined and organised. I remember they would occasionally argue, like all parents, but I guess that's because they were working hard and raising a family. It was an awful lot to do. She's a lot mellower now.

My mother is the stronger personality; she has always been the strength that keeps my father on the straight and narrow. He's a very disciplined businessman, but he's less disciplined on the social side! Even as a young boy I was very aware that my mother was a very strong woman, absolutely the rock of the family. My father is a one-off. You might suspect that a Scottish haulage firm owner can be a pretty fiery and loud character, but in fact I've never heard him shout. He might raise his voice slightly if he is really pissed off; naturally, if someone said something nasty about his family he would get very upset, but generally he is not the type to shout and scream or get aggressive, not at all, he's not like that.

To this day they are a great team and they still go everywhere together. In 2006, they came to Melbourne for the grand prix and my mother said something that really struck me: 'Your father is my life.' It was just such a sweet moment, especially when you think they've been married for forty years. I unashamedly admit that I aspire to this sort of relationship when it is time for my own family, because my parents have been my blueprint.

CHASING COWS AND
TICKLING TROUT

When you are a kid, your surroundings seem so big. Having travelled the world with Formula 1, Twynholm now looks like a small, rural village, exactly what it is. Back when I was at primary school, though, just going round to your friend's felt like a big adventure, even though there are only really three main streets in the village. I went to Twynholm Primary School between 1976 and 1983, which was only about half a mile from my home.

There were only seventy pupils at the whole school. My father had gone there and this is also where I met my oldest friend, David Cawthorne, who came late from another school and has been my closest friend since. Pre-dating various lurid tabloid headlines about me as a 'F1 Ladies Man' in later life, back in primary school I was a popular guy with the ladies. I remember a girl putting a clothes peg on my willy in the little doll's tent in class once. Fortunately that didn't become a fetish of mine!

Even as young as five, I used to wander off out of class sometimes. I would call it 'a healthy desire to skive', but one time it backfired on me badly. There was a tag system for the toilets, where you were given a little medallion and only one boy and one girl were allowed in at any one time. On this particular day, I'd wandered off around the schoolyard but, unfortunately, by the time I realised I needed a pee and ran back, all the tags were being used . . . so I pissed myself. I didn't want anyone in class to know, so I sat in my short trousers with a puddle of piss beneath my desk. I thought I might get away with it, but the little girl sitting next to me helpfully piped up, 'Miss, David's peed himself!' I was horrified and said, 'No I haven't!' But as there was a growing lake of urine under my chair it was to no avail. These things can scar you for the rest of your life!

I remember being the second-fastest runner in my class but, other than that, I was just average at primary school. Among the brief flashbacks is one incident that might sound a little goody-goody, but which was something I was genuinely bothered by at the time. As is the case with most schools, there was this one boy who wore NHS glasses, big, thick, black specs which, at the time, was a sure-fire guarantee to get bullied. It just seemed so easy for certain kids to pick on him. One day, we were all playing this game called 'Band Tig' in the yard, which involved chasing someone until you caught them, then you would have to hold hands and chase someone else until you caught them and so on, until you were all holding hands apart from the last person, who was the winner. Everyone was playing and having a great time except this boy, who was just blatantly left out. I felt very uncomfortable about this, it seemed totally wrong, so I gave my place in the line to him. That stands out in my mind, not because I was a do-gooder, but because my future motor-racing career would take me into circles that can be very self-consuming – occasionally I will see something on the TV or elsewhere and it makes me think, 'Fucking hell, my life is so disposable . . .' Being a race driver is such a specific way of life and certain events in the 'real' world really shock you to the core. That boy standing there in that playground, alone, left out, is a very vivid memory for me.

Away from school, we enjoyed a pretty idyllic country child-hood. We were allowed out on to the streets and fields on our own, something which even most city kids back then could not do. We'd cycle or run over the fields or go to farms and just play. One game we played was 'guddling' which involved trying to catch fish with your hands – maybe if you were really canny, you'd build a dam to collect them in a pool of water first. Wellies were essential everyday items. You'd sometimes chase cows, but when you met the farmer he wouldn't be shouting, 'Get off my land!' like some irate caricature, he'd just pass the time of day with you and let you be on your way. Also, we were only three miles from the sea, so we had all that to enjoy as well. Compared to life as a Formula 1 driver, this all seems like a million miles away, a real country bumpkin existence, but it was an innocent, pure, outdoor life and I really loved it.

One old lady who played a cherished part in my childhood was Granny Ingram. She wasn't actually my granny; in fact we were not blood-related at all. As I said, my parents travelled a lot on business, by necessity, and Granny Ingram was a friend of the family who would come and baby-sit. Even when I was quite a bit older, she would come and sit with me. She came from a big family in the village and her sons still live there.

To me, even when I first met her, she looked seventy, yet she never seemed to grow any older. I knew her from when I was a wee boy until she passed away in the late 1990s. I never really got the chance to thank Granny Ingram, which is a terrible thing, but my family were always very good to her. Dad took her on a plane, which she'd never done before, down to London and back. We spent a lot of time with Granny Ingram; she looked after us really well and it was great, because she was a bit more easy-going than my parents. My mum was really strict, so if I had to be in at nine o'clock and I ran in the door at five seconds past, I'd get a bollocking. By contrast, Granny Ingram would let us stay up late, eat chips and fried food. She was 'naughty', as she used to say, with a mischievous twinkle in her eye.

I've always enjoyed a cup of tea. She used to call me a 'tea jenny' because, even at that age, I loved drinking tea. I used to make the tea for my parents in the morning and even now when I go home to see them, I'll walk in the house and the very first thing I'll do is put the kettle on. Then the next morning I will take them tea in bed. With Granny Ingram, I used to wait until my parents shut the door on their way out and then I would turn to her and say, 'How about a nice cup o' tea Granny?'

My secondary school was Kirkcudbright Academy, which I went to from 1983 until 1986, just about three miles away from home. At the time, that journey felt like a full-blown expedition; venturing that far away from Twynholm, it might as well have been the other side of the world. Sometimes we'd cycle, but most days a school bus would pick us up at 8.15 a.m., which was an adventure in itself at first.

Even going up to the big school was daunting. Cawthorne is only three months older than me, but that meant he started at the secondary an academic year before me. We still saw each other after school in the evening and I'd hear all these tales of antics up at the big school. When it came to my turn to go there, I was shitting myself, thinking I'd get my head kicked in, because we were known to have the trucking business and people might see the family's money as a target, something to pick on.

Living in a very small village like Twynholm has both its good sides and its bad. There were only a few hundred metres between the company offices and our home, but pretty much all the neighbours and most of our family lived in between. So everyone kind of knew each other. As the main employer in the village, my family name was very well-known locally, we were 'the wealthiest family in the village'. My dad would always drive a lovely Mercedes, for example. You would get a mixture of reactions: certain people were happy to know that your family have done okay but, on the other side, some people assumed you were a snobby family because you've got a bit of money ... which, in reality, could not be further from the truth. My mother is the most grounded, hardworking person you could meet and my father is a hard-worker who talks to anyone.

Money makes people do funny things. I always remember my mother rightfully took her child benefit when we were kids, but several local people would whisper and snipe about that, because we were perceived as being a well-off family. But she had every right to that money. That's just a small-town mentality. We spoke about it and I said, 'That's why you pay taxes, to have roads, health care and child support. You are entitled to it . . . why not?'

I was always a little bit of the outsider rather than the ring-leader at secondary. I don't remember really any magical moments during my time at that school. I think I was a bit timid, I'd felt more comfortable at primary. I'm still the same today – I prefer smaller groups of people, I always have. I just like who I like and I'm very comfortable with those smaller circles.

Apart from Cawthorne, there was a girl called Zoe Halliday, who was the daughter of the local hairdresser – she's now got several beautician shops on the back of seeing her father run a business. I'd hang out with her a lot. I was also mates with Michael Gillespie in my year, as well as a guy in the year above called John Jameson, who famously dated J.K. Rowling. He's an accountant in Edinburgh now, but every year I get a funny letter from him saying words to the effect of 'If only I'd stuck in there before she made the big time!' They come to the odd race, like at Silverstone or Barcelona, and Michael came down to Monaco for his stag weekend, but I won't speak to them on the phone in between times. I've never been a big 'phone' person. I don't keep in touch with people very well; I don't even keep in touch with the family that often when I'm travelling. I'd say those are the only people I really keep in touch with from my school days; I don't really have strong bonds with anyone from my teenage years apart from Cawthorne.

Back then, my domestic routine each morning before school was the same: I'd make the tea, take it to my parents, then my mum would get up and make breakfast and then off I'd go to school. Even though we were well off and were known to have money, my parents were determined to teach me its value. Of course, as a self-conscious teenager that's not always what you want to hear. My mother was, after all, from a working-class family and so she would knit grey jumpers for me, which I have to say I was mortified about, because all my friends were wearing labels like Pringle, all these 'big' designer names. The bottom line is, no matter how superficial the clothes on your back are, at that age if you are wearing the 'wrong' item, it makes you *different*. I did mention the possibility of getting some Pringle knitwear to my mother, but she just said, 'David, this is a much better jumper and, besides, I've spent hours making it.' So that was that.

Although my parents owned the haulage firm, I did do odd holiday jobs – there was the power wash at my father's garage and we'd get a bit of pocket money cleaning people's cars. Other times we'd help tidy up, you know, clean the cupboards out, that sort of thing. I also remember not getting as much dinner money as my friends. Some of these kids' dads were unemployed, but they were coming to school with much more than me, sometimes double. I could never work that out. The problem was my mother knew what a set meal at school cost and she didn't want to give me extra to go and spend on rubbish. It's all valuable lessons in life, of course, but at the time, this stuff makes a big difference to your school day. I sometimes have a rueful chuckle now and again though, because over the years I've burned my way through literally millions of pounds with nothing to show for it. Perhaps I've spent all these years making up for the time when I had less dinner money!

One aspect of my childhood that was certainly second-to-none was the family parties. My father is a special case who just loves to organise functions and parties. Growing up in the bungalow, there were always people round. It wasn't even a big house back then (my father has extended it massively since those days), but he put a little dance floor down and people would party away all night. My mother is a great cook, so she'd spend all her time in the kitchen getting things ready. They were brilliant at entertaining.

It was quite a big deal when I was finally allowed to join the adults' party night for the first time – although this was on the strict understanding that the minute I acted like I kid I was out. After these parties, my father was supposed do the dishes and usually did, but if he was feeling a little worse for wear, I could boost my £1-a-week pocket money a little by doing the washing up for him.

As the business grew, my father's parties just got bigger. So instead of small numbers around the bungalow, he ended up throwing lavish company dances up in Edinburgh, ostensibly to thank all of his customers, but actually just another excuse to have a great time, he just loves it. Once I got to Formula 1, he would invite important customers to races and, because I would sometimes turn up at parties and meet his guests, a lot of my conversations with my father involve organising a party!

I wasn't really one for going to many parties from school, though. The family's profile was probably one factor, as

IT IS WHAT IT IS

I've said, and my reticence to get involved in big groups of people another. But perhaps the main reason I felt more of an outsider at secondary was that I was very rarely around on weekends to play football or any of those sorts of things with the other kids.

Why was that?

Because I was always busy, off round the country ... racing karts.

THE LONG ROAD AHEAD

Scotland has a proud Formula 1 history. Two of Britain's eight world champions in the modern era have been Scottish: Jim Clark and Jackie Stewart. Apparently, the first ever Scot to win a grand prix – Innes Ireland, driving a Lotus at the 1961 US Grand Prix – was from a nearby veterinarian family based in Dumfries and Galloway. But it was the obvious icons of two-time world champion Clark and three-time champion Stewart whom I was more aware of as a kid. My father always spoke very fondly of Jim Clark, he loved to watch him race, so I guess his was the first name of a racing driver I heard. Clark was from a farming community, Duns, in the eastern Borders – unlike me, both his and Jackie Stewart's mothers were not keen for their sons to become racing drivers.

On one occasion, Clark entered a rally that ran very close to our village and my father managed to get his autograph on a cigarette packet, which remained a treasured family memento. Dad used to love talking about him and the fact that he 'knew' a grand prix driver. Clark won those two titles then sadly died in a Formula 2 race at Hockenheim in 1968, but not before he'd won more grands prix than anyone else in the sport's history at that point. He was a loyal man too, only driving for Lotus throughout his entire career. He was a Scottish farmer so, of course, it might seem entirely feasible that a quiet boy from Twynholm could make it into Formula 1.

Yet, as a kid, I wasn't the little boy waiting at the door to go to the grand prix. I enjoyed listening to my father talk about Clark and Stewart and all these famous cars and races. I remember my father even went to a couple of British Grands Prix, but I didn't. I wasn't interested enough and I never asked to go. The first time I ever went to a grand prix was when I raced in a Vauxhall Lotus support race in 1990. I'm not a big 'watcher'; I'm not very good at going to sports events. I never went to watch the local football club. Even now, I've only gone to odd events as an adult because I've been invited as a so-called sports 'personality' or whatever. The way I look at it is, if I can't actually do these sports in person, I'd watch them on the telly in the comfort of my own home.

In many ways, nothing has changed: it was always my father, not me, who was the 'Formula 1 historian', so to speak. Obviously I'm aware of who's won multiple world titles and what have you, but I'm not some bespectacled stats obsessive. I know a bit of the sport's history, but it's not something I study or watch. When I'm not racing I don't really watch anything to do with racing.

When I was a kid, the grand prix was on BBC2 on a Sunday night, and even then it was only highlights. My mum didn't really like watching it back then, but my dad and I would sit there and watch people like Mansell and Prost. Obviously drivers who were not even alive when you are born make a more diluted mark on your psyche, so people like Mansell, Prost and Senna were always somehow more tangible, naturally. Sure, I got up and watched the grands prix on telly with my dad, even if they were on in the middle of the night, so I was following the races, but I certainly wasn't going to them. I know that many Formula 1 drivers were originally the little kids travelling to grands prix and getting autographs from all their heroes. That was never me; when I was growing up, I had a picture of 'Page 3' model, Samantha Fox, not Ayrton Senna, on my wall.

I tried rugby, but it didn't take long for me to realise it wasn't for me. One day I was playing a match on a public pitch and I fell in some dog shit. It was vile, so I cleaned it off my legs as best I could with the sleeve of my shirt. Then, when we came to scrum, I turned and politely apologised to my team-mate who was about to put his head right on this smear of dog shit. He just put his mouthpiece in, growled and scrummed down with a loud grunt, his face rubbing all over this dog shit. I remember looking down and thinking, 'Okay, these are different people to me! They are cut from a different cloth, excuse me, am I allowed to take my leave?'

My father had always stayed involved in karting, despite his own career having been cruelly cut short. He sponsored a few guys and was keen to see me race. So, for my eleventh birthday, he bought me a kart, a simple 100cc machine with no gear box, that now hangs from the roof of the David Coulthard Museum in Twynholm – which my father has created from boxes full of memorabilia which he's collected over the years . . . surely proof that he's a compulsive hoarder.

Many of my future rivals started karting when they were

barely at primary school – Mika Hakkinen began at the age of only five – so I certainly wasn't an early learner. Unlike the grand prix, I had been to quite a few kart races (including some at Silverstone), but I certainly wasn't the kid forcing my father to take me racing; it was presented to me as an option and I chose to take it. So I never dreamt of being in F1 – I'm very much like that today; I know hard work is the only way of realising a 'dream', not speculative daydreaming, so I don't waste energy on dreams.

My father ran karts for several years before I started racing them myself, but he didn't really have much success to speak of. The main driver he helped was Brian Smith, who was the main driver for 'Coulthard Racing', a team which ran 125cc and 250cc karts, all paid for by my father.

My first race was in the spring of 1982, at a local track called The Cults in Stranraer, about an hour from where we lived. The first heat saw me lapped a couple of times; the second heat saw me lapped only once by a few racers; and in the final heat I wasn't lapped at all. My father has since told me that was the day when he thought he saw something in my competitive nature and driving talent that would take me to Formula 1. It's hard to imagine that kind of foresight, but that's what he says.

And you know what? He was right. Within twelve years, I was sitting on the grid in a Formula 1 car in Barcelona about to start my first grand prix.

I won my first race shortly after my first outing, scooping the best novice trophy at The Cults. I was really pleased to win and the competitive streak in me enjoyed it, but at that stage I didn't yet have the passion for racing. That came a few years later.

I clearly remember a picture of me in my motorbike leathers collecting my wee trophy, proud as you like. It was a second-hand set of leathers, like old-fashioned motorbike leathers in two-tone blue with white stars on them and you zipped them straight up the centre of the chest. I'd bought them from the then-Scottish champion, Craig McWilliams. They were all padded and a bit too big really, but the theory was I could grow into them. I'm sure my father could have afforded to buy me a brand-new set of my own, but this was all part of my parents teaching me to value things and money. I didn't care to be honest, I was really proud when I went up for that trophy in them. Besides, they were a perfectly good set of second-hand leathers and they'd belonged to a champion.

I also vividly remember coming back home after the race with my father. We'd already had a pool and a games room built on the side of the bungalow, so the latter became the trophy room. We put up some shelves and placed this little trophy up there: it bore the legend, 'Stranraer K Club, Best Novice, May 1982'. A start had been made.

When I first started, we would have maybe one race a month at Stranraer or at Larkhall, just outside Glasgow; I also used to race at Rowrah, which is in Cumbria at an old quarry, as well as tracks at Crail, Boyndie, Golspie and others. I was driving all the time – when it wasn't on a track, I'd be found turning the family car round on the drive, just getting behind the wheel whenever I could. Often when we went to circuits, I would drive my mother's Honda around the track. I wasn't so tall at this stage, so we used to put an industrial, gallon-size tub of oil on the seat so that I could see over the steering wheel ... anything just so that I could *drive*.

Not wishing to sound dismissive, but one great thing about karting at that young age was that I never had to go to church on Sundays, I was always racing. Although Mum and Dad weren't particularly regular church-goers, I did go to Sunday school when I was younger and learned from the Bible, and I can see the set of rules it offers, or at least a guideline for how you might live your life. I can also see that some people would really appreciate and enjoy that but, for me, it was never something that made an impact. I'm not at all religious and I find the preaching of overly zealous religious types hard to stomach. So yes, karting was perhaps the ultimate excuse to get out of going to Sunday School.

My karting started to get pretty serious, pretty quickly. I was still only eleven, but I was learning quickly. One of the first things I was taught was never to look behind. It might sound a bit simple, even obvious, but a lot of kids will look behind to see where their opposition is. You have to focus on going forward, going as fast as you can. Occasionally you would get overtaken because you wouldn't be aware of someone catching you and they'd pass you on a corner, but generally it was a simple, direct and – for me at least – successful philosophy. Conversely, if I was behind someone and they were looking back at me, then psychologically I was lifted; I felt like I was eating away at their lead, pulling them in. Then if they looked a little later and I was closer still, you could almost see the whites of their eyes and them thinking, 'Shit, he's closer again!' It was so easy to pressurise people who spent half the race looking backwards; I never did – if you can't see the enemy, you can't worry about them.

By this stage, my karting had graduated to club championships, so you had to be a club member and would compete in about ten or eleven races a year – although the inclement Scottish weather sometimes reduced how many races were actually staged to just a handful. Initially I raced that kart with no gearbox, in a formula called Junior Britain. Back then, you could race Junior Britain from as early as eleven years old until you were sixteen, so obviously there were some big, hairy sixteen-year-olds racing against kids four or five years their junior. They've changed it now so that it's split into different categories and that seems much fairer.

Back then, however, I was in at the deep end with kids much older than me, and often with several hundred races under their belts. There was a minimum weight, so the little kids had to add a lot of lead on their karts (although for my final year in Junior Britain I was actually over the weight and so at a considerable disadvantage). I found I was good and I quickly started to win races and, eventually, club championships.

The routine was to head to Stranraer early on Saturday morning for practice sessions, then work on the kart all day and stay over in my father's motorhome ready for the race on Sunday. My father was sponsoring other racers in long-circuit racing, so the motorhome was invaluable, we lived in it. I would eventually race karts for six years and during that time the motorhome was like a bungalow on wheels.

After seeing a dominant Allan McNish – who is a year older than me and from Dumfries – win a lot of kart races ahead of me in 1982, I graduated to the winner's spot the following year – in what was only my second season in karting. Once I had a taste for winning races, there was no stopping me. In 1983 and the two years that followed it, I won the Scottish

Junior kart championship, a very definite step on the ladder. So I was winning a lot of races in Scotland for long periods of time, but in the world of motor-sport, the reality is that my home country is a small place; in England it was much more competitive, so it was quite a culture shock when I first started competing in the south.

My father is someone who gets feelings about events; he sometimes seems to know what is going to happen in the future. He often said, 'I knew you were going to win that race,' which some people might put down to simple optimism or belief in my abilities. Yet, one day, when I was just fourteen, my father said something to me out of the blue, which would later prove true: 'David, when you are in F1, you should live in Monaco.'

The next step up, in what was to prove a constant progression of formulas, was the so-called Super 1 series, which at the time was the premier British kart championship. Dad helped out with the karts and Brian Smith helped tons, too. My father wasn't particularly mechanically minded, so we always needed someone to tune the engines and set up the karts and that sort of thing, which is where Dave Boyce, the main mechanic, comes into my story. He is a fantastic character who played an absolutely crucial role in the early days of my career (and my life as well as that of Cawthorne), and we are still friends to this day.

Dave had a brilliant reputation in karting and was already running Allan McNish. He's said that when we first introduced ourselves to him, he thought to himself 'the package is not just the kid', because he really took to my mother and father and liked the way they handled me and were bringing me up.

We ran a Simon Wright kart with a TKM engine and the tyres were quite a hard compound for this style of racing – compared to the much softer tyres used in European karting. This made finding the ideal set-up quite tricky, so it was a very demanding series and, looking back, brilliant for learning my craft and preparing me for the tyres we use in Formula 1. The Super 1 Series was held over eight to ten different tracks in England. They also ran a winter series too, which could be vicious what with the combination of the mileage and the weather. You can imagine driving from Scotland all the way to Rye House, near London, on a Friday night after school in the deepest days of winter, only to spin off at the first corner. I think during my first year in England I crashed at nearly every race. You really had to want to race and, of course, to win.

The sheer logistics of competing in England were exhausting, for all of us. My father would work hard all week and then pick me up from school on a Friday night, still in my school blazer, and we would drive south to race. The distances were gruelling – London was over 350 miles away. We pretty much lived on the M6 for years. As we'd been used to local club racing in and around Scotland, the added effort of facing a fifteen-hour round trip, or more, just to get to the starting line was a big burden for everyone.

Weeknights after school were no less busy than race weekends. Each night during the week, there was a strict order of things to do. So on the Monday night, I'd unpack the motorhome and clean it ... I'm an expert toilet cleaner, let's say that. I'd roll the seatbelts up so they were all in one precise place and brush the carpet all in one direction so it was immaculate. Then my father would inspect it, not at all in a harsh way, but just to say it was a good job. I enjoyed getting the tick at the end of the day from him, saying, 'Yes, David, you did that well.'

Tuesday night would be the night to strip the kart and clean it; Wednesday night would be taken up with saddle soaping my leathers, cleaning them, shining my helmet and anything else that needed attending to; then, on Thursday night, I would pack the motorhome up ready for that weekend; and then, straight out of school on Friday night, we'd be off once again and the whole circus would come full circle. Each race weekend would involve a Saturday practice, then on Sunday morning you'd wake up and have pre-heats, then eight to ten laps and then a final of probably fifteen laps. Then the motorhome would be packed up again before we'd drive home on the Sunday night ready for work and school again on Monday morning. I'd always be massaging my father's shoulders on the drive home or rubbing his eyes with damp flannels or holding blocks of ice on his head to keep him awake. My mother was fantastically supportive, too. During the week, she would make delicious soups and food to freeze for the journey and the race weekend.

On occasions, there would be eight of us in the motorhome, hammering down to the south: myself, Mum, Dad, my sister Lyndsay, my mother's brother Uncle Richard, Dave Boyce, Brian Smith and Cawthorne. Uncle Richard had been involved in racing as a race official in Stranraer. Cawthorne used to help the mechanics and keep the times; mother knitted and made all the food; everyone chipped in. Cawthorne went everywhere with us and he's since told me that he saw my father more as his 'favourite uncle'.

Brian Smith had to stop racing for my father's team after he had a bad accident at a track called Cadwell Park in Lincolnshire and broke his back. Thankfully he wasn't paralysed, but it stopped him racing, so instead he became a mechanic for me. It was Brian who painted the Scottish saltire on my helmet, which he actually did while still recuperating from his big accident. Brian painted the word 'Budgie' on the helmet, too – at this time, no one called me DC, my nickname was Budgie after the purple bike of the same name I owned. Later Brian used my initials with the 'C' inside the 'D'. It's funny to think that all those years later people started to call me 'DC' in Formula 1. My Uncle Richard still calls me Budgie!

Despite his misfortune with the accident, Brian still had a burning passion for racing and it was great to have him around. I always used to think of him when we trudged back home to Twynholm after eight, nine or more hours in the motorhome, late on Sunday nights – he still had another hour's drive to his house. If my mother had stayed at home and the return journey was particularly long or late and we didn't return to Twynholm until the wee small hours, we would often just sleep in the motorhome so as not to disturb her. If we were all awake, we would haul all the gear from the motorhome up the steep drive to the bungalow – 'No one ever comes up to the house empty-handed!' my father used to say. Then, I'd get up the next morning and head off to school. I lost count of the times I did my weekend's homework on the Monday morning bus to school.

It wasn't just the travel that was shocking – the standards were that much higher. Looking back at all those endless miles staring at cat's eyes in the road, I actually think it made me far more focused than my rivals. If you think about it, I had to be so much more disciplined, dedicated and driven as a teenager to undertake a nine-hour drive to get to a race (as did my family, of course). A lot of the kids who raced karts from down south lived an hour or so away from a track and it was easy for them to roll up on the morning of a race and compete. I couldn't do that. My entire week, pretty much my every waking moment, revolved around racing. Just the pure logistics of getting to a race made it impossible to approach it any other way. But, in turn, that meant I was more prepared, more focused and more eager to make all that effort worthwhile. That was undoubtedly an advantage I had over my fellow karters.

Over the coming years, whatever time we arrived back, whether it was late on a Sunday or early Monday, we'd have this tradition of going through to the 'trophy room' and finding somewhere to put the silverware we'd won that weekend. Pretty soon there were well over one hundred trophies – eventually they were moved to the museum.

Even at this relatively early stage, I was very particular about my karts. Sometimes Dave might change the steering wheel position a few centimetres or even millimetres and I would always know and ask him why; he couldn't get anything past me! He's told me I was the most particular of his karters, and that most of my peers would just climb in and rush off. He wasn't complaining, he actually said it made his life quite easy because he knew that if anything was wrong, I would be able to tell him exactly where the problem was.

One thing I always avoided doing was making an excuse – when we came in to analyse lap times, I would just say, 'Yup, made a mistake there ...' What's the point otherwise? How else could the team improve and move forward? We worked really well together.

There were so many races it is hard to recall all but the most obvious highs and lows. I do remember going to Clay Pigeon, near Yeovil, one time – a drive of over eight hours – it seemed like an eternity, only for me to spin off on the first lap (I would do the same in 1995 when my grandparents had flown out to the Canadian Grand Prix no less!). Another time we had a puncture in the pouring rain on the M6 and it seemed days before we got to the track, and again I spun off on the first corner.

At one circuit, I spun and stalled and had to bump start the kart myself, before catching up with the leaders and winning by some distance. I was fiercely competitive, not aggressive, but I certainly wanted to win. There was a big controversy once when my Uncle Richard, as the race official, finished a race a lap early and I won. I think he was so excited he just waved the chequered flag! There was a protest afterwards from other racers, but the win stood – I had a huge lead anyway, so his presumptuousness made no difference. Looking back now, those days feel full of innocence.

I say that, but it was all very serious, too. At one race at Rye House, in Hertfordshire, I won but was then disqualified for running a yellow flag. My mother suspected foul play and was furious; particularly as all the stewards on the course that day said I had done nothing wrong. She was livid and marched up to the clerk of the course's hut to protest. After the race, she took the decision to a tribunal at the RAC headquarters in London, complete with an expensive lawyer to represent us, and had the disqualification overturned.

One trip to Italy was notable for some dubious tactics by the Italians at the World Karting Championships. I was already known for racing very fast in the rain, but when I crashed in the heats, the Italians saw their chance – they knew rain was forecast for the main race, so they brought the start forward, meaning not only was it a dry race, but also that we barely had enough time to get the kart ready properly. Cheeky.

Another time, we were testing at Stranraer the week before one particular big race and, on the far side of the track, away from the crew, I hit a kerb at high speed. In doing so, I knocked the mounts off so the engine actually fell out, pulled the fuel line out and then sparked, which set the kart on fire. I jumped out of the kart before I could get burnt and stood there, crying and dejected. It was one of the few times in racing that I was scared, although it was as much down to shock as it was fear; it was all a bit dramatic for a teenager. I wasn't injured, but my kart was in flames in front of me and a big race was looming. The main reason I was upset was because I thought it meant I wouldn't be able to race that weekend. Fortunately, the kart went off and got resprayed and rebuilt ready for the race that weekend. I won that race, too, along with plenty of others and, by the end of 1986, I had won the Super 1 Championship.

If my father was happy because I'd won, then I was happy. Often he was not happy. As I said, sometimes we would drive after school and work on a Friday night for maybe nine hours, get up the next day, practise, then on the race day I would come off unexpectedly. If that happened and it was a racing incident, my father would never have a problem, in his eyes that was just racing. But if he suspected I wasn't trying my hardest or was not putting in the effort, it was an altogether different reaction.

On a few occasions he called my bluff, although I think they were not entirely idle threats. On the few times he felt I was not focusing all my effort, he confronted me. 'We are wasting our time, we may as well put the kart back in the van and go home,' and I'd be saying, 'No! I'll try harder next time!' Once, at Rye House, I remember having to sit him down and convince him to let me carry on. I actually started crying, I was devastated, and he said, 'You can cry all you like, that was rubbish . . .' Dave Boyce intervened – as he often did – and tried to mediate between us. I eventually persuaded Dad to give me another go and the very next race I won by miles. The funny thing is, my father will still phone me up sometimes when I've had a bad race in Formula 1 and say, 'David, that was rubbish!'

Looking back, at that age there are times when you are not totally focused. When something is available to you on tap, as it were, which karting was, you can also take it for granted. It was perhaps inevitable that we had the odd 'blow-out'. Obviously, the lifestyle of racing every weekend as a schoolboy was quite rigid and, generally, I didn't stray far from the track. Inevitably, perhaps, as I went through my teenage years, I did occasionally let my hair down more away from the track too, whether that was with girls or the odd swig out of a bottle of cheap cider with Cawthorne. One time we got hold of a bottle of Pimms – a real man's drink – and I got pretty legless. Cawthorne dragged me back home, put me to bed, walked into the lounge and said, 'Hello Mr and Mrs Coulthard,' then legged it. Twynholm is hardly a den of iniquity, don't get me wrong, but with all the money and time that was being invested in my career, father wasn't too impressed on more than one occasion.

Back in those teenage days, none of us really drank that much, but one weekend in Dorset, Cawthorne got completely pissed. We were sharing a room and, at some point in the night, I actually woke up to find him pissing on me. I wasn't overly pleased, so I got up, went and had a shower and came back to find him snoring loudly, fast asleep. It was only in the morning when I showed him the wet sheets that he believed he peed on me. You see, my life was just as glamorous back then.

Just as had been the case that day he scolded me at Rye House, there was a point back in Twynholm when my dad obviously thought I wasn't taking the karting as seriously as I needed to, so he sat me down and said, 'If you want to do this, I'll support you all the way, but if you are just going to play at it, there are other family members to think of and we can do other things with the money.' I guess I was probably fourteen or fifteen at the time.

I thought for quite a few days about what I really wanted to do. I could carry on karting and discipline myself to be absolutely dedicated; or I could go out on the piss and chase girls and party, like a lot of my teenage mates were doing (quite naturally). I came to the conclusion that I was being given an opportunity that my friends weren't and I was not about to waste it. I do want to make it clear that my father wasn't overpowering at all: he wanted me to do well and I wanted to race. I couldn't have asked for more from him.

In the winter of 1986 into 1987, Dave switched from Wright karts to Zip karts, a manufacturer that was much less proven in the Junior series. He's made the analogy of moving from Ferrari to Minardi. It was a risk, but Dave knew what he was doing and I always had absolute confidence in his decisions. Besides, we won the title in 1987 regardless.

That's not to say we didn't have our teething problems. Of course we did, and it took a long, hard winter of testing to get things right. We never spent big money on the karts and always worked on them frantically, we were so focused. Dave Boyce will tell you that the raw talent in my karting was not blatantly visible to him at first, but that it rapidly started to manifest itself as I gained more experience – I understand he now tells people I was 'the best junior karter he's ever seen', which is very nice of him.

Dave took me karting all over Europe too, not just the UK, so the mileage was even more gruelling. Most of the overseas races were in Europe, but we even travelled as far afield as Australia. One particular race Down Under was very interesting and shows just how competitive and quick-thinking karting was at that level. The kart I drove had a double-frame chassis and, in this one particular race, a lot of rain was predicted. We actually cut the chassis, which had the effect of giving the kart much more flexibility and therefore more grip . . . in the wet. If it starts to dry out, you are finished. On this day, unfortunately, that's exactly what happened and, after leading for some time, I was eventually overhauled by a chap called Jan Magnussen, who was the karting world champion at the time, and finally came in third. You take a gamble and sometimes it works, sometimes it doesn't. At one point on the same race weekend, the temperatures were so high we were having problems with the fuel supply, so we packed some ice in an oil tin and passed the fuel line through this makeshift cooling system to prevent it evaporating before it got to the engine.

We had some great fun among all the hard work. The afore-
mentioned world championship in Italy in 1986 was of particular note, but not for karting historians. For it was there that
I lost my virginity – not in the back of a motorhome, as my
racing-obsessed father would have it! It was to a girl called
Caroline who had a set of knockers on her that – as a teenage
boy – you'd never seen the like of. Her nipples were like Scania
wheel nuts. The magic moment was in her hotel room (for
some reason I can't recall I was actually staying in a tent!). I
rarely went out on the evenings at race meets – it was always
'9 p.m., bedtime! Got to be up early tomorrow ...' – but, on
this occasion, I was out on the town. Well, more accurately,
we'd gone to a disco called Lido de Jesolo and Caroline basically
came in, grabbed me by the ear and hauled me away to be
'taken'. It was my turn. I think she'd done my friend the night
before. Then, horribly, as I was going into the hotel my mum
and dad were checking in, so I shat myself and had to hide.
She took me upstairs and, three-and-a-half minutes later, I was
smoking a cigarette. I went to Italy a boy and came back a man.

For years I'd had these conversations with my Uncle Richard
about losing my cherry and he kept giving me all this 'advice',
saying stuff like, 'Aye lad, once you've had one, there'll
be no stopping you, they'll just be coming along one after
another ...' To a teenage virgin, this was the stuff of dreams,
literally. Anyway, the night after Caroline, I somehow ended
up in a Transit van with two Dutch girls. I can clearly remember
in the middle of all that Netherlandish activity thinking, 'It's
true what he said, it's fucking true!'

We often went on holiday to Barbados and, one particular
year, my father and Cawthorne shot some 'fake' cine-footage

of 'the famous Formula 1 racing superstar David Coulthard' hounded by paparazzi and being interviewed around the island. 'Aren't you that famous race driver?'; all that sort of stuff. It was a real laugh and I think Dave Boyce still has a copy of it to this day. When I think of that, I can see that my father was only half-joking. It was always known-stroke-expected that I'd be racing Formula 1 some day.

Karting was relatively injury-free. I rolled the kart once, but that was a result of already having a broken collar bone from playing football at school, just a few weeks before that dubious karting world championships in Jesolo, Italy. I was at the doctors getting my collar bone strapped up when my father came in giving it the, 'You bloody idiot! I told you not to play football, because the race is coming up!' He was pretty pissed off. I was just having a kick about with my hands in my pockets when I tripped up, fell over and broke my collar bone; the very next day, my brother broke his collar bone in a sack race at the local village sports day, so we were both walking round the house with identical injuries! It's bloody painful breaking your collarbone, I can tell you, because they can't pin it or put it in a plaster, they just have to let it heal. My mother got two deck chairs out and we would sit in those, reclined in equal discomfort, waiting for our bones to heal. I couldn't lie down, so I actually slept in one of those bloody deck chairs for a week. I literally couldn't lie down.

I'd broken my collar bone before when I fell off the back of an Italjet motorbike aged eight. My brother and I had got these oil drums out in the fields with a plank running up the side and we were jumping up this ramp, stunt rider-style. I was on the back one day and he was racing around incredibly fast when he aimed the wheels at this ramp, as if he was going to jump over with me on the back. I thought, 'Fuck this!' and jumped off, twisting the helmet around sharply and breaking my collar bone in the process. When I broke it the second time, it happened to be in the same place as the first, which is unusual because normally the repair that forms around the break strengthens the bone. The combined result of these two breaks is that I'm all lopsided.

My father was used to us rattling about on the bike and he was never scared of that. It was only when I got to the age of about fifteen that he was more specifically concerned about teenage pranks causing injuries that might get in the way of racing. He once sat me down and told me to keep out of fights and not get involved in anything at school. 'You keep fit for the racing son.'

Other than that, teenage injuries were mostly from life rather than racing. They built a twelve-foot fence round the house to keep my brother in, because he was wild. I caught my shoelace on that one day and fell face down and broke my left arm – that was a bad break because it was at the joint, so it's an awkward one to heal, even to this day it doesn't hang straight. I've had as many injuries from life as I have had from racing, so although I may be a little battered, compared to so many of my contemporaries, I'm hardly the Six Million Dollar Man.

Dave Boyce took me karting all over Britain and Europe, so we spent huge amounts of time together. It's funny because Dave hasn't changed the way he treated me then to the way he treats me now, because he has this fantastic way of treating kids like adults. Dave is a very bright engineer and is certainly a very intelligent racing man. In many ways, he should be at the helm of a number of people, maybe even a high-profile race team, certainly running a big business and earning a lot of money. But he likes working on his own, so there you go.

The karting was starting to get very serious at this level and more senior racing people would be watching the results to scout for future talent. Fortunately for me, I'd won those three Junior kart championships, then those back-to-back Super 1 championships, something that had never been done before. Add to that three consecutive Scottish Open Championships and I was certainly getting in the habit of winning races.

Karting was never a cheap sport to compete in and so people took it very seriously (it can cost around £50,000 a season at certain levels); nowadays that is even more the case. Karting has changed drastically, of course, like a lot of modern sports. I always remember being embarrassed when I went up to collect my trophy and at all the dinner dances at the end of the year where they award your club's trophies, I was always quite shy. Today, I see young kids in karting, bowling up for their trophy with their cap on sideways and they're up there giving it out for the cameras. It just shows what a different time it is. Dave Boyce tells me that some kids even turn up to races with 'their lawyers'. He calls it 'chequebook karting' nowadays – apparently some of these kids have budgets in excess of £100,000 a season. You have a lot more driver-development programmes now and that was only really starting when I was racing the early formulas. It has changed the environment entirely.

When I think back at how young, naïve and relatively shy I was, I would be a fish out of water in the modern scene.

Motor-racing, even for teens and pre-teens, is so pressurised nowadays; it's just become another part of the MTV culture really. I grew up in a time where kids were supposed to be seen and not heard.

The modern nature of competition is so purely focused on winning at any cost. Yet I like to think – idealistically, you may say – that you can win with a certain style and honour. Some people would shoot their granny to cross the line first. They just want to win, regardless of circumstance. I would rather have a good race and finish second than win in an unsporting way. Don't get me wrong, I like to win, very much so and I am intensely competitive. If you are a racing driver and I'm given an equal opportunity to yourself on a track and you happen to be better on the day, I'd shake your hand and say, 'Well done,' and for the most part feel relatively philosophical about the result. But as I congratulated you, I'd be thinking, 'I'll try harder. How can I turn that around next time?' I've always been motivated to improve. I carry a fear of failure.

When I was karting, I used to grade each and every race. When the motorhome was packed up, I'd write down all the statistics in a little book. The obvious ones were there – position in the race, fastest laps, all the usual – but I would also have my own separate column, which rated *performance*. So sometimes I'd come first, but only score a six for performance; other times I'd come third, but rate my performance an eight. It was all about whether I made mistakes or whether it was a clinically correct race. That mattered to me then and it matters to me now. I never gave myself ten out of ten, even if I won the race or took the championship. Even when I won those back-to-back Super 1 British kart championships I know for a fact the folder

44

with all my writing in it does not have a single maximum mark out of ten. So yes, I am self-critical, without a doubt. That's why I can be critical of others in certain situations where I am applying myself and they appear not to be. I don't think that is unfair.

However, that brutal drive to win without conscience is almost alien to me. So, for example, I could never have been a championship boxer. When a boxer goes into the ring, he has to have an unswerving and absolute self-belief; otherwise it might prove fatal – literally – to his chances of success. I have never had that flawless self-belief. I think that's why it's often been a slight embarrassment when I get all the adulation and congratulations after a successful race, because I'm not doing it for that, nor am I doing it to prove anything to myself, I am racing just to do it. I'm certainly not doing it for the money, either. That is nice, of course, but it is a by-product. When I started, you needed people to be motivated by far more than the money or the *image* of being a driver.

I'm not saying I wasn't very committed, I was. In fact, there was a phase when I was perhaps *too* disciplined. As a Formula 1 driver, I like to think that I train hard, usually two or three hours a day spent on fitness alone, whether that is mountain-biking, gym work, specific muscle conditioning, whatever. I eat carefully, rarely any biscuits or cakes, although I will have a sweet cup of tea and maybe a chocolate bar after a race when I am dehydrated and in need of a quick boost. The team supply a personal trainer who follows me around the globe and assists in keeping me in excellent physical shape.

However, back when I was karting, I trained very hard, too. I always took fitness very seriously whatever level of racing I was at and whatever amount of facilities were available to me. We had the pool at the house and also a little gym machine for doing leg exercises. We also had dumbbells and other bits and pieces, so for my age and level of success, I was incredibly fit. My father would always say, 'Have you done your exercises?' He knew how important it was. It is a racing myth that I used to watch the television with my helmet on to strengthen my neck muscles, but I did used to do exercises with my helmet on. Sometimes that might have been in front of the TV, but I wouldn't just sit there in front of the telly wearing it as a matter of course.

By my mid- to late teens, however, the focus on fitness – or rather weight – took a slightly more sinister turn. I'd always been very conscious of my weight and had made an effort not to eat biscuits and junk food. People complimented me on how disciplined I was with food. I basically had to keep my weight like a professional jockey. I was nearly the same height as I am now – six foot – but I was only just over nine stone (my current race weight is still just 72.5 kilos).

I was getting too tall. At the time of writing, I'm still one of the tallest grand prix drivers on the grid; it's always been difficult to fit in the cars comfortably, but I'd rather be over six foot, because I've got the rest of my life as a reasonably tall male. I don't want to be a dwarf. I see some of the drivers in the paddock and they just look like mini-men to me, and they will still be mini-men when they have retired. That may be convenient for a career in racing, but it's half a man!

I digress. The problem was that, as I got taller, I started to become a lot heavier than some of my counterparts. There was a very brutal indication of your weight once you got to the track – the lead they added to each kart would come off if you were heavier. I'd started off as a little boy with lead all over the car to weigh it down, but as I got bigger the lead started being stripped off until there was none on at all and I was running heavy.

I first noticed a preoccupation, for want of a better word, with food when I would open a tin of biscuits and look at them, then just leave them there after thinking about the negative impact they would have on my weight. This soon accelerated to the stage where I simply would not eat these things.

Before I knew what had happened, I was bulimic. Or rather, it was a severe form of weight management. I did this for a couple of years around the age of sixteen. In my mind, the only way I could keep my weight down was by making myself vomit. It was very easy, too. I have since found out that I have a herniated valve on my stomach that doesn't close properly, which essentially means that I can voluntarily make myself bring the contents of my stomach back up. Some people can't make themselves sick even if they try, whereas I can do it without putting my fingers down my throat, because my stomach is effectively open. As I write this, I could decide to do it and that would be that. This herniated valve is not uncommon, apparently, and is often found in people who suffer from constant indigestion, but obviously the way I utilised this medical condition during my late teens was not ideal.

I don't remember being a wafer, though. At first I was just very, very lean. I became skin and bone, but I weighed myself every morning, noon and night – in the evening, if I was half a pound heavier, I'd get in the pool and swim some laps or skip for an hour to try to burn off what was actually probably just water or a few ounces. I saw that as being very disciplined. Some people would say it was obsessive behaviour, but you don't achieve a certain level of success without some form of dedication.

Making yourself vomit to keep your weight down is obviously not something I would recommend to any aspiring race driver, or indeed anyone else with sensitive issues about their size. I can't help thinking a lot of jockeys must do the same. Within sports, however, I would suggest that those that achieve at the very highest level, can relate to what I have admitted here.

Looking back, I would recommend karting to anyone. Even if you have no aspiration for your kids to do anything in racing, putting them in a kart at a fun park at the right age – which can be as young as six or seven – is a brilliant idea. They will have a great day, but in the longer term it will prepare them very well for driving safely on the roads. I've seen it with children of my friends: they send out really young kids in a kart and they learn so fast. The kart will slide on a corner and they will just automatically, instinctively make an adjustment without being taught anything. It's like learning to balance on a bicycle, once they learn it they never forget.

When they grow older, it will definitely make them better road car drivers. This is something I've had many thoughts on over the years. It's not exactly hard to pass your driving test and then, suddenly, at the age of seventeen you can burn down the motorway doing 100mph in your old MkII Fiesta. The problem is, for many kids the first time they have a big slide is also the last time they get out of their car – in a box. If you have a big slide and it happens to be at the edge of a big hill or next to a tree, then sadly it's all over. However, if you've got a bit of awareness, it might save your life.

In a driving test you do very little in terms of 'losing control' of a car. You practise an emergency stop – which in many ways is dangerous in itself out on the road – then you can pass the test, go out and borrow your dad's Porsche if he's rich enough to insure you and then go fucking kill yourself, wrap yourself and your mates around a tree at 140mph. It happens.

I am involved in many businesses outside of Formula 1, but one of the ideas I've had that relates to racing is to take a bunch of cars around schools. If a company like Red Bull funded a batch of Smart Cars, you could take them to schools or colleges for sixteen-year-olds, free of charge, and show them some basic safety stuff. Schoolyards are always big and a Smart Car is small, so it could be done after school or even during the day, so long as everyone turned up and learned something. Better to run over a cone than a kid. I could do some of the classes and organise a team of people to teach them the basics. There's always funding issues with ideas like that, but given the number of deaths on British roads from teenagers in cars, it really is something that would make a difference.

I personally don't feel I was given enough road experience before I set off on the motorway in my red Renault 5 Turbo. That was a fast little car for an inexperienced driver. My first car was actually a van, so there had been little to worry about with speeding. It was a red Mercedes 508D van that my father had previously used for his Coulthard Racing team. It was great, it had a couple of bunk beds in the back, a wee kitchen, all that sort of thing. I could load it with friends and go out, it was perfect. It wasn't very fast, but it had two gear boxes, a

four-speed and a five-speed box – there must have been problems with it at some point – and the five-speed got you an extra
ten miles an hour out of it, but flat out it could only reach
75mph and even then it would make a noise that rattled your
bones. My father's still got the shell of that Mercedes in the
garage of the haulage business – he's a collector-holic, and it is
entirely down to his hoarding tendency that there is the David
Coulthard Museum in Twynholm crammed full with my first
kart and other cars from various series. It's funny really to
think of that red Merc wagon now, given my relationship in
future years in Formula 1 with that car manufacturer. I used
the van for a year before my father got me a Renault 5 Turbo. I
think it was his way of keeping me calm on the roads.

To get back to my point, I'd been racing for six years or so
when I got the actual car, so compared to my school-mates I
knew what I was doing, relatively. Looking back I used to
drive flat out around the villages as if it were a race track, but
somehow I survived. I normally did it at night, but I was still
taking a risk. That said, I don't consider myself to be a hooligan
tearaway teenager. By then I probably had an instinctive ability
to control the car, but the reality is you can't control what is
coming the other way or other hazards – if someone has broken
down and left no lights on the car on a single-track road, for
example. If I'd had less experience of karting, I would almost
certainly have wrapped myself around a tree somewhere.
Unlike Formula 1 cars, road cars like that are just bean cans on
wheels; any high-speed crash causes them to disintegrate, often
long before you hit the tree. But either way, you're dead before
you are out of your teens.

I see a lot of sportsmen do the same thing. They start to earn a lot of money at a very young age, so the supercars get bought and off they go in vehicles that can top 200mph. But they might only be twenty years old. Even more mature sportsmen make the mistake. Look at Naseem Hamed, who was jailed following a crash in his Mercedes-Benz SLR McLaren. I once saw a magazine article featuring sportsmen's car crashes and there were some horrific pictures in there.

I did put the Renault 5 in a ditch on one occasion, and got it towed out by a local builder. Luckily I'd only broken the front panel. Then I drove it down to my dad's garage, got a power wash to try and blast all the mud and shit off, but then got a bollocking from my mother for turning up late for lunch! 'Your lunch has been out for hours, David!' Believe me, since that was all that happened to me as a fast teenage driver, I was lucky.

I bought another Renault 5 Turbo a few years ago as a trip down memory lane and driving it around the back roads near Twynholm scared the shit out of me. I was driving along thinking, 'This is fucking mad!' Those Renaults could reach over 130mph and if the road was straight enough I'd get pretty close to that on many occasions. At the time you don't know any better. Thankfully, my karting at least gave me some basic skills to get me through those teenage years.

To prove my point, I think maybe Cawthorne might have benefited from a bit of karting. He's always been a crap driver and, unlike me, didn't pass his driving test first time. He eventually passed in his mum's Volvo and we were on the way back home when he scraped it down the full-length of another car. His dad could be a bit fiery at times, so I volunteered to break the news.

I knocked on the door.

'Er, hello Mr Cawthorne, I've got some good news and I've got some bad news ...'

'Hello David. What's the good news?'

'Well, your son has passed his driving test!'

'Excellent, and the bad ...?'

'He's crashed the car ... goodbye!'

... and off I ran.

YOUNG GUNS AND OLD BOYS

When I was at school I presumed I'd work in the family business, so when I left I enrolled in a business computing course at Dumfries Technical College, just to qualify myself to go into business. I never fancied driving one of my father's trucks or working as a mechanic in his garage. I'd done reasonably well at school, earning eight O-levels, as they were called then, and one 'Higher', but I knew I was not cut out for the academic world – although I would later be awarded an honorary degree from Paisley University!

I used to drive the twenty-five miles to and from college in the red Mercedes van and then my Renault 5. However, I only did a month or two of that course because I was away racing an awful lot and starting to win most weekends. I was able to keep the prize money, which was often as much as £150, and since I was winning so much and living at home with virtually no bills, for a seventeen-year-old, I thought I'd made the big time.

By contrast, my brother did go into the family business. I didn't really know my brother that well when I was a teenager.

He had the chance to kart race before I did, and he was very quick, probably more talented than me, but he just wasn't competitive enough. He liked to show off, but didn't like to compete; I didn't like to show off, but I did want to win. He generally didn't come to the motor-racing events the family attended, however, and had his own interests.

However, as I got into my later teens, we definitely became closer and now we are good friends. He's really into his motor-bikes ... I don't remember ever seeing him in a kart or a race car since those teenage days, even during all the years we went to motor-sport. He's got a few motorbikes, including a couple I gave to him. Once a year he and I will go on a cruise on the motorbikes; he's got three kids with his wife Monica, on whom he dotes – they live next door to my parents.

My brother was a bit wilder than me in his younger days, but at sixteen he headed off to do his mechanics apprenticeship – just like our father had at that age – albeit at a different firm, Curries of Dumfries. Father knew the owner and wanted Duncan to learn early. My father used to joke that when he was a kid they'd wake him up in the morning and the first thing they'd do was batter him for all the things he was going to do wrong that day. My brother started driving the small trucks, then the big ones and now he's running the business, so he's got a good all-round knowledge and is building up more and more experience of dealing with the customers every day – after all, it's a bit of an art and when you can do it like my father it's because you are a bit of a showman.

My sister Lyndsay raced too, and she was *very* fast. Again, she wasn't as dedicated as me, but she was very quick. Looking back, twenty years on, I think it was almost mapped out: my brother would take over the business and I was going to be a racing driver. My sister was always far more inclined away from commerce and studied to be a care assistant. I started karting when she was only five so, in a way, I've been an absent brother to her, because I was away most weekends and I left home before she was even in her teens.

My brother and sister always supported me too, even though they would not go on to race professionally themselves. I don't remember any jealousy from my brother at all; he simply chose not to come to races and would usually be at home. He just wasn't competitive in that respect and didn't want to race. Lyndsay always supported me and came to races, they were both great.

Now my brother pretty much runs the business and my father generally just keeps a watchful eye on things (when they are both working in the offices, people phone in and ask for either 'Daddy Dunc' or 'Young Dunc'). We have tried to get my father to slow down for years. Eventually, I bought a place for them in La Manga in Spain and that seems to have encouraged him to spend more time relaxing and less time working. He has a tendency to be a bit of a Doomsday merchant, worrying about losing big contracts and things like that, but I realised quite early on that this was what drives him to keep going, to keep sharp. To this day, I'll phone him and say, 'How's the business father?' and he will launch into one, 'Oh, the bloody government, this-and-that ...' and I'll say, 'Yes, but are you making money?' to which he will reply, 'Well, yes, of course ...' I laugh sometimes, because he's a bit like some farmers in that way, a person who might tell you that nothing is working for them, before driving off in a Range Rover Sport.

I really admire how my father has made such a success of the business. Even when he took over at that relatively young age, it was clear he had an uncanny ability to form warm relationships with people, so much of his business was based on personal contacts and social skills, interacting with people. A lot of the people he's had business dealings with over the years – even the really big companies – have ended up becoming family friends. The people skills he has have proved applicable with much of my later dealings in racing motorcars. He is acutely aware that he provides a service to deliver that load from A to B in that time frame and, more importantly, that there's always someone who can do it for £5 cheaper. That might not sound like a lot, but over the course of a year, with a thousand loads, then it starts to save money. So you've got to give something else, and he does: as well as providing a first-class service and insisting on all of his vehicles being immaculately presented, he *entertains* them. He wines and dines them; he takes them to grands prix; he makes them feel special and builds a personal relationship with them. Human interaction is everything in business. Father is an absolute expert in that. I've watched him and learned so much from seeing what he does best.

I'm not sure how many hundreds of thousands of pounds my father spent over the years to get me to F1, but it was an ongoing situation and a huge amount of money was required. Given that he had another son and a daughter, as well as a wife and a business to support, it was an incredible commitment.

So, in many ways, the relationship with my father has been more of a business one than a normal father-son relationship. Having said that, I don't know what a 'normal' one is, because he was effectively managing my career from an early age, so it was often more business than anything else. That is in no way a criticism, though, not at all. The effort my father put in has actually created a very strong father-son bond, and even though we speak a lot less now than when I was living at home, that closeness is still there. That doesn't mean I call him up every day. I might on occasion go weeks without calling him, but I really have a great deal of respect for the way he was able to run a family, a business and help create a career.

If you think back to his position and what he was doing for me, it was incredible. It was the ultimate in long-term investment, believing that ten years down the line I would be in Formula 1. The strength of his belief is reflected in the fact that he kept all my helmets, suits, most of the karts, trophies and other stuff, which he seemed to see as 'memorabilia' even back when I was just a teenager coming through the ranks. I would struggle to invest in something that might not come to fruition for a decade, because God knows how much things can change in a decade.

My mother has held the whole family together and helped massively to make my racing possible, looking after her husband and three kids, cooking, keeping the house, coming to races, and somehow still finding the time to be with her own family and do fundraisers and all that sort of stuff. It is amazing, I really don't know how she did it, she was a rock. They are both incredible people. Looking back as an adult, I can clearly see and fully appreciate just how important that support was. As a kid, you just get on with it; you don't think of the level of commitment, money, time or demands on a family, you are just a kid racing karts. But now, I can appreciate how incredible their commitment was.

What is amazing is the way they encouraged me, despite everything they had going on in their hectic lives, knowing that if I did make it to Formula 1 – or indeed various racing formulas – my job would ultimately take me away from Twynholm and, by definition, away from them. As parents they always put me first.

Very occasionally, in among all the flights, travel, testing, races and madness that goes with being a Formula 1 driver, it is easy to – not forget, never that – but not to give my parents as much attention as they deserve. When this happens, I quickly remind myself of what they did for me and get cross with myself for perhaps rushing Dad off the phone or something like that. For instance, as I was actually writing this book, my father called, chasing me to get some replica helmets sorted, which I knew were in the system and being processed. He is a very persuasive and persistent man, he just pushes and pushes and pushes, that's how he gets things done, he just doesn't let go and that is why he is so brilliantly successful with the haulage business. That day, I had other things going on in my mind rather than worrying about his helmets. So I was a little bit brief, you know, 'I cannae talk about that right now, I'm just in the middle of something…' But, in fact, his happiness should be my *primary concern* and the first thing I should worry about. His and my mother's, my family's, happiness: nothing else really matters. I will never forget what they did for me.

When you look back at career stats on a piece of paper, it all looks very planned and deliberate. However, I have to be honest and say that when I first made the jump from karting to Formula Ford for the 1989 season, I didn't really want to. Left to make the decision myself, I wouldn't have done it. I was really enjoying karting, but my father wanted me to go into cars. I wanted to do another year of karting, but he was like, 'No, this is the right time, David, you should go in to cars now.' It wasn't just the karts themselves, which I loved; it was the people. Once I made the jump into cars, for instance, Dave Boyce would no longer be involved in my racing – don't forget I was seeing these people several times a week and for long, long hours, testing and racing all over Europe, so for a teenage boy it was quite a big change.

When I first sat in a Formula Ford and took it around the track at Knockhill, it confirmed my worst fears. The new car felt so unresponsive compared to a kart. I was used to driving a kart that was nimble, quick, very reactive; in many ways a good kart is very similar to a grand prix car. Yet these Formula Ford cars felt big and soft, with a 110bhp engine, which felt like there was no power, plus they shook all over the place. It felt worse to drive than a kart and certainly wasn't as enjoyable.

What made it more uninteresting was that, on race weekends, there were no heats: you'd qualify then wait around all day, do one race, then go home. I was used to a frantic weekend of karting: practice on Saturdays, more practice on Sunday, then heats, then the final, it was non-stop. Formula Ford felt so dull by comparison.

However, deep down I knew perfectly well that at some point I needed to make that step up, but it was just so disappointing that the cars felt so sluggish and unrewarding. I managed to eek out a couple of final kart races, but Formula Ford was ultimately the way forward. If you have reached the top of a particular job, genre or in this case series, you have to change the scenery. If you swim in the same pond over and over, you'll keep bumping into the same sharks, as they say, so if you want to progress, you've got to make the move. Senna and all sorts of guys started in Formula Ford, so it was accepted as the second rung on the ladder.

To make the move, the first thing we did was drive all the way down to Norfolk to the Snetterton race circuit to speak to Ralph Firman, the owner of Van Diemen, who had famously made Formula Ford cars for years and years. We were asking him who should run us in Formula Ford, how do you do it, all sorts of questions, and he recommended a guy called David Sears, who had a unit just over the road from the race track.

Unfortunately, he was out to lunch and we needed to get back up the road to Scotland. It was a very long drive and we really couldn't hang around. So we drove from Snetterton back home and, as we passed Carlisle, decided to go and meet a guy called David Leslie Sr, who had a Fiat dealership in that town – my dad had raced karts against him. David Leslie was a very accomplished racer and his son, also called David, was part of the operation, too – he was a kart champion himself and would go on to race in Formula Ford himself as well as the British Touring Car Championships, among others.

One of David Leslie's drivers at the time was Allan McNish, who I pretty much grew up racing against – although, when I first started, Allan was by far the most well known of all the Scottish karters. He went on to race in many series, including Formula 3, Formula 3000, he won Le Mans with Porsche and, after testing for McLaren and Benetton, he was the race driver for Toyota at their F1 debut in 2002. He was always a couple of steps ahead of me. We agreed a deal with David Leslie – it was relatively straightforward, because for Formula Ford you need just a driver, a mechanic and a truck to get you to the circuits (that said, I think the budget was still about £50,000 which my father had to find through sponsors such as Eternit – this covered Leslie's wages, but also all the considerable expenses of running the team for a year).

With so many Davids, we ended up calling ourselves DC, Cawthorne, Father David and Young David. Through Ralph Firman, Father David negotiated the use of an old 1987 Van Diemen for me to practise in around Knockhill, in Fife, and then we bought a brand-new, bright red Van Diemen RF89 in the winter of 1988 to race in the following year's campaign. We stopped karting as late as the October and that autumn and winter Father David and Young David taught me how to race Formula Ford.

I got to grips with the new car very quickly, but I still didn't like it. My memories of Formula Ford are of slow, soft cars. You'd hit a kerb and, because there was suspension, the wheel would wobble and move on you. It also reminds me of bitterly cold, freezing days of endless testing at Knockhill over the Forth Road Bridge – where it was so cold they didn't race during the winter at all. We tested relentlessly over the winter, at pretty much every circuit that would be included in the forthcoming season. I have to admit, at my first test I hated it; I really wanted to pack up, go home and return to karting.

However, we persevered and it grew into a fantastic experience for me as well as a very successful year competitively. We competed in two series, the Dunlop Star of Tomorrow and the

P&O Ferries Championship, both fourteen races apiece. The tracks we used were established names such as Silverstone, Brands Hatch and Donington. I won the first race of the season by almost seven seconds, against Kelvin Burt, who had been sweeping all before him the previous year, and we never looked back. I won the next four races, too. Eventually, at season's end, I'd won both the junior championships that were running, with twenty-two out of twenty-eight races won. That was effectively the springboard on which the rest of my career was built – I also started to attract my first snippets of press coverage in magazines such as *Motoring News*. I wasn't interested in the adulation, but I was aware that coverage would help my chances of being spotted by major players higher up the motor-racing ranks. I also started to learn more about the mechanics of the cars, which was another progression that would obviously benefit my racing.

As my father owned the trucking business, he bought an old twelve-and-a-half-ton truck from a Suzuki motorbike team, got his mechanics to kit it out with living accommodation at the front, bunk beds, a little kitchen and a workshop at the back, and got his body workshop boys to spray the livery – it was basically a more advanced version of the van we'd had in karting. We got sponsorship from a building product supplier called Eternit, which made roofing tiles and stuff like that. We did a launch and had a beautifully turned out racing team, which consisted of David Leslie Senior, a mechanic who worked in the garage with them and occasionally his brother-in-law, who was an old boy called Walt. David was in his sixties back then, so too was Walt. So many times it would be the two old boys and me. We spent a lot of time together, what with the two series to compete in and all the winter testing. We'd drive miles and miles with each other in this truck, never going above 65mph – sometimes we wouldn't talk for hours and other times we'd chat away constantly about all sorts of things. Invariably, we'd win the race and then go home back up to Scotland.

We'd set off from Carlisle, head down to whichever track was being used, win the race, then drive back up to Carlisle; then, first thing on a Monday morning, I'd drive the hour's journey back over to Carlisle to strip the car, clean it and do anything else that was needed. Sometimes I would stay over at Father David's, and he still laughs that I was the only young driver he worked with who offered to do the dishes.

When we were on the road, I used to cook for the old boys. We'd all sleep in the truck, with David and Walt in the bunk beds which folded down into a sofa and me up in the top of the front of the truck. There was a little kitchenette there, so we had everything we needed.

When we raced at Silverstone, I would get up early, go and wash my face and hair in the sink in the toilets – the truck did not have a shower – and then come back to get the breakfast on while they got the car out of the truck, fuelled it up and prepared to go testing. It was always a full Scottish breakfast, tattie-scones, eggs, all the rest of it, because I'd always have a cooked breakfast on the Sunday when I was racing karts, it was a tradition. I'd go out and test all morning then come back and have lunch, either sandwiches made by me or some soup my mother had prepared for us.

In Formula Ford, you only had the one car, so you knew that if you had a big shunt it could end your season, or certainly curtail your chances of the title by the time any major repairs had been carried out. That said, although they felt so soft to drive, as I said, they were actually very sturdy cars and you'd need to try really hard to destroy the chassis. I think I had only two minor crashes that year, both causing just minor body damage. Throughout my career – and I don't want to tempt fate! – I've never really been a 'big' crasher, which is fortunate I guess. I really enjoyed that Formula Ford year and, after the last race of the season, I cleaned the car off and put it in my father's museum in Scotland.

It was a very cost-effective partnership, and Father David was totally confident in my abilities. That was very enriching for me at that stage, a great boost. He is an amazing character, a real wise head and a man of very few words. Scots would call him 'canny'. I remember he was once asked about my chances for the forthcoming seasons and he said simply, 'He'll no' win them all, but he'll win most of them.' It turned out I did.

As well as being the first formula I did in cars, my year in Formula Ford was also the very first time that I was shocked at how fast some people raced. Not actually in the Formula Ford series – as I said, that felt slow – but as a result of an incident at testing at Silverstone. It was an open test day, so you had all sorts of different formulas out on the track. At one point, a Formula 3000 car literally flew past me, going several seconds a lap faster. At the time, that was the formula just below F1. I was incredulous. I vividly remember seeing this car disappear around a corner and thinking, 'How the fuck does he have the reaction time to drive that fast?' It was absolutely shocking.

In many ways, that could have been very demoralising, because at that point it was hard to comprehend that anyone could race that fast, never mind even faster in an F1 car. But what you learn is that everything becomes relative – you may have more horse-power, but you also have more grip, and the cars are so much more capable, as indeed are the drivers. You become acclimatised to the faster speeds and your cars are much more advanced. Over the years, I have found the jump up into faster cars, getting used to the new speeds, handling, how much quicker the corners come up on you and so on takes about half a day. As an example, when I finally made the leap into Formula 1, I'd been in Formula 3000 for two years. So instead of driving the straights at 180mph, I was taking them at 200mph, which actually isn't all that different (unless you hit something!).

Some people at that time did a year of junior Formula Ford then went on to do another year in the senior category of that series, but I had designs on moving on. Before I did, I went to the Formula Ford Festival at Brands Hatch, which attracted the international elite of this series. Against a legion of better-equipped works cars, I managed to finish third, which I was very pleased with, it was a fantastic result. Previous Festival achievers included Johnny Herbert and Jenson Button. That season we'd won the majority of the races, we really were blasting people off the track and the eyebrows of the motor-sport elite were starting to be raised.

That season in Formula Ford was indeed a springboard for several reasons. It made me mentally adapt to racing cars not karts and after all the success we enjoyed, perhaps for the first time I started to think that the dream of racing an F1 car could actually become a reality. Further, my success got me noticed. Formula Ford enjoyed limited coverage in the motor-racing media, so my name was being used in articles and in results. Teams in higher formulas watched Formula Ford for future talent. It was a great breeding ground. And, perhaps most significantly that year, I won the McLaren/*Autosport* 'Young Driver of the Year' Award. The prize? A test in a Formula 3 car but, most importantly, also a test drive in a McLaren Formula 1 car ...

STEPPING UP THE STAIRCASE

Imagine this: you are an eighteen-year-old aspiring racing driver, the phone in your dad's garage rings and ex-world champion and living legend Jackie Stewart is on the other end of the line. This happened to me at the tail-end of my season in Formula Ford. At first I thought it was one of my mates impersonating Jackie and winding me up, I was just a young naïve kid at that time. I'd met Jackie and his son Paul very, very briefly at a few Formula Ford races, which were occasionally support races to the higher Formula 3 championship; he had also been at the Café Royal for the *Autosport* award ceremony, where I'd scooped my forthcoming test drive in a Formula 1 car.

Jackie had designs on creating a three-tier race team based in Milton Keynes, catering for Formula Vauxhall Lotus, Formula 3 (which Paul was racing) and Formula 3000. He set up Paul Stewart Racing (PSR) and called it his 'Staircase of Talent' and, over the years, it has proved a very successful concept – many of his drivers have gone on to successful Formula 1, Sports Car or Indycar careers. Allan McNish is a Le Mans winner; Gil de

Ferran has taken the chequered flag at the Indy 500 and two Champ Car titles; and Juan Pablo Montoya – the chubby chap and potential future Michelin model – has also raced and won in both F1 and Indycar.

Jackie obviously knew I was Scottish, knew my results in Formula Ford and so gave me a call. For him, it was simple. For me, it was a big shock. I could have fallen over.

Jackie would prove a huge influence on my career, much more so than people like Jim Clark for example, because he's actually been active in my career – not in a managerial way, but in the way he has advised, helped and influenced me. PSR had been established only as recently as 1988 but, by 1989, Paul was moving up to Formula 3 – at that point the feeder formula for F1 – and so the following year they offered me a contract, which basically scheduled drives in each of the formulas.

I started off on Jackie's staircase of talent and would go on to compete for his team in each of the levels. That first season was a free drive, meaning that I didn't have to provide the racing budget for the season, that all came from PSR. I also had the opportunity to put sponsors' badges on the suit, such as my father's company and another couple of small sponsors which, in theory, paid for my living accommodation and stuff like that. And with the contract to race for Paul Stewart Racing came a very big development in my life: I moved out of my home in Twynholm and into a shared house in Milton Keynes.

I remember setting off from Scotland to make the journey down to Milton Keynes, a trek of several hundred miles. I still had the Renault 5 turbo at the time, but that was too small so I borrowed my mum's BMW, which had a real nasty body kit on it, crammed it full with all my stuff and then set off. It felt weird because, although I had made the trip down south hundreds of times over the years for racing, it was always with someone else driving, I'd never actually driven down myself. I actually said to my father, 'What roundabout do I get off on the motorway for Milton Keynes?' and he said, 'There aren't any bloody roundabouts on the motorway, you silly boy! Here's the map, on you go.' After several hours and only a few wrong turns, I turned up in Milton Keynes and that was it, I started living away from my childhood home.

I never went back.

At first, I'd visit home for a couple of days as often as I could. I'd do the drive in the middle of the night, because I don't like traffic. If you left Milton Keynes at eleven at night, you could comfortably do the 300-odd miles in four hours without going crazy. I'd go home on a Monday, spend Monday night, Tuesday night with my parents, then come back down again on Wednesday morning, because at that stage I'd rather have been at home than hanging around in Milton Keynes. I lived with a couple called Brian and Dawn Parias. Brian used to race karts and Dave Boyce knew him. They used to call him 'Fatty Parias' because he was a chubby chap, but they were lovely people and really looked after me. I lost contact with them eventually; it's one of the things I'm not very good at in life, keeping in contact with people. Not because I don't want to, it's just my life moves onto another phase very quickly and I simply don't have the time or the energy while doing what I do.

They'd moved there from up north to run their own business together out of Milton Keynes, which at the time was undergoing a period of huge investment and growth. Brian and Dawn had a very young son at that time (they have two grown-up sons now) and, when I look back, it was great of them to let me live with them during such a hectic period of their life. I didn't want for anything. That family took care of me and, I suppose because I was only a kid, I didn't really appreciate what they did for me at the time as much as I might have. I was paying them £50 a week for the smallest room in the house, but for that Dawn was cooking all my meals and doing the laundry. They were a young married couple, so I am sure there were other things they'd have wanted to do with their time.

Eventually, after about a year, I moved out of Brian's house. During the course of my three years with Paul Stewart Racing, I lived in various houses sharing with mechanics and other racing personnel; then eventually, in 1993, I rented my own house, also in Milton Keynes. For this entire period, I lived, breathed, ate and drank racing cars. I used to go the factory every day – it was never more than half a mile away – and I'd stay there for hours, looking, learning, taking everything in. In 2006, I drove past one of the houses I'd lived in during my spell in Milton Keynes, because it is a stone's throw from my current team, Red Bull's factory. It was a little detached house with the garage fixed to the side so you can walk into the kitchen from the car. When I lived there, people in the same cul de sac never spoke to me, so perhaps I've had a bad example of that lifestyle. Funnily enough, when I got to Formula 1, all of a sudden if I saw one of my ex-neighbours in Milton Keynes, they'd be like, 'Hey! Alright Dave!'

It was during this spell living down south that my father started to have less day-to-day involvement in my racing career. Obviously the geography made his physical presence largely impractical, especially when combined with looking after his business in Twynholm. Ultimately, I would get my own managers and his role would become increasingly diluted. I think this transition was probably more difficult for my dad than it was for me. To my mind, it was a natural progression of moving down south. I can see how it must have felt odd that he had been involved in every race and every day and then – quite suddenly – that involvement was not there anymore.

The biggest influence on my career was Father, for sure, and for someone who doesn't actually know about cars technically or the structure and politics of a team, his passion and drive was incredible. He encouraged without being pushy – we've all seen pushy dads and dominant parents, but my father was very happy to be in the background, despite being so heavily involved. He was my guiding light.

My time in Milton Keynes also introduced me to one of my closest friends, my team-mate in Formula Vauxhall at PSR, the Brazilian driver Gil de Ferran (who is now sports director of Honda). Gil was a little older than me, so he was good to be around; neither of us had a lot of money and would often share accommodation when we were at races in Britain and Europe (we even sometimes shared a room in Milton Keynes). We rarely argued, apart from when we'd had the odd coming together on track – such as at Zolder that first year, the opening continental race of the season. On the very first lap he was in front of me and I ran into the back of him, cut his tyre and the resulting puncture retired him from the race. Meanwhile, my car was relatively untouched and I went on to finish on the podium. I remember him hanging over the pit wall giving me the wanker sign and the V's, he was so angry. The race was in

Belgium and we had to share a car all the way back home to Milton Keynes – and he didn't utter a single word to me for the entire journey! Apart from that, we have been great friends for many years now and it is a pleasure to be godfather to his daughter, Anna.

We were in Belgium because the UK series was supplemented by European races for the Formula Opel Lotus Euroseries. Despite being many observers' pre-season favourite, I didn't win the first UK race of the season, at Donington. The main incident of note in that season was a big crash I had at a European series event in Spa, Belgium, where I broke my leg and subsequently missed a few races in recovery – the only time in my career I have missed races through injury. In the process, it scuppered any hopes I may have had of winning the 1990 championship. I was nudged into a spin on the first lap by another car and hit the barrier fairly innocuously, but the impact left me facing the wrong way and stranded. When the car of Alain Plasch also spun, he unluckily – for both of us – smashed straight into me.

I found out later that my parents had a pretty horrible experience because of this accident. The radio communications were poor and there was no conversation going back and forth between where the crash site was and the garage. Even when I was receiving medical attention, my parents, who were waiting anxiously in the garage, had no idea what state I was in. In fact, they have since told me that when they first arrived they were told to 'expect brain damage'. That's a pretty bad mistake to make when you are talking to someone's parents.

There was a certain poignancy to the crash for my team principal Jackie Stewart, too. It was there at Spa in the 1960s that Jackie had suffered a life-altering crash. He spun off and ended up trapped in a ditch. Incredibly, he was stuck for thirty minutes and only managed to escape the wreckage of his car with the help of two fellow drivers and a spectator's toolbox. He later labelled that old version of Spa 'a circuit of many dangers' and was so shocked by his predicament and how much danger the lack of safety precautions had put him in, that he started campaigning for better standards in motor-sport – over the years Jackie has probably done more for the sport's safety than any other driver.

Fortunately, there is a rather more light-hearted memory that stands out for me from that day at Spa. My mother – and I bet I'm not alone here – used to say to me, 'You should always wear clean underwear just in case you have an accident.' Well, that day in Spa, I did have an accident and I was wearing possibly the most weathered and battered pair of pants known to man. Why? Because they were my 'lucky' pants. Yes, the urban legends are true, drivers do have lucky pants, lucky gloves, and so on. Not all drivers – and not all their underpants – but our lives can be very ritualistic and, at this early stage, the ritual for me involved my lucky underpants.

My Aunty Elaine had bought me a couple of pairs of pants when I was in karting and they were really comfortable. I wore them for a few races and won every time. So I kept wearing them – having them washed in between races, I'd like to point out. After about two years of racing in them, they were worn through, littered with holes and looking really unsavoury. But I kept winning, so I kept wearing.

After the crash in Spa, I was taken back to the medical centre and, in front of Jackie Stewart and my parents they started to cut off my race suit. I was lying there, leg broken, still stunned from the crash thinking, 'Shit, my lucky underpants are about to greet the world ...' They cut my suit off and there I lay, in all my glory, my pants with more holes than cloth left, my bollocks hanging out of one hole, my dick falling out of another, it was a sorry sight. My mother was mortified.

I retired the pants after that debacle. It seemed only fair to put them out of their misery. And no, they are not at the museum in Twynholm ... actually, I have to admit, for years I carried them with me to every race. I have a little bag I take to races with odd little keep-sakes in. I don't really consider myself to be superstitious, but I had a St Christopher from my great-grandmother, some gold coins that someone else gave to me and those lucky underpants. Fast forward another six years to my time at McLaren, a team famed for its clinical precision and immaculate presentation, and those lucky pants were still in my little bag. Then, one day, a McLaren employee was cleaning my things, saw these pants – which in all fairness were by then over a decade old – and threw them away. I don't remember if I won that day or not, but I do recall my bag seemed a lot fresher.

Now I have about forty pairs of Australian hole-proof under-wear, which are very comfortable. Normally I wear boxer shorts, but when I'm driving I wear jockies. When I go to Melbourne I stock up on new pairs, always grey. So there you have it, F1 – a sport of space-age technology, lightning-fast motor cars and ... lucky underpants.

The leg didn't feel that painful after my crash at Spa and I even went home before realising there was something badly wrong.

They put me in a plaster after the crash, but as soon as I came back to the UK I went to see the F1 doctor Sid Watkins and he immediately cut this off, telling me that if I left it on I wouldn't be able to race again for ages. He bandaged it and said that was the best way of getting back in the car quickly. So the whole episode at Spa – broken leg, warnings about brain damage, Jackie Stewart looking at my lucky pants – was a slightly bizarre scenario. I managed to recover in time for the season finale at Donington, only to be disqualified for supposedly making a false start. My year in Formula Vauxhall Lotus with PSR had been a modestly successful campaign, although I only actually won two races. I finished fourth in the domestic series and fifth in the European one.

One of the problems I've had in writing this book is that I've been racing for so long I don't remember how driven I was back when I was just a teenager. By the time I was nineteen, because of some excess sponsorship my father was able to get, I had £30,000 in a bank account, which was just there as a contingency for when my racing needed it. Nana Coulthard had always given us £20 at Christmas, which was a lot of cash back then, and she very kindly supported my racing at times – when I was in Formula 3000 she contributed £30,000 towards my costs for the season. There came a point at PSR when I needed to contribute towards the drive, so without hesitation I withdrew all the money, every penny of that £30,000, and put it into the team. I went from having that money beside my name as a young man to not having any money at all, which perhaps shows my commitment. I never gave it a second thought.

*

The other obvious highlight of the year was my prize for winning 'Young Driver of the Year', that feted test drive in a McLaren MP4/5. Only Ayrton Senna and Alain Prost had driven this particular McLaren before me, so I was in the most illustrious of company. What is quite interesting to me is that I went to that test alone, my father wasn't there. Looking back, given the enormous influence he has had over my career, that seems surprising, but I believe he was just trying to give me some space to stand on my own two feet. I was just nineteen when I went along to Silverstone from Milton Keynes for the test. I went to the track, drove the car for a while, then went home and rang my dad to say, 'Yeah, that was fun.' My father had, after all, got a sizeable transport business to run and he has never been a 'paddock father'. He has been to lots of races over the years, hundreds, but he's never actually been that involved in the paddock. So, that day, I just went and did my thing and then came home. It was nice to drive the car: it is what it is.

The next progression on Jackie's 'Staircase of Talent' was to graduate to the prestigious Formula 3 series. Jackie himself had started his single-seater career in Formula 3 back in 1964, so this was a known path to F1 – he moved up to the top grade just one year later. Like the Formula Ford and Formula Vauxhall Lotus previously, I would spend only one season in this next step up the ladder.

Given my results in previous formulas, I was widely expected to win the Formula 3 championship, even though PSR was up against some heavily funded and highly successful teams. The white and blue Ralt RT35 was distinctly Scottish in flavour and was backed by predominantly Scottish sponsors, including my father's business. With Gil de Ferran replaced by, firstly Eduar Mehry Neto, then Andre Ribeiro, all eyes were on me. I was expected to win the championship. Unfortunately, although I came close to doing so, it all fell apart at the season-closer.

There were some solid performances, including winning at Silverstone in the wet after qualifying only seventh – poor qualifying would prove a millstone that followed me round for much of the season. I managed another four wins and headed to the final race of the year at Thruxton in a reasonably controlling position. If I won and my closest rival, Rubens Barrichello, finished lower than fourth, the crown was mine. Things didn't start well, with Rubens on pole and me back in seventh, but I'd won from that position before and felt confident. I had made my way up to third when the car in second – Hideki Noda of Alan Docking Racing – cut across in front of me and bent my wing, ultimately causing me to retire. Barrichello only finished sixth, but that was enough to give him the title, which was more than a little annoying, not least because I had won more races than him that year. To lose the championship in the last round was bitterly disappointing, even more so because it was the result of that coming together, rather than purely by being beaten to the line.

To counter my new-found tag as being average in qualifying, one of the positives to emerge from the season was my reputation for super-quick starts. I would often sit on the grid in sixth or seventh, but would be leading or in second by the first corner – like that day at Silverstone. Likewise, at the next round, I was on the second row of the grid, but reached the first corner in the lead. You can analyse it all you like, but starting so

77

quickly is just something that comes naturally to me.

Brighter moments had come with my mid-season victory at the European Marlboro Masters of F3 in Zandvoort in Holland, but perhaps the highlight of that season was when I travelled to Macau and won the so-called Formula 3 'Grand Prix' against the world's best drivers in that series (thus becoming the only driver ever to win both the European Championship race and the Macau race in the same season). That was a great race to win (it was actually a pair of races with an overall winner) and to this day the victory there is one of my all-time favourites because you had to beat everyone; you beat the Italian champion, the French, the German and so on. It was the cream of the crop from your formula on an amazing street circuit and the history books shone brightly on the previous winners, including Michael Schumacher and Senna. This was a race watched by the whole of motor-sport.

The win in Macau was particularly sweet as – aside from the prize money, which all helped with a new, expensive season approaching – it swiftly followed the disappointment of not winning the championship in Britain. To go out in rainy November to such an exotic location and triumph over all those elite drivers was very energising and extremely satisfying. It felt like I'd won the championship itself. At the time, it felt more important somehow than the title I'd lost out on, because Macau was something I was doing purely for the love of racing.

Macau was symbolic of how I view my life back then. Although at the time there was pressure, financial headaches, hard work and stress, I look back on that period of my life and career now with very fond memories, because it was so pure, so innocent. It was pre-bullshit, pre-media, and it wasn't for money: it was for the love of racing with a small group of people who believed in you.

No doubt, no politics, no media. It was as pure as racing gets.

As the winner in 1991, I was invited back the following year, even though by then I had moved up to Formula 3000. I knew I wouldn't win because I was out of that formula by then, but it was a great fun to go back. The race was also notable because it introduced me to my first serious girlfriend, Andrea Murray. I saw a picture of her in advance and knew she was going to be my 'grid girl' at the race. I really thought she was very beautiful and looked forward to meeting her. As soon as I got there, I chatted her up and she became my girlfriend – we spent four years together.

So I stepped down to Formula 3 to do that one-off race and was paid a couple of grand, which was the first time I was paid to race – as against earning money by winning or getting a podium.

That was 1992. By 1996, I was a Formula 1 driver, sitting in a 200mph McLaren.

I was ready for the leap into the F1 feeder series, Formula 3000, and with my still-glowing track record, expectations were growing. Unfortunately, the first of my two years in Formula 3000 at Paul Stewart Racing was a pretty sorry season. I was racing alongside Paul Stewart himself, but it was hard work. We had a decent chassis, but a new engine made by Judd, and the package just wasn't working very well. In the first round at Silverstone I started on the back row, twenty-fifth on the grid (ironically alongside Hideka Noda who had just crashed into me and ended my Formula 3 championship hopes). We had three DNFs, two being accidents, one being electrics, and only three top-five placings out of ten races. By the end of the season, I had scraped in a lowly ninth in the championship with only eleven points. Our budget was not insignificant, but we were regularly outperformed by lesser-financed teams. Although I closed the season promisingly – with podiums in the last two races at Nogaro and Magny Cours – overall it had been a pretty demoralising campaign. I had not won a single race all season for the very first time in my career. It was a blow to PSR too, as they had designs on evolving into a Formula 1 outfit and winning a Formula 3000 title would really have cemented that ambition.

I had my own designs on F1, of course, so you can imagine how delighted I was when I managed to get a bona fide test (rather than a prize) for the Benetton F1 team at the end of my first F3000 season with PSR. While I was racing Formula 3000, my manager at the time was a guy called Tim Wright from the huge sports management firm, IMG. The same agency also represented Senna and Prost way back and had some dealings with Michael Schumacher. I was being noticed, so it was arranged for me to do a test, providing I paid the insurance on the car, so that the team were covered if I crashed. We managed to get Crookes Health Care, who supplied pharmaceuticals to retailers like Boots, to fund the insurance. I think the figure for one day's cover was something like £20,000.

Unfortunately, the day arrived and it was wet and horrible. I couldn't exploit the Benetton's limits, so the performance of the car wasn't a shock. It was still brilliant though and it could have been worse – I have heard of some drivers raising the funds for a day and being totally rained off. The testing didn't ultimately lead to a full-time contract with Benetton, but it did contribute to me getting a later call to do some testing with Williams in 1993, courtesy of Iain Cunningham, a great friend who would go on to become my business manager for several years, more of whom later.

Further problems lay ahead with funding. Basically the money ran out to fund my climb up the staircase any further with PSR – we were talking about a figure in the region of £500,000 to £750,000 for the next season, which I would have to find with my father's help from sponsors etc – so I went off to a team called Pacific Racing – meanwhile my seat at PSR was taken by my old friend, Gil de Ferran. Although constant funding issues were very frustrating at the time, looking back there were silver linings to my predicament. It kept me hungry. I was always looking for the next bit of funding, the next opportunity.

At Pacific Racing, I was partnering Michael Bartels and the atmosphere in the team was friendly and focused, even though money was very tight (although there was enough to pay for a luminous pink, blue and orange livery!). The season-opener brought me in a modest thirteenth, but that was followed by a brace of second places before I topped the podium at Enna in Sicily, on a blistering hot day. Gearbox problems and poorer finishes meant the rest of the year was only average, but we had done very well on a small budget. Despite the much lower funding, I more than doubled my points tally compared to the previous season at PSR, got a win under my belt again and could have even challenged for the title – I managed to finish a very respectable third in the 1993 championship, behind Olivier Panis and Pedro Lamy.

Both of those drivers headed off into the sunset and a place in a Formula 1 team.

Many people don't realise I won at Le Mans when I was only twenty-two. It is obviously a very famous race, which I knew quite a bit about because my father used to go. He'd head off with a bunch of mates and they'd lubricate the few days abroad with plenty of beer and racing talk. He'd come back and tell me stories about what had happened and he'd buy the papers and read all about who had won. So it was a known race in our house.

I was in my second F3000 season in 1993 when the phone rang one day. I was still living with some mechanics and was actually looking for new digs. In the course of these various conversations to find a new place to live, it was mentioned that one friend worked for TWR, Tom Walkinshaw Racing, a team that was running a Jaguar XJ220 at Le Mans. Next thing I know, I get a call to ask if I wanted to race with them! I was doing reasonably well at the time, I had a track record in the lower formulas and so on, but it was still a surprising call to receive.

So off I went to Le Mans and donned my Jaguar outfit. My team-mate, David Brabham, son of world champion Jack, had the car literally drop on his foot after a jack failed at one of the pit stops, so it was just down to me and a driver called John Nielson to do the rest of the twenty-four hours. We also had a car fire and a fuel leak, but managed to get through all of this and continue regardless. They stuck me out mainly at night because they thought as a young guy my eyes would be better! To cut a long story short, we clawed back the Porsche team's massive initial lead and somehow won our class, which was the GT classification (intriguingly, there were two other XJ220s running, one being driven by none other than my old friend David Leslie Jr). I stood on the podium in front of a sea of British people and British flags and was lucky enough to enjoy the whole Le Mans experience. I'd dreamt of going to Le Mans, but I have to be honest, I found the whole event a bit boring.

I just remember it going on and on and on. You're not driving at 100 per cent because you've got to drive to an exact lap time to conserve fuel, so you are confined by strategy in a very limiting way. We won and collected the trophy and then, a week later, we were disqualified for not having the right catalytic converter. This piece of kit was standard on the road car, but had not been put on the race car. So I never got my prize money because TWR were never paid either, which I thought was a bit harsh. I kept the trophy though!

So I got to race at Le Mans. I know I might sound a little complacent or disinterested about what is one of motor-sport's most famous races, but it really was just one of those things I did on the way up. I'd done 'extra-curricular' activities before. For example, I'd also done a touring car race for Vauxhall in 1990, the year I broke my leg. Although I signed up for two races and they were paying me £500 to do each one – a vast sum to me at the time – I broke my leg after the first race and never competed in the second. I wasn't that bothered to be honest, because it was a front-wheel drive and I didn't really enjoy either the feel of the car or the race. It was like driving in a completely different way to what I was used to and I had little interest in pursuing it because my path obviously lay elsewhere. I was delighted: breaking my leg meant I didn't have to do both the touring car races – I guess that was the only positive. I found Le Mans similarly underwhelming. I know that many drivers dream of Le Mans and touring cars and many end up on those formulas or series at some point with great excitement. For me, if I am perfectly honest, it was just another step on the ladder to the F1 paddock.

TESTING AND BACON AND EGGS

One of what I consider to be the few 'pinch-me' moments in my life came in the Williams Formula 1 team garage at Imola in 1993. I was there as a test driver. I'd just come in to the garage and was sitting around waiting for the next lap to be called when I looked across and saw Alain Prost sitting in the other car.

I was only twenty-two years old, I had never been in a Formula 1 car in a competitive situation and here was a legend who I had admired all the way through my career, within arm's reach. The driver I looked up to the most was Prost. I liked the smoothness of his style, he was very efficient and not an aggressive driver. While I appreciated Mansell's talent for what it was, I wasn't drawn to him. Like millions of people, I had a great admiration for Prost.

I can honestly say that, at that precise moment, it didn't matter that I was yet to compete in a race. There I was, testing for Alain Prost.

That was a big moment.

*

Back when I was at Paul Stewart Racing, I'd become friends with a very proud Scot, Iain Cunningham, who would prove to have a very important role in my career. Iain's father is a board member of Ballantine's Whisky, an old established Scottish family. Iain is an only child and has been passionate about motor-sport all his life. Frank Williams went to school in Dumfries, so there was a connection there and Iain worked for Frank before moving to PSR, which is where our friendship started. I have learned an awful lot from knowing him and being his friend.

Iain then moved back to Williams and I've since found out he would regularly talk to Frank about me being a great driver and that he should keep an eye on my progress. Iain loves classical music and so does Frank, so they were good friends and spent a lot of time together – so Iain's endorsement of my future potential would have been taken very seriously. Consequently, I was delighted when I was offered a freelance contract testing for the Williams Formula 1 team in 1993, the same year I was still in F3000 for Pacific and charging around Le Mans. I categorically believe I got the test drive at Williams because of Iain knowing Frank so well; he had his ear and was a trusted aide. Normally marketing guys wouldn't be sitting there talking to the boss of a team, but because there was history between them, there he was championing my cause, and I am very grateful for that.

I loved testing. When you are a known driver with a seat for the season, testing can be demoralising, challenging and exhausting. But when you are an up-and-coming driver with everything to learn and you want to prove yourself, it is luxury.

In my time, I have tested for Mansell, Prost and Senna. Testing for drivers like that is a great experience, because you have none of the pressure they are under, but you're seeing all the inner workings of a first-class team: how they set up a car, how they go to work on a car and so on. It's just fantastic.

The test driver basically does all of the donkey work prior to the race drivers getting in the car – for example, in my first year testing for Williams, I did twenty-five separate full-scale testing sessions. The actual race drivers obviously test as well, but they can only afford to do so on a limited number of days each year, because of their commitments and travelling to the actual races – if you are racing in Australia, you are obviously not going to fly back for a three-day test at Silverstone, so the test driver steps in. Thus, the grinding lap accumulation and early testing is down to the test driver.

Every metre of every lap is recorded and you can look back on the computers at the dampers, throttle position, steering angle, gear selection, all of those things and a thousand more. The driver has to direct the engineer to so much data in order to give them a snapshot and discover where there might be a problem or potential for progress. So, as the test driver, you become like a conductor, because although there are all these computers in the garage, you are the one out there driving the car and the engineers can't see what is happening out on that track.

The test driver will do anything: driving up and down an airfield; what we call 'shaking a car down', which basically means a systems check; doing start practices to validate clutches; doing brake assessments; driving a car down a city street as a promotion for the sponsor; going to the factory to sit in a wooden mock-up of the chassis to see if the driver can fit; just doing all the mundane work that would be relatively tedious for the race driver – he tends to concentrate on performance-related issues. Once the test driver has picked out these various issues, the race driver will validate or work on the key ones. Test driving is essentially like any apprentice work.

If you think about it, however, there is a central flaw to the system, in that you are paying a relatively inexperienced driver to test the car. By definition, he will not, therefore, have the ability to spot things in the same way a more seasoned driver would. The system is essentially flawed. From my point of view, that is why I have done so much testing throughout my career, even when I was the main driver, because I've always wanted to feel the car for myself, rather than rely on someone else. You can rely on data analysis for some aspects, naturally, such as brake wear or overheating, but there is no better way to test a car than take it out on the track yourself.

Teams build up a trust with a test driver or main driver, too. I still do as much testing today as I did when I first started. It's vital. I can validate issues with more qualification, I think it is fair to say. Recently I was in Barcelona testing eight sets of different tyre compounds for Michelin – now there might only be one or two tenths of a seconds difference on the first lap, but I want to feel how *that* tyre performed on *that* lap. How do I think that tyre will operate on lap fifty in Budapest when it's hot and the team are telling me to push? No engineer, tyre expert or mechanic can tell you exactly how that will feel if they haven't been on that track in

Racing was in the blood, as this image of my father, Duncan, at the age of twelve shows.

Aged just thirteen months, and already I am being strapped into my seat.

In the garden with my elder brother, Duncan Junior.

On holiday in Barbados, in April 1982, just after my eleventh birthday. L-R: Duncan Junior, my father Duncan, Lynsay, my mother Joyce and me.

Lynsay, me, Duncan Junior and my father at home in 1984.

Celebrating winning my first Scottish Junior kart championship in 1983 with (above) sister Lynsay and cousin Donna Marshall, and (right) with Brian Smith and Dave Boyce.

Some of the gang who supported me in my early years racing, here at Silverstone in the early 1980s.

My twenty-first birthday party in Kircudbright, March 1992. (Above) Dave Boyce and David Cawthorne, and (right) me.

My debut year in cars, the 1989 Formula Ford season. At the end of it, I won the McLaren/*Autosport* Young Driver of the Year Award. (PA Photos)

Mike Gascoyne and Dave Ryan look on as I take a test with McLaren in 1989, part of my prize for being Young Driver of the Year. (LAT)

A very early interview with Murray Walker, 1991.

With Iain Cunningham (centre), a great friend who worked for Frank Williams, and so helped me get a test drive for Alain Prost (left).

OPPOSITE PAGE
(Above) A great example of having the team all around you. Jackie Stewart's PSR team was his 'Staircase of Talent'.

(Below) In action in the 1991 F3 race at Silverstone; at the end of the season I was ready to take the next step. (PA Photos)

My only win in the 1993 Formula 3000 season, at Enna in Sicily. (LAT)

Driving the Jaguar XJ220 in the 1993 Le Mans where we won our class – but it was all a stepping stone to where I wanted to be: Formula 1. (LAT)

With my father in his very tidy office, early in 1994. Little did I realise how my life was about to change. (PA Photos)

race conditions themselves. You have to rely on the engineers, and they have to rely on you.

Not everybody has a test driver because of the cost – it's not just his wages, there is also the considerable expense of running extra cars. Generally, the more successful teams have a three-car travelling circus going to the races, as well as a group of people at a test track working in tandem.

Some people are known to be good test drivers; some are known to be good qualifiers; some are at their peak only in a race. Before his 2007 drive for Super Aguri, Anthony Davidson was pretty much a permanent test driver. He did a couple of races for Minardi but, prior to 2007, it seemed entirely possible he might never graduate from being a test driver. It's a harsh sport and sometimes, if your face doesn't fit, being quick is not enough.

In my first year as a test driver, I was not paid by Williams; in the second, I got £20,000, payable as a regular retainer rather than the previous year's freelance arrangement. I was living in Milton Keynes and had relatively few expenses – pretty much all I ever did was race and test and train. It felt like an awful lot of money. By comparison, the third driver at Red Bull in 2007 will likely be *paying* as much as six or seven million euros for the privilege of that third place. His sponsors get some branding on his suit, but he has to bring that money to get the drive.

Testing is gruelling, that's why so many lead drivers don't do too much of it. The hours are very long. The first meeting is a briefing at 7.45 a.m. and you are usually still working around 7 or 8 p.m.. You regularly do over one hundred laps during testing days. That is knackering, let me tell you. What a lot of people don't realise is that test days are open to the public, or at least people who know sponsors or someone involved in F1. The garages at Silverstone, for example, are across a small tarmac'd lane from where I park my motorhome. It's only a few metres, but you can get swamped by fans and autograph hunters. I feel bad because there are people who have been coming to the grand prix circuit for years asking politely for autographs and you just feel so tired, but I can stand out there for ages sometimes just giving everyone the pictures and so on. Back when I was younger and had more time, I probably stood and talked to them all, but now I just put my head down, sometimes I don't even look at people I'm signing for because if you engage with every single person it adds a minute or so to every signature and if you've got maybe fifty signatures to get through . . .

Meanwhile, the team are sitting there with a multi-million-pound set-up, twiddling their fingers, waiting to go back out on the track. They are far more clinical about it, necessarily: I'm not there to sign autographs, I'm not there for a personal appearance, I'm there to work, that is my office.

It used to really eat me up if I turned someone down for an autograph because I didn't have the time to sign something. Now I am able to compartmentalise it more, as I know I can't give lots of time to everyone, I've got to save something for myself: after all, I'll be in a meeting at 7.45 a.m. and at 9 a.m. I'll be doing 200 miles an hour.

Of course, closed testing away from the public would be a lot easier for the drivers, but the sponsors get a lot of value out of letting clients and associates see this side of Formula 1 – on race day you don't get anything like that, the restrictions are much more severe. Open testing encourages the sponsors to invest more in a team, which means everyone benefits, including that driver who takes forty minutes to sign autographs every time he walks to the garage. So it comes with the territory.

The same could be said of the TV coverage. I've met various sports people who've said they couldn't imagine being interviewed like we are on the grid. In effect, if I am putting on my helmet and an interviewer approaches me, that is the same as being in the Real Madrid dressing room and talking to David Beckham while he is still lacing up his boots. It would be unheard of. But in F1 it's accepted, because it has a value in getting the sponsors on the grid.

I remember when Senna first came to the track when I was testing for him at Williams. He'd crashed in his first test for the team and hurt his neck, but on this particular occasion I was already out in the car when he turned up later in the day. I saw him in the garage and assumed he wanted to go out and run a few laps, but what he actually wanted to do – unbeknown to me at the time – was to check out what I was like as a test driver. I ran the car as usual then came back to the garage and went through the usual analysis with the engineers. I didn't know, but Senna was listening to all my comments and explanations of the car's performance, purely to see if I was, in his opinion, good enough to be his test driver, because it was the first time he'd worked with me. He must have been happy, because he buggered off at lunchtime.

Back on that day when I stood there like a startled rabbit, looking at Prost in the Williams garage, I didn't approach him or speak to him. I've never wanted to make a fool of myself. I'm very aware of the chain of command. Maybe that's because I was brought up in a fairly strict household where the children knew their place and you never spoke out of turn. I never did the Boy Scouts things past Cubs age, and certainly never the TA or anything like that, but I always like to adhere to the chain of command. I know how to respect the boss. In testing, I was always quiet and respectful, just got on with the job in hand.

So, despite my shock at seeing him, I didn't speak to Prost at all that day.

But it was a big moment.

Some people are very comfortable to walk up to anybody at any time, but that's not me. It's just something I've always carried with me. I never needed to run up to these people I admired, ask for an autograph when I was a kid or speak to them about racing in my later years, that wasn't my style. Just to see them from a distance was enough for me to acknowledge they were alive and real. Even though I was Prost's test driver, even though I was in the same team, in the same garage and all of those things, it was not in my nature to walk up to him and take up his time in that way. So for quite a while, I'd never actually spent any real time talking to him.

Iain Cunningham could see this and kindly organised for me to have breakfast at a local hotel with Prost when he was testing at Silverstone one time. That was quite a surreal moment. I went to a local hotel to meet him. I can't honestly remember a great deal about the day, except obviously I was a little nervous. Iain wanted me to meet Prost and talk with him about opportunities in the future, but it was all a bit strange because Damon Hill was there, too. Being considered a veteran of F1 now, I can look back and see that if a young gun came for breakfast with me, it might feel quite awkward, but Prost was very polite. I don't recall what we actually spoke about though, probably just bacon and eggs.

IT IS WHAT IT IS

At the end of 1993, despite the Le Mans win, despite mixing with the likes of Alain Prost and testing for Williams, my problems were looming large. As 1993 drew to a close, I did not have a race drive for the following season. I had a new retainer contract to continue testing for Williams, but with Ayrton Senna and Damon Hill as their two drivers for 1994, there was unlikely to be any room for promotion there. After one poor and one modest season in F3000, my glittering CV was now starting to look a little less dazzling. Motor-sport is all about momentum and names come and go as fast as the cars. As the winter of 1993 headed into the New Year, I was acutely aware that I needed to think, and fast.

Thus far, my journey up the ladder to an F1 driver had been reasonably smooth. Yes, the Formula 3000 seasons had been relatively disappointing, but that was racing. Yes, there were always pressures with money, but my father – although he was no longer involved in a day-to-day capacity with the racing itself – performed regular miracles in finding funding from lots of places. By the time we got to Formula 3000, the cost of a season was heading towards £750,000, as against approximately only £60,000 for Formula Ford – and my father even managed to find that money in three months. One year, the Inspector of Taxes took my father to court, claiming that he was using business money to fund a family pastime – my father won. The only person he could not defeat was my mother, naturally – one day when the suggestion was put forward about possibly looking into borrowing money against the house, she refused point blank to consider it, her argument being that this was the family home and it was not going to happen. It didn't happen.

I have since found out that my father would go to one customer and borrow money to fund me then, when that was due to be paid back, he would borrow off another customer to pay off the first one. Companies like Highland Spring Mineral Water have been big supporters over the years. It may have potentially been a house of cards, but my father's belief in me meant that he knew, in his mind, that it would all be paid back one day. And he was right. He paid off every single penny he ever borrowed. However, by 1993, it was becoming increasingly difficult to find the vast sums of money needed to continue racing, the financial expectations were just beyond even his amazing help. This was the moment my father finally had to sit me down and say he could no longer finance my career. He said, 'Look, son, I just can't fund you anymore. I can't get that kind of money together.' I wasn't disappointed. I knew he couldn't continue and it was unrealistic to expect anything different.

It was time to find the money myself.

One place I got short shrift from was Mr Frank Williams

himself and I still laugh now when I recall this meeting. I called his office and requested an appointment with him in private. He knew me as a test driver who usually wore jeans, so when I turned up in a smart, crisp new suit, he bluntly said, 'What are you wearing a suit for, David?'

Frank sat there unmoved as I proceeded to explain that I was very ambitious, hardworking, a solid test driver, keen to learn and so on and so on. We talked a little about him going to school in Dumfries, but I really wanted to make my point directly. I highlighted that another season in Formula 3000 would inevitably make me a better test driver for his own team and that being competitive all year would keep me sharp. He sat there and waited for me to finish what was a pretty rambling presentation, then said, very quietly, 'So, David, what is it that you are actually asking me?'

I had been put on the spot by one of Formula 1's most influential figures.

'I'd like you to sponsor me to race in Formula 3000 next season please.'

Frank just said, 'No.'

... and that was that.

It might seem bizarre, but at this relatively lofty level of racing, I was essentially starting the year scraping around for a budget and a car. I knew I needed to keep racing at that level, not least because there wasn't an obvious slot for me in Formula 1. I could not afford to remain still.

Frank Williams might have rejected my bid for sponsorship, but he did put me in touch with a Dutch businessman called Henny Vollenberg, who had made a lot of money from his own freight company, as well as an associate called Jan Willem, who I recall had various shops selling bikes and so on across the continent. I travelled to Holland and he agreed to help with the next season's funding. Eventually, through the various contacts of my father, my manager, Frank Williams and a few other friends, we somehow created a package for that first race.

Basically, by begging, stealing (allegedly) and borrowing, we'd got together a rudimentary set-up. I went with a team called Vortex, which was managed and part-owned by a guy called Ronnie Meadows who, in 2007, is team manager of Honda Formula 1. Ronnie was keen to get hold of a driver who was racing because he was *good*, rather than because he could pay for his drive. There is obviously a key difference. So we hooked up together and somehow got hold of a chassis, struck an engine deal with Cosworth and gradually got our package together for me to race the team's second Reynard Cosworth. I only signed the deal two weeks before the season started, so there was no testing, no forward planning and barely enough time to have my seat fitted.

The first race of the season was full of anxiety, because we were not sure where the money for the next race was going to come from. My personal kitty was certainly pretty empty: I had the contract to test for Williams, which luckily paid £20,000 for the year and was very welcome money indeed, but that was a drop in the ocean. These were financially very difficult times. On the day of the opening race, we actually paid the race engineer cash in a brown envelope, it really was hand-to-mouth racing, as shoestring as it gets. Incredibly, at that season opener at Silverstone I managed to finish second, the team's best ever performance – they'd never even had a podium before.

But there would be no celebration.

No one cared who won, lost or did not finish in that race.

No one cared what happened in any other race in the world on that Bank Holiday weekend except the Formula 1 Grand Prix in Imola.

On 1 May 1994, Aytron Senna was fighting off a vibrant Michael Schumacher at the San Marino Grand Prix. The safety car had been called out and, after the restart, Michael was driving brilliantly quick, leaving Senna battling hard to keep him at bay. During lap seven, Senna's Williams car smashed into a wall at 190mph on the Tamburello corner, a bend usually taken pretty much flat out. He was critically injured and later died from his injuries. Millions of people watched his accident live on global television.

The previous day, I had received a fax from the Williams team wishing me well for the forthcoming F3000 race at Silverstone. Autographed on the page was Ayrton Senna's name, with the words, 'Very best to you.'

I can tell you exactly where I was when I heard Senna had been killed. I was walking across the paddock to the motorhome and I stopped at the Avon truck, which was a tyre supplier for Formula 3000 at that time – they had this big screen there which showed the start of the grand prix and Senna's crash. I watched his car hit the wall and I can vividly recall thinking, 'Shit, that doesn't look good.'

The details started to filter through into the paddock and rumour about the severity of his injuries was quickly confirmed and then the grim news of his actual death spread. Later, I remember a guy called Jim Dunn, who works for *The Scotsman* newspaper, walking up to me and saying, 'Do you think this is your opportunity ... blah blah?' It was his job to ask questions, but I can honestly say the thought had never crossed my mind, it really hadn't. You'd have to be a pretty cold-hearted bastard to hear that your team-mate has been killed one moment and then think, 'Yes, that's my opportunity, this could be to my benefit.' I did not consider or think about how it would affect my position and career. It was just very, very sad.

In the immediate aftermath, I did not phone Frank Williams. I didn't go to the funeral either, just because I didn't think it was appropriate. I held great, great respect for Senna as a driver, of course I did, but my relationship with him was a professional one. I wasn't family, so it didn't seem appropriate to be at the funeral. Then, when I saw what a media spectacle the funeral actually became, I realised it wasn't just a small, private family affair after all. For me, it was a little bit strange to see Alain Prost carrying his coffin, because they clearly weren't buddies. Could I imagine that Senna would want Prost carrying his coffin, his fiercest rival, a foe whose battles with, and mutual animosity between, had been famous the world over? Maybe he would. Maybe he had underlying respect for him, I don't know. He was a deeply religious man, so maybe he saw it coming at some point and had thought about that. I don't know.

I went about my business, as I was paid to do. The next grand prix was Monaco, where Williams only ran one car with Damon Hill at the wheel. The following week I was testing in Jerez and was told by the Williams team other drivers there would be coming to test, like a kind of shoot-out to see who gets to drive. There were whispers about Riccardo Patrese and a few other names. I was fine with that. Formula 1 is nothing if not a competition; it is about winning, about being better than your rival.

There would be no rival.

No one else turned up.

Frank Williams flew down to Jerez and literally as he came through the gates I crashed the car! That was the first time I'd ever crashed a Williams and I couldn't believe my timing. Shortly after, I saw him in the garage and he said, 'Despite what you have just done to my car, I'm hear to tell you you'll be racing in Spain next week. That's our decision.'

People often ask me how I reacted to being told I was about to become a Formula 1 racing driver, did I jump up and down or cheer after all those years of racing, travelling, testing, training? I reacted exactly as I do to most things – when I was a kid, I was never the type to rip open a present and shout, 'Wow! An Action Man!' I'd just open it and say, 'Great, thanks.' That was my character then and it still is to this day. Obviously the context of Senna's death would have made shouting and cheering seem somewhat inappropriate, but I would never do that anyway.

I simply said, 'Oh, okay Frank, thank you.'

So that was that.

I was a grand prix driver.

On the Thursday afternoon before the Spanish Grand Prix, the Williams team announced to the world's media that I was being promoted to race driver. I was offered the drive on a race-by-race basis at this stage, starting in Spain, round five. Although there was much debate in the media and, indeed, in the paddock, about who should step into Senna's seat, the normal procedure would be that the test driver was effectively the reserve driver. However, despite this, it was perceived by many in motor-sport to be a sizeable gamble by Frank.

It is often said that Ayrton Senna told Frank that if anything happened to him, he wanted me to have the drive. I don't know if Senna foresaw his death, I know he was a deeply religious man so maybe he did. I also don't know if he ever said those exact words about me to Frank. What I do know is that Senna's manager, Julian Jakobi – who had signed the contract for IMG when I joined their management team – told me this story a couple of weeks after the funeral: Julian, Senna and Frank had a private conversation in which Senna stated he thought I was good and that I should get 'an opportunity'. Knowing this conversation had happened felt like Senna would have endorsed Frank's decision to go with me over the more obvious and established faces available to the paddock at the time.

In the days preceding my F1 debut, I hardly had any chance to get more familiar with the car I would soon be racing at Spain. The shunt Frank had witnessed in Jerez had been a big one, sufficiently so that I needed an hour's physio afterwards before I could get back in the car. Then, within minutes of going back out on the track, rain had halted the session. This meant I'd only had a handful of laps in the actual race car ahead of my first competitive Formula 1 grand prix.

Even when I had apparently been handed the F1 dream ticket, it was almost snatched away from me. The Senna death – and that of Roland Ratzenberger on the same weekend, who had been killed after his car hit a concrete wall at 200mph – had raised serious safety concerns. This was exacerbated a fortnight later when Karl Wendlinger was put in a coma after a dramatic smash in Monaco. The sport went into shock. These were the first deaths for twelve years and suddenly we had two dead drivers and one in a coma. The carnage years of the 1950s and 1960s – in 1957–58 twelve drivers died, *half the grid* – had given way to a new modern era of safety and most people had started to think of Formula 1 drivers as indestructible.

Not so, it seemed.

A power struggle ensued between Bernie Ecclestone, head of the Formula 1 Constructors' Association and Max Mosley, president of the FIA, the sport's governing body. There were arguments about the time needed to implement various proposed safety changes and, to cut a long and political story short, most of the team owners boycotted the Friday morning warm-up in Spain. From a personal point of view, I dearly wanted to run the car and get some miles under my belt. I'd literally done one lap shaking the car down in Jerez. I'd driven the old Williams, but not the actual current one. Eventually, after much speculation, it was thankfully confirmed that the race would go ahead.

Even then it wasn't straightforward. Prior to the actual race, Andrea Montermini had a huge crash, which shook a lot of the drivers up. I have to be honest and say it had pretty much no impact on me whatsoever.

I was raring to go.

The first time I drove the Williams in anger was in qualifying at the Spanish Grand Prix, my first ever F1 race. As I finally sat in the blue and white Rothmans Williams, awaiting the signal to head out on to the track for qualifying in a Formula 1 grand prix, it was a great moment. The team radio hissed at me and it was Patrick Head.

'Okay, David, we're not looking for anything dramatic, just take the car round, keep it off the kerbs, make sure you qualify.'

I couldn't resist . . .

'Thank you for that, Patrick. Remind me, when I pull out of the garage, do I turn left or right into the pit lane?'

THE LOGICAL EVOLUTION OF A
CHILDHOOD OF RAINY DAYS

People often ask me how amazing it must feel sitting on the grid with all those other Formula 1 cars, waiting for the start of your very first grand prix. It's a fair question, but one that I can only answer in what must seem like a subdued way – you don't think of it like that, *it is just another race*. I think this is why sometimes the public and media see new, young drivers and remark how calm and collected they seem to be in their first season. It's preparation, we don't know any different; we just get on with it. If you are wired and over-excitable at your first race, then you are going to be wired and over-excitable throughout your whole career. And being wired in a Formula 1 car is probably not the wisest thing you can do to yourself.

You have to remember, by this stage you've done hundreds of races, thousands of laps, and the step up to Formula 1 isn't a huge quantum leap, it is the next rung up the ladder. Also, from a physical point of view, by 1994 I was very well prepared; I did a lot of training every day and my body was ready for the rigours of Formula 1. Where a lot of people get caught out is in not being physically prepared. Then what happens? Simple, the body starts to give up on you and immediately you are limiting your capabilities.

Of course, there was a genuine concern that the second time I was to drive this car flat-out would be in my debut grand prix. Yet, I'd been in daily professional contact with the likes of Senna and Prost and had constant meetings with every level of the team, so it didn't honestly feel any different to my everyday job. The thought that maybe 150 million people were watching never entered my head. Why would it? I had a job to do.

My parents were probably more excited with the prospect. I phoned them after Frank had told me he was offering me the drive to tell them the good news. They've since told me they sat up late with a drink that night, chattering about what had happened – the last thing my father said before he fell asleep was, 'This is only the beginning ...' I later found out Dave Boyce cried when I ran in my first grand prix, as did my mother, who to this day keeps her fingers crossed for the entire race.

It happens less so now, but when I first started I was repeatedly asked the question about how did I feel knowing my career in F1 started because another man had died. I always said the same thing: of course, I would never have wished the start of my career through the death of another, that's a given, but it's a harsh reality of life and the business I am in that drivers come and drivers go. Usually they move teams, but sometimes they are killed or seriously injured. This was my opportunity and rather than reflecting on the loss of a great champion, I had to concentrate on my job. If I had done it half-heartedly and worried about something other than the car and the race, that would have been very disrespectful to the late Ayrton, so I just got on with it.

After qualifying ninth, I warmed up as fourth fastest and, in the race itself, I managed to battle up to sixth by charging around on the first lap – why change the habit of a lifetime? At one point it had looked entirely possible I could score a points finish, before escalating electrical problems ultimately ended my debut with retirement. Struggling against a dominant – and soon-to-be-champion – Schumacher, Damon Hill won, but for me the after-race news was even better – Frank said my performance was 'magnificent' and later confirmed that I would definitely start the next race, in Canada. My father still has a lunch menu I signed for him and my mother at that very first F1 race – he says, for him, that race is *his* highlight of my career and the menu is his favourite memento.

When we got to Montreal, the pits were buzzing with speculation that former world champion Nigel Mansell was considering coming back to Formula 1 for Williams, slotting it in among his current Indycar commitments (there was also talk of Alain Prost, but he would not consider coming out of his recent retirement). As a novice racer in the formula, with one 'DNF' to my name, this was obviously disconcerting news.

I got the race at Canada and did well, qualifying and finishing fifth – my first ever points score. I overtook Damon in the first corner which, given the pressure he was under as No. 1 driver after what had happened to Senna, probably wasn't very welcome. It certainly wasn't personal, I just wanted to race – ahead of me were Alesi, Berger and up front, Schumacher. Later, when my tyres overheated and I started to slow, Damon was on the team radio asking them to get me to move over. Eventually the team made the order and I obeyed. There were a few angry words sent my way after the race. That's motor-racing. It is what it is.

I scored my first point in only my second grand prix, but what the public didn't know was that I had lost the feeling in my foot during the race. Not long into the early laps, I realised I couldn't feel my foot under braking, which when you are driving at 200mph isn't an ideal scenario. I had a choice: (a) park the car and give in or (b) make do and struggle on. I did the latter, there was no option as far as I was concerned. I knew that if I stopped that was it, game over; if you try to finish, but the injury overwhelms you, then at least you've tried your hardest (I had a similar experience once when the underside of my seat was actually touching the track and I suffered quite a nasty burn to my buttock from the heat and friction). On this occasion I just couldn't feel my foot. It was a bit like severe pins and needles and I didn't really know how much pressure I was putting on the brake and I didn't quite have the same strength or control . . . but you adapt. It's amazing what you'll do when you feel you don't have a choice, because stopping was not an option. If you give up, you give up, end of story. That wasn't going to happen.

One odd story from Canada that still makes me laugh is the fact I was being paid £5,000 a race (my test driver's salary was separate). That felt like a lot of extra cash to me at the time (Damon was on around £500,000 for the season). That wasn't what made me laugh. It was the fact that in Canada, the withholding tax payment that had been agreed between the government and the FIA was £7,000. So it cost me £2,000 to come fifth!

Despite having my saltire painted on the car above my name, I was then informed that at round seven, in France, I would not even be racing. Nigel Mansell would be, after all. Renault and Williams had won a title with him in 1992 and some observers could see the argument in his favour. My concern about a long-term future with Williams was allayed somewhat when, although sharp in qualifying, Mansell retired his Williams just after halfway.

Round eight, Silverstone, and I got the call again – Mansell had Indycar commitments in America that would see me race alongside Damon from round eight in Britain through to round thirteen in Portugal, before Nigel would return for the last three races of the season. I hadn't been in the car for weeks, but I was fastest in the pre-race warm-up at Silverstone; then, disastrously, I suffered a hydraulic failure which stalled my car and so I had to start from the back of the grid. In the race itself, I spun early on, but managed to finish fifth.

During the race itself, along with all the drama, my team radio buzzed into life and a voice said, 'Dave, Dave …' 'Yes?' I asked, waiting for the next team order or perhaps some helpful feedback from the telemetry. 'Er, can you do a 2.30 pick-up in Towcester?' Somehow, a local taxi firm's radio had picked up my frequency and they were calling a driver who just happened to be called David. It seemed impolite not to answer properly, so I said, 'Sorry, I can't, I'm a wee bit busy right now …'

*

The spectre of Mansell was still on my shoulder. Even though I had a run of six races coming up, it was still not clear who would get the seat for 1995. Within a few months, I could feasibly have just been a test driver again. People often ask me if it was intimidating to be a newcomer vying for the seat with such a famous name like Nigel Mansell. The newspapers suddenly started writing long articles about me and I felt the spotlight of media interest far more than I ever had before – *The Times*, for instance, wrote that I had 'ice in the veins'. What's more, Senna had been widely tipped to take the 1994 title, so Williams' aspirations for that season were very high. All these elements left plenty of room for feeling intimidated, if that was your personality.

Being thrust into such an environment with Mansell was indeed an unusual situation for a young driver to find himself in. For a start, I had a great deal of respect for Nigel, not just for his achievements, but also from first-hand experience of him in the past. I'd met him when I was younger, racing karts and cars, doing various motor-sport events across the country, and he was always very supportive. I remember he wrote a really nice letter to my sister when she was in karts. As I said, she was very fast and there was even a TV crew filming her at one point, you know, the 'young girl coming through the ranks'. Mansell had sent her a letter and that, along with my growing career, meant that he knew of me and, of course, I knew of him.

So it was slightly awkward to be thrown into this debate about who was going to get the seat for Williams in 1995. I remember in Jerez he'd got me on the pit wall with all the media around – he was always the showman – and was saying words to the effect of, 'Make sure you've got other options in your back pocket because at this level teams need experienced drivers . . .' I replied, 'Okay, well, can I borrow your wallet then?' He didn't find it very funny and nor did his assistant, who leaned over to me and piped up with, 'That's not the sort of thing you should be saying at this time in your career . . .' I was just reacting to Nigel giving me advice I hadn't asked for.

Any whispers Riccardo Patrese might return as a possible Williams replacement for Senna were promptly hushed when he declared he wanted no further part as a race driver because he was so saddened by the loss. The car I would debut in F1 was a Williams FW16, known to be twitchy and quite a handful to drive, 'loose' at the back. It was exactly the same car in which Ayrton Senna had died – which could have made some drivers nervous.

I can honestly say I never saw it like that. The way I saw it, a small window of opportunity had opened up and I had a job to do. That focus, combined with my youth, made me incredibly determined – remember, I was only twenty-three. And, at the end of the day, we are racing drivers; that is what we do. I was being offered the chance to race for one of the best teams in the pinnacle of motor-sport.

Doubts? Fears?

None whatsoever.

I didn't need to be asked twice.

You never think something's going to happen to you. It is a quite logical process for me: how can a car fail or crash, and then drive again perfectly well later that day? Because the engineers and mechanics have examined the car; they've come to understand the failure; these vehicle parts are designed and engineered to sustain certain loads and, therefore, if they understand why a part failed, they will understand how to fix it. Logical. At the point it re-enters the track after a failure, that car is as good as ever. So, why should I be fearful of getting back in the driver's seat? No reason. Besides, a quality team that knows its limits won't run the car if there is the slightest doubt. If I was in the pits testing and a mechanic said to me, 'We don't understand it, we think it should be okay, but we don't know,' then I would say, 'Well, you should know because that's your business, that's your job.' In that circumstance I wouldn't get in the car.

At the same time, as a driver you have to accept that failures happen, always. You hear a lot of talk about F1 being very safe nowadays, and indeed it is. Even in the thirteen years I have been in the sport, the safety has developed exponentially. But you still get failures and if that is at high speed, it can be a concern. Sometimes people say, 'Why does a suspension fail when you've had suspensions for so many years etc etc?' You do occasionally get carry-over parts from the previous season's car, but usually there are hardly any duplicates. Given that there are thousands of parts on one car, you can see where reliability issues occur. Plus, a lot of these parts are made of carbon fibre and hand-shaped, hand-glued and then baked in an autoclave (which is effectively a big oven), so anything that is made so uniquely, especially at certain joints, has room for slight variation ... and, ultimately, failure.

What they do to alleviate the chance of failure is test the loads, really just like the safety tests in the aeronautics industry. An airplane manufacturer will take a wing and keep bending it and bending it until it breaks; the theory is that the margin between the stress-level at failure and during normal flight is so large that the chances of a failure of that magnitude are negligible. Same with our cars. Yet, sometimes the glue hasn't set properly, and a part can fail as you corner at 150mph. Call it chaos, call it probability, but failures happen and they always will. It's how you deal with them as a team and as a driver that separates you from the rest of the paddock.

I'm not a heroic person, I'm not a risk taker. I trust in the team and they give me no reason not to trust them. I accept that people make mistakes. Mechanics sometimes fail to tighten something up. Best intentions can sometimes still lead to a failure. But you don't stress over walking downstairs in case you might trip over a broom. It's the same; it's unnecessary worrying about something that might not happen. End of story.

It was a very interesting time when I first started racing for Williams – the run of six races from round eight to round thirteen in 1994 was an incredible experience for a twenty-three-year-old. Damon was over a decade older; I'd been his test driver and then become his team-mate, so there was a certain dynamic as a result. We got on okay, but we didn't spend a great deal of time with each other. We are probably more comfortable with each other today, because back then he was focusing on trying to win the championship and his battles with Schumacher, while I was focusing on trying to win a seat in the team. Before Hockenheim he had received death threats and with all the safety issues flying around – exacerbated by Jos Verstappen's Benetton Ford being engulfed in flames during a catastrophic pit stop – he must have had a lot to think about.

On the track, the partnership with Damon, such as it was, did not come without a few complications and it certainly had its share of tense moments. On a few occasions, I was ahead of him. He was competing for the title with Michael, so that, coupled with the fact I was so much younger and less experienced, didn't always go down too well. He obviously struggled with the fact he wanted to be the number one guy and get the support of the team and I was the young gun starting out and making my way and didn't care about him. He was battling for the championship and I was taking points off him. To be fair, it couldn't have been easy for him, but at the time I just wanted to win.

I briefly led a grand prix for the first time ever at Spa (although because of the race dynamic, I did not realise at the time and only found out later). Damon and I had a fall out at this race because Rubens had qualified on pole in the Jordan because of a wet qualifying session. Remember, I had raced against Rubens many, many times in the feeder formulas, so I knew his nuances. I was only trying to be helpful when I said to Damon, 'Be careful of Rubens at the start ...' But Damon took that as me winding him up; the new blood patronising the seasoned racer, I suppose. I wasn't doing that at all, but it was in front of all our engineers and he really didn't take kindly to it. I tried to explain myself and repeated the advice, then he said, 'You fucking say that one more time and we are going to go outside.'

Damon could be a quite intense guy. All the engineers went silent and we were just stood there, opposite one another.

'Well, that's fine, Damon ...'

'Don't expect any help from me then ...'

'Fine, if you want to go outside, we'll go outside. If you are inviting me out then I accept the invitation ...'

And we bickered back and forth for a minute or so until it just faded away. It wasn't so much handbags at dawn as we didn't even manage to get our purses out.

When we got to Monza, the title race was hotting up. Schumacher had been disqualified at Spa – stripping him of a win – over irregularities in the wooden plank on the underside of his car. The result was that, suddenly, Damon's chances of winning the title were reignited. Monza was, therefore, a highly charged race. I was faster than my team-mate in first qualifying, but suffered an engine failure and started in fifth. I was driving very fast and – knowing it this time – led the race for several laps. Then, with me still in front of Damon, Williams asked me to move over – after all, I was only doing random races and Damon was after the title. I said, ' ... he's not close enough ...?' but they insisted, 'You have to move over.' I said, 'I will when he is closer ...' I felt the gap at this point was too great to move over without it looking ridiculous. Damon eventually overtook me when I did move over and went on to win the race, but for the duration I stayed right up his gear-box to show I was clearly faster. Damon was on the radio telling the team, 'Tell him to back off, get him to back off!' Unfortunately, I ran out of fuel on the last corner! That was quite a scary experience in itself – the Italians are famous for track invasions and have been known to rip off wing mirrors, wings, parts of the car and so on. My father has a can of fuel in the museum in Twynholm that he worked out has the exact amount of fuel in it that was needed to get me across the line. It is the tiniest amount, literally a splash.

Although I didn't finish the race, I was classified sixth, despite not actually having crossed the line! I'd made a point though: I was much quicker than Damon that day. The high-light of the year came in my final race at Portugal's Estoril circuit, where I came second, thus enjoying my first ever podium finish – I had led again, but once more obeyed team orders to move over for Damon. He duly won just ahead of me, which was Williams' first one-two of the campaign (and the first British one-two since Damon's father won Monaco in 1969 ahead of Piers Courage). This was a vital signal to Frank that I meant business for 1995. I felt I was settling into the car and was growing in confidence. You can imagine how disappointed I then was when I then had to sit back and watch Nigel Mansell replace me for the final three races of the season. Fortunately, his tenure in the Williams seat would prove very temporary.

At the first of Mansell's three next races, the European Grand Prix at Jerez, I was asked to commentate for the TV coverage and I just happened to be on the mike when he spun off. I covered the microphone and rather loudly expressed a few words that neatly detailed my enjoyment of this incident and how it might have a positive effect on the complicated politics that were shaping my career. But not necessarily in such a polite, succinct way.

Mansell had spun into the gravel that day and apparently didn't want to test before the next race in Japan; when we got to Japan, Nigel suggested quite strongly that I was a distraction walking around the pits and garage. Some of the team even jokingly made up a sign with a picture of me and a red crossed circle over my face, effectively saying, 'Coulthard Forbidden!' They were just winding Mansell up, I guess. I have the greatest respect for Nigel, but he was just not as committed as I was at that time.

Also, I think the great thing about youth is that you don't look at the big picture; you only look at what is right in front of you. Thinking back now, about battling with Mansell for the seat, I just think, 'How did a young lad manage to get the job over Mansell who's an established world champion?' Well, I got it because I was hardworking and dedicated, available and cheap, and could do the job; he was not so available, obviously dedicated, but he was also hard work.

So, come the end of the 1994 season, my first in Formula 1, I had scored fourteen points from eight races, several of which were at tracks I had never raced before. Yet certain aspects of the results disappointed me, because I knew I could have done so much better. A nice accolade was being voted 'Scottish Sports Personality of the Year' and ITV's 'Young Sports Personality of the Year'. But, of course, all that really mattered was winning races.

The simple fact is that as a result of being offered the seat with Williams at the Spanish Grand Prix in 1994, I never had to find the money for the next Formula 3000 race that I'd been struggling to finance prior to Senna's death. I don't think we would have been able to fund any more races in that feeder series to be honest; if that had happened, I would have probably spent the rest of 1994 testing for someone, an opportunity may have presented itself in touring cars or I may have dabbled with sports cars. Without Frank Williams gambling on me that day, there is every chance I would never have raced a Formula 1 car.

PURE AS THE DRIVEN

After my second place in Portugal at the thirteenth round of the 1994 season, my home for 1995 was still undecided. In fact, at one point, the only contract I had in my files was a piece of paper regarding testing for Williams. I did not have a driver's contract. I felt I had performed well in my first partial season for Frank and other teams were making their interest known to me. It seemed only fair that I should try to secure my future.

We were in negotiations with Frank to sign a three-year deal; I was looking for longevity and stability, as any driver would. Then, seemingly at the last moment, Frank said he did not want to do that and instead talked about only a one-year deal. This was too short-term. To be fair to Frank, there was a lot going on. I think maybe he was pissed off with Damon – I'm surmising here – because he was after a more lucrative deal, and there were lots of legal complications because of Senna's death. There was a lot of stuff happening. Nonetheless, I had to protect my career in the way I saw fit, and talk of a one-year deal caused enough concern for me to open up discussions with Ron Dennis of McLaren.

I first received a phone-call from Ron in the latter stages of the 1994 season. He invited me to dinner at the Quaver Park Hotel near the circuit in Jerez – where Mansell was racing for Williams and I was making myself visible in the pits – and, at that meal, we talked about the Mercedes Benz engine deal he had secured and the potential for the car. Naturally, conversation turned to my prospects, too. Over the ensuing months, McLaren positively courted me to join the team. They romanced me, at times I felt like I was embraced as a member of the team really before I actually was. The result? A complicated and lengthy contractual wrangle between Williams and McLaren, with me at the very centre of the argument.

What happened was I signed a letter of intent to race for McLaren in 1996; at this point, Williams had a multi-year agreement based on a test contract; we signed the McLaren contract on the basis that we believed the Williams multi-year test contract was unenforceable as a race contract. Williams disagreed. There was an inevitable conflict, even though Frank was not yet offering me a drive for 1996. He took the complex situation to the Contracts Recognition Board in Geneva – a facility created by the teams to avoid going into a lengthy legal process in the British courts, whereby all the teams sign up and agree to be arbitrated by the CRB in any contract dispute.

Clearly the contractual situation needed clarifying, so Frank took the matter to the Board in Geneva. That particular day was a very odd experience; there I was, sat in this lawyer's office of the CRB next to the representatives of McLaren ... when I was still driving for Williams, who were sitting opposite us. The CRB eventually announced that Williams were entitled to secure me as their driver for 1995.

Of course, looking back, my management company, IMG, were on a percentage of my racing salary; thus if one team offers substantially more than another then there is a logical business thought process for them to side with that larger offer. In this case, McLaren's bid was, I believe, around four times greater than Williams' offer. Furthermore, as part of the long-winded negotiations, McLaren cleared my racing debts, which by the time I was at the CRB had mounted to over £300,000. These are not insubstantial amounts of money we were talking about. So, let me be clear, I'm not saying there was no benefit to me, of course there was – within the space of a few days I went from having relatively little in my bank account to being a contracted millionaire. It's funny, because among the many things Ron Dennis has said to me over the years, one of the sentences that stood out was, 'Money is only important if you don't have any.'

At the time, youth and naiveté got me through again. You're living those scenarios for the first time and so you don't realise it's a ridiculous position to find yourself in. Nonetheless, the whole McLaren/Williams contracts disagreement was all quite a shock to me, to be honest. Prior to this, I simply wasn't aware that any sport could be so complicated and political. I'd always had a relatively naïve view on life, on Formula 1 and on sport in general. I always thought it was sport, sport, sport, win, win, win, that was all that mattered. I was never motivated by money: the first year I'd tested for Williams I hadn't been paid and it hadn't been a major problem for me, not because I had money in my bank account, but because I had been given an opportunity and for me it was always about that and the chance to go racing. Youth is a powerful ally in circumstances like these, because I didn't really think about it while it was happening. You don't realise how absurd it is until you've come through it.

When you are embroiled in all of this, racing cars can seem like the last thing anyone is focusing on. However, in a sense it is exactly what people are thinking about, because they are trying to get the best drivers for their cars.

The end result of all this politics was that, at the start of January 1995, Williams announced that I was to race for them in 1995 alongside Damon Hill. As I said, my salary increased from £50,000 to half a million. Not surprisingly, my personal circumstances soon changed. I had been living in Milton Keynes with my model girlfriend, Andrea Murray – Cawthorne lived with us too, and got the train to London for his job every morning. After that, we'd moved to a house in Chiswick for a year, which I shared with Cawthorne. You might think that two old mates sharing a house near central London would have been a riotous time, but actually I didn't see very much of him. He was working hard at his career in the insurance industry and was out first thing every morning and back late at night; I had my girlfriend at the time and was also working hard at my career. Home has always been important to me. Then, in 1995, I did exactly what my father had told me to do way back when I was just fourteen. I moved to Monaco.

For my first full season at Williams in 1995, I was stepping up on to the podium for almost half of the season; my best result to date had been that second place at Portugal, which was my last race of the 'part-time' 1994 season, so I was very excited to be on the grid for the opener at Brazil with a full seventeen-race schedule ahead of me. I qualified in third and gained a place during the race to take second on the podium (a temporary disqualification over a fuel measurement was eventually lifted and the standings remained). I led that season-opener and ended up the only driver to finish on the same lap as Schumacher, the eventual winner. In four races I retired with mechanical failures and did not finish four other times. Thereafter followed a series of podiums and top-five placings, mixed in with a few electrical and gearbox problems.

Of considerable note was my first ever pole position in Argentina. It was the first grand prix in that country for fourteen years, so there was a lot of media attention on the weekend – the track lost F1 in the 1980s after its surface had actually started to break up during the 1980 race. This loss had come as a blow: this was a proud motor-sport country, which had produced several greats, including Fangio. This particular weekend was the first time I had out-qualified Damon (I was fastest on both the Friday and Saturday), although I ultimately ended up parking the car after my electronics failed.

This race was seen as a signal that the championship was not now between just Damon and Michael, my name was being mentioned in the same sentence, too. Williams also stated there would be no team orders for this season. I had already been asked by some journalists what my thoughts were about winning the world title, but I hadn't even won a grand prix yet. I still had a lot to prove. I bagged pole again in Italy ten races later, the second of my career, but after a spin on the parade lap and a restart in the spare, I still did not finish due to a collapsed front wheel bearing. When I scooped a second consecutive pole at Estoril in Portugal two weeks later, this time events would finally go my way. It was my twenty-first grand prix and would turn out to be my maiden win.

Estoril lies fifteen miles west along the coast from Lisbon, and is built on a pretty barren plateau. It was historically a very good track for Williams – between 1991 and 1996, the team had won five out of the six races there. Ayrton Senna won his first ever grand prix there too, so I was in illustrious company. I led from the front, followed closely by Hill, Schumacher and Berger. I posted the fastest lap of the day and eventually, after some dramatic pit stops, won by seven seconds.

It wasn't an easy ride, though. About fifteen laps into the race, I was already absolutely exhausted because I'd really gone for it and driving a Formula 1 car at that tempo is very, very physical. Schumacher wasn't far behind me and was flying and I remember thinking, 'If he keeps this pace up I can't keep going and I'll crash,' but then, thankfully, around the nineteenth lap he started to slow down – that slight dip in momentum allowed me a few precious seconds to catch my breath and get a second wind. The adrenaline surge and rush of excitement in the first few laps of a grand prix is extreme; you race away from the grid and it is such a blur, and in those few laps it is all too easy to make mistakes, come under pressure and cave in, just generally be overwhelmed. I am still proud that I was able to gather myself and continue on to victory against the most successful driver of all-time. I'd also earned Frank Williams a big kiss from my mother.

I crossed the line with both hands thrust in the air, my steering wheel untouched. For that first win, I had Michael Schumacher second and Damon Hill third, so that's a pretty good victory for a twenty-four-year-old – it also made me one of the youngest grand prix winners of all-time. If you see podium pictures of the day, I'm obviously looking elated, and they're both pissed off. There you go.

It was such a pure driving experience at that early stage of my career. Damon was under immense pressure; his battles with Schumacher, being the leading Brit, all of these things intensified the heat of the spotlight on him. In a sense, it was quite the opposite for me. I remember it very much as a pure and innocent time. I was a kid who just turned up do a job, then went home. I was very good at that point in my career because I was just *driving*; I wasn't worried about team politics or anything like that, because I hadn't become aware of them yet. The more you realise the situation you are in, the more you contemplate your surroundings, the more likely it is you will suddenly jolt upright and think, 'Shit!' At that second, you lose something; you are not driving so purely.

I had four pole positions in a row towards the end of that season, which is quite impressive for a young guy – yet I was so comfortable and eager to compete, it was like, 'Of course I've done four poles, that's what I'm here to do.' I don't mean that in an arrogant way, it was just a very simple, direct period of racing. In many ways, that was the best time of my career; because I was young and just driving on instinct, there was nothing dragging me down. I wasn't thinking about what I was doing, I was just doing it.

Plus, I was around brilliant minds like Patrick Head, co-founder of the Williams team, and Adrian Newey, a superstar designer in the sport. From an engineering point of view, it has to be recognised that he has been at the helm of some great successes for Williams. Patrick is one of the great, eccentric British designers, larger than life, a great personality. He wears his heart on his sleeve, absolutely speaks his mind and is not embarrassed to do so. That can be hard sometimes when his face is red, his veins are popping out of his neck and he's telling you you'll never drive for his team again! But at least you know where you stand with him: he is blunt, direct and honest. I appreciate that characteristic, it's straightforward. When we were getting into the contractual complications with McLaren and Williams, he was quite a formidable personality, let me say that. Yet, he is also man enough to come back to you after a disagreement and say, 'Well, look, I was a little het up at the time, and we all say things that we can regret . . .' and he moves on. He is a great character and I have an enormous amount of respect for him.

Of course, one major factor that made the 1995 season so enjoyable was the fact I was in a very quick car. Maybe it was the fantastic circumstances surrounding the team, perhaps also the wide track, slick tyre, 3.5 litre formula suited my driving style very well, but without a doubt that particular car was a dream to drive. It just responded to change; you could make the minutest adjustment and immediately feel the difference. I remember once making a half a millimetre ride height adjustment and feeling a difference the very next lap. It suited my smooth driving style perfectly and when you were in the zone, it was a beautifully balanced car. In fact, I would say that year's Williams was the most enjoyable Formula 1 car I have ever driven.

In 1995, I had a big shunt while testing at Silverstone, which knocked me unconscious. It was my first really big impact in

Formula 1. I hit the barrier at Club Corner which, at the time, consisted of old wooden sleepers from train tracks. My head slammed forward and smashed into the side of the chassis, which cracked the helmet and knocked me out.

For every crash I have had – and all the ones I have avoided – I always think I am going to recover the situation. People often ask me how scary it is in the micro-seconds before impact. Well, I can honestly say, because I just think I am going to recover, I don't realise I have had a crash until after it's happened. So, in essence, it isn't scary at all. Even when I know I'm going to hit something, I know the chances are that I'm going to be okay.

There is no flapping about in the cockpit, screaming, 'Oh my God! I'm going to die ...' You just don't do that. You have a situation to control and things to do to achieve that.

Immediately before the impact at Silverstone testing, my memory remains patchy, just a few snippets here and there. After I came round, I remember getting out of the car and walking to an ambulance – as opposed to being stretchered – which took me to the medical centre. Oddly, I kept looking at my watch on this ambulance journey, because I thought they would ask me the time and, if I couldn't tell them, they wouldn't let me drive again that day. They'd already asked me how many fingers they were holding up which was no problem, so I was trying to figure out how they would stop me continuing the test. So I kept looking at my watch, which told me it was a quarter past ten. Strangely, I thought I'd been out there testing for several hours, but in fact the session had only started at ten, so I'd actually crashed on the very first run of the day.

I don't remember the accident as such, the lights going out or being unconscious or whatever, but on reflection I remember the moments up to it thinking, 'I'm turning this way but the car's going that way,' and being confused as to why it wouldn't go where I wanted it. This was in the tiny window of time between my steering failing and the car hitting the wall, maybe less than a second? All I was doing was trying to recover the situation.

One consequence of this big accident was I phoned my mother. I said to her, 'Mother, I just want you to know that if I'm ever killed in a race, the chances are that it will be on television and there is every chance that you might be watching at home. If that is so, I don't want you to think that my last moments were full of fear, or that I knew I was going to die . . .' That experience at Silverstone showed me that it would not be like that. Halfway through the conversation, my mother said, 'Stop, stop, I don't want to have this conversation,' but I was like, 'Mum, it's important.' It was a struggle for her to listen to that, but I am glad I made that call. For me the Silverstone testing accident had been a revelation. It made me imagine the journey to death: perhaps it was just like getting knocked out, but for eternity? The only difference here was I woke up. There was no pain, no fear, nothing alarming.

It transpired that a mechanic had not fully tightened the bolt where the steering column joins the steering rack; there's a bolt that goes through, normally from the top, with a split pin or wire so it cannot come out. Essentially, this bolt was not properly secured, so when I'd sped around the corner, the nut had fallen out, then the bolt (being upside down) just literally dropped out, so I lost all steering and smashed straight into a wall.

I was fine, so I headed back to the garage and, shortly afterwards, they found out what had happened. The mechanic was in tears in front of me. He was an experienced mechanic who'd been around for years and he was very upset because, after all, I could have been killed. He had made a mistake.

There was, of course, a wider context to this incident. When Ayrton Senna died in a Williams the previous year, there was a huge amount of forensic and investigative attention on the steering of his car and a resulting high-profile court case involving Frank and Patrick. Much of the debate hinged around whether there had been a steering failure as a result of the impact on the wall or before the crash. As I understand it, the defence for Williams were able to prove – from data and so on – that there was steering load right up to *before* the impact, therefore there was a connected force between the driver and the front of the car; the argument being there would have been zero load if the column was broken before the impact. It was never proved that the steering column failed. The entire accident is subject to speculation and conspiracy theory to this day, it's like the 'Who killed J F K?' of Formula 1.

In my opinion, the reality is there are a lot of factors involved in a crash: was it cold tyres causing low pressure, was it the car touching the ground, was it driver error, did a tyre deflate? There are so many things you cannot prove after an event. *However*, in the case of Senna's crash, they can prove there was steering load up until the impact.

My accident at Silverstone in testing came in the following season and there was sufficient concern over the sensitivity of the incident for Frank Williams to come up from the factory to see me and apologise for what had happened in person. It was kept quiet thereafter too, and I have never discussed this matter in public until now. Given how fond and admiring I am of Frank Williams, it was quite shocking that he came and apologised to me, 'I'm really sorry about that David,' and yet in the next breath he said, 'I'm also here to tell you officially that we won't be offering you a contract for 1996.'

I normally have one car-failure or mechanic-error accident per year. In 2006 I didn't, but that is the exception to the rule. Apart from Silverstone, one big impact came when I was taken off the circuit after a tyre deflated in Barcelona, before the rear suspension failed, the rear wheel and wing came off, I naturally lost all my braking and down force and found myself hurtling towards the barrier head on. That's one of my biggest testing crashes. Every year, as far as I can recall, I have had one big crash in testing, where something would fail on the car and put you in the barriers. I just accept it as part of winter testing.

There is a lot made of how different drivers react to accidents in different ways. I'm pretty unfazed by them, even when they happen as a result of something that is not my own fault. I've always got back in and driven the same day if the car can be physically fixed in time. I always think, 'Well, I'm still alive. I'm not broken. It is what it is.'

I know of some drivers who simper off home if they've got a head cold. I have only missed two races, after I broke my leg in 1990, other than that I have never missed a race. I raced for much of the 1994 and 1995 seasons with tonsillitis and eventually had to have my tonsils taken out to ease the discomfort, but I never missed a race. So only two races missed. That's not bad if you consider I've taken part in over 200 races over the years.

People talk about Mansell being 'enigmatic' to work with, but when he was offered a test drive with Lotus – essentially his big break – he had a broken bone in his neck but kept it quiet so as not to jeopardise his chances. I've never raced with a broken neck, but I've had to clamber out of a Formula 1 car to vomit from food poisoning, then climb back in and get out on the track on more than one occasion. That is commitment. Not because I'm trying to be gung-ho or appear macho or strong, but I don't want to let the side down, because these guys are committed and so you get on with it. The only thing that has ever stopped me testing is when I've tweaked a nerve or cricked my neck, because you just physically can't drive – that's happened maybe two or three times in my career. That is something that has happened to every driver at some point, because of all the extreme forces placed on the neck when driving.

The funny thing is that over time you realise that feeling poorly does not preclude you from doing well on the track. There are days I've felt great and performed badly and there are days I haven't felt good physically and done quite well. There was one time in Belgium I was up most of the night coughing and spitting up blood, didn't sleep at all, didn't feel good, then sloped off to the circuit, went out and won the race. To this day I have no idea how, but I was probably so pissed off I wanted to get in, get the job done and get off. There you go.

*

By the middle of the 1995 season, the paddock rumour mill had said I as going to be replaced at Williams by Jacques Villeneuve, who had been breaking records in American Indycar. He even tested at Silverstone in August, so for me it was clear what would happen. I said at the time, 'Three into two doesn't go.' I was, however, already lined up to drive for McLaren (Mansell briefly raced for my future team, but that partnership dissolved after only four grands prix).

After my maiden grand prix win in Portugal, I ended the season with two more podiums in the European and Pacific Grands Prix, then two disappointing DNFs at Japan and Australia. At the season finale, I suffered a rather odd incident when my car hit the pit wall, after the electronics had mistakenly sensed a stall and raised the revs, slamming me into the brickwork. Nonetheless, despite this rather subdued finish to the year, I was delighted to achieve third in the championship with forty-nine points, behind Damon and the title winner Michael.

I thoroughly enjoyed my time at Williams and I have the utmost respect for Frank Williams in particular. Aside from the racing, the contract problems and all the intense atmosphere of competition, being in Frank's team was also good fun at times. He might seem very stern in TV interviews, but he was constantly winding me up. The Scottish saltire on my helmet is not actually acknowledged by the FIA, I am down as a British driver; that is my nationality; Frank loved this and would often tease me about it.

The Williams engineers were not averse to a prank or two either. Back when I was testing for the team, at the Paul Ricard circuit, the mechanics rigged up my rental car's screenwash plumbing pipes to spurt water all over me when I turned the engine on. I got drenched and, worse still, didn't have a spare pair of trousers.

Perhaps one of the best examples of Frank's humour goes right back to when he announced I was to be the new driver for his team. The massed ranks of motor-sport journalists were sitting there and I was obviously keen to make a good impression. When asked why he'd chosen me, I was looking forward to hearing his opinion. 'Well,' said Frank, 'David has been given the drive with Williams Formula 1 because he has a very pretty girlfriend ...'

Despite Frank choosing his moment after the Silverstone testing crash to tell me he did not want me for 1996, what I respect about Frank is that he will admit to lying to you. This will sound like an odd, back-handed compliment, but if he does lie to you, he acknowledges it afterwards and gives you the reason why he lied. He admits to withholding information, but for a greater reason. The next day you can walk up to him and say, 'Frank, you told me so-and-so yesterday and that wasn't the case,' to which he will reply, 'Yes I did, but I had to in order to protect the company and the 300 employees I have and if I told you the truth that would have compromised the team.' So he admits to those situations and I respect that. In my experience, there are other people – and I will avoid being nasty by naming them – who will back up a lie with another lie, then back that up with yet another lie, and so on. You can stand in front of certain people in the paddock and know they are lying to you ... they know you know as well, but it doesn't stop them!

Frank Williams took a big gamble with me and I'd like to

think it clearly paid off for him. After one particularly dramatic win in Italy in 1997, Frank said I was 'one of Formula 1's elite guard, a rare example' to other drivers. Those are kind words indeed. He's been taking gambles with young drivers for years; he is continually giving opportunities to very young talent, it's a brave asset of his and he has rightly reaped the rewards. I sincerely and wholeheartedly appreciate all of the opportunities Frank Williams has given me.

A SEVERE ATTACK OF
THE TRUTH

I am known as something of a 'neat freak', and I admit I am certainly very tidy. I like to see everything in its place. We all have different motivations and I'm a great believer in success: it's not about money or position; it's about whatever goal you set on a particular day. I get a great amount of satisfaction if I am around the house all day, cleaning and tidying and sorting things out; that to me can be a successful day, because I've achieved my goal.

Some people say it's a little obsessive, but it is what it is. I don't stand for anyone making a fucking mess, like if someone uses the toilet and pisses on the seat, then wipe it off. Accidents happen, men are not always that good at aiming, but have a bit of decency please, clean it off. I don't have a problem getting my hand down a toilet and getting rid of skid marks that someone else has left because there isn't a toilet brush. Besides, if I don't do it, some other poor fucker is going to have to.

I am well versed in cleaning because of my years in the motorhome. Spending my teenage years racing certainly made me more inclined to be clean and tidy. During the week, I would clean my helmet repeatedly, spend hours leather soaping my suit and would polish my kart into a perfect finish. Likewise the motorhome was always spotless. I might not be a mechanic, but I certainly know how to strip and clean a car.

Everything was immaculate; it was all about preparation. I recall when I was an eighteen-year-old in Formula Ford and the car had these aluminium panels on it – by the time I had finished using a special polish on those it was sparkling. I'd even get that car up on a hydraulic jack and polish the underside to within an inch of its life; it was gleaming. Some people said this was ridiculous because no one was going to see it. But I made the point, jokingly, that if I ever rolled over, my car would have the shiniest underside. For me, this was all just part of the detail, the preparation, the application. It was always about being as equally prepared, if not better, than any of your track rivals. I believe it gave me a psychological edge.

Having said that, I also think I was predisposed to being this particular about cleanliness before racing, because my sister and I used to share a helmet in the early days and she certainly didn't clean stuff like me! She'd just throw her leathers in a corner after a race and that would be that; for me, getting home was just the start of more cleaning.

It has been suggested to me that the clinical nature and near-surgical environment of Formula 1 has fuelled this obsession with neatness and cleanliness. It is a profession based on precision and exactness. There may be something in that for sure – if you walk around a team factory it is like some hermetically sealed laboratory. The factories take cleanliness to an extreme. The electronics department are 'dust-free' environments. If you think about it, if you think of a motor mechanic, you think of oil and dirt, filthy overalls, grubby fingers, all that. A Formula 1 factory couldn't be further from that, it's like something from another planet.

Everything is aircraft standard, aircraft quality. There's no playing of radios, calendars of Page 3 girls and fags hanging out of the corner of the mouth. This is not your local car dealership 'service centre'. Nor should it be. If a sponsor is going to spend twenty million bucks with a racing team to get their name globally known and he walks in to a factory to find people chewing gum and smoking a cigarette, that is not a great impression. If they walk in and everyone is dressed immaculately and working in a hushed environment with not a speck of dirt anywhere, then it feels entirely more appropriate. That is why all the teams try and 'out-present' each other.

Polishing my helmet – no pun intended – is a specific ritual I have. The race helmet is possibly the most prized of all the artefacts a racing driver has. At its most rudimentary level, it is your safety device. When you are starting out, you only have one helmet for several years and they can be a pricey piece of kit, probably the equivalent of buying a top-of-the-range iPod or similar, I suppose. I cherished mine, and I cleaned it religiously again and again and again. I enjoyed cleaning it. By the time you get to Formula 1, you are getting through probably a dozen helmets a year, and these ones are a little pricier than an iPod!

I have other routines and rituals – if someone took my gloves off me while I was in the car waiting to race, I'd be unsettled, but would probably just grab a pair of mechanic's gloves and get on with it. However, I have got used to wearing a new helmet regularly through necessity. Although normally I'd never dream of wearing someone else's helmet, I had a problem with my visor at the 1996 Monaco Grand Prix and just couldn't see properly in the conditions, the visor just kept fogging up. In the end I used one of Michael Schumacher's.

Michael very kindly let me keep the helmet after the race. He'd finished second in Brazil with that helmet, so it's a unique piece of history – two grand prix drivers wearing the same helmet and finishing on different podiums. There's another side of that story, too. Ron Dennis has one of the biggest helmet collections in motor-racing and he thinks he has the original, because he went to Michael's manager after the race and asked for it. But he'd pissed Michael off over something, I can't recall what, so I spoke to Michael and said, 'I'd like the helmet and can we make a replica of the helmet for Ron?' So we did. Ron has a replica and I have the original. He'll find out when he reads this book. He shouldn't have pissed Michael off.

Fast-forward to 2006 and Michael came to me again and said he wanted to swap a helmet with me. This was before he'd announced he was retiring, so my immediate thought was, 'Well, if he's doing the helmet collection thing . . .?' So I gave him a helmet and he gave me a signed one of his.

Helmets are treasured and it is quite rare for me to give race ones to anyone. The helmet has always remained more important to me than a trophy. The odd person has one of my helmets. I only gave David Cawthorne one recently – we've known each other since we were five and perhaps part of that relationship is taken for granted. Sometimes you forget, you're hardest on those you love the most and you make an effort with people you hardly know. So he has one of my helmets.

So, yes, I do spend a lot of my time in this acutely clean

environment and maybe that has fuelled my preference for cleanliness. But again, it certainly wasn't like this in the pissing rain changing a fuel line in Stranraer as an eleven year old. I think it is just my way.

Perhaps of all the teams, McLaren are the most immaculate. Everything is exact, precise, spotless, gleaming. So it was here, in January 1996, that I headed off to their Woking headquarters to start what would become a nine-year relationship with that team, the second longest in Formula 1 history behind only Michael and Ferrari. I have already said that McLaren positively courted me to join and I was pleased to find that when I arrived, after everything that had happened with Williams, I was treated with great respect. There was a very definite honeymoon period, too – for example, I was given a beautiful Mercedes car for my use and was treated in a very engaging way. This lasted probably until some time in 1997.

Unfortunately, my early performances were beleaguered with technical problems, throttle, hydraulics, engine failures and so on. The car that Mansell had briefly driven the year before was being modified after many problems, but development was still littered with issues. The sixteen races in that 1996 season were entirely ordinary for me, my team-mate Mika Hakkinen and the team. From scoring forty-nine points with Williams in 1995, I slumped to just eighteen; from third in the title race behind Hill and Schumacher, I dropped down to seventh; I was not on the front row once; McLaren could only manage a modest fourth in the constructors' championship. I bagged only two podiums compared to eight the previous year, although the second at Monaco was in a race that saw so many crashes, spins and incidents that only three cars finished ... and I still didn't win. Pretty much the only highlights on race days for me were my repeatedly fast starts, often leap-frogging me up four or more places, race after race.

All this was despite McLaren bringing in Alain Prost to advise the team as a 'consultant' (Mika was openly unhappy about this within the garage). The idea was that Prost would run the car at tracks, effectively testing it (although that obviously wasn't his job title), then report back and assist the team with improvements and progress. He was certainly a heavyweight acquisition given his achievements, a very powerful and experienced backroom asset.

You can imagine how this felt a little strange for me. Prost was, after all, my hero, growing up as a kid. Only a few years after I was all breathless in the pits at seeing him as I prepared to become his test driver, here he was, effectively being my test driver. He was obviously being paid a lot of money, rightly so, but it later transpired – unbeknown to Ron, I believe – that he was going to set up Prost Grand Prix, which ultimately failed spectacularly.

Looking back on that pretty dismal first season with McLaren in 1996, all the signs were there to worry me right from the start of the season. I went from leading the closing race of the 1995 season in Adelaide in a Williams to sitting on the grid for the season-opener in Melbourne in 1996 in thirteenth place ... before retiring.

Then, suddenly, the penny dropped.

I had moved for money ...

... and in many ways, in the short term, it was the wrong move.

*

I spent nine years at McLaren, as I've said, it was one of the longest driver–team relationships in Formula 1 history. Of those nine years, six were with the same team-mate, Mika Hakkinen. It's one of the longest pairing of two drivers in F1 history. Normally drivers stay perhaps three or four years at a team and then move on. On the surface, those facts about my tenure at McLaren suggest a serene near-decade of teamwork and compatibility. My time there certainly brought me some fantastic highlights and many memorable moments. Unfortunately, at times, the McLaren years were also some of the most difficult of my career.

In 1995, Mika had a 130mph crash in qualifying at the last race of the season in Australia that very nearly killed him. When Ron Dennis visited him in hospital, he was wired up to ventilators, his body broken by the impact, deep in a coma. I started racing for Ron at effectively the very next race, the 1996 opener. On paper, I had every reason to feel confident – I had won a grand prix, Mika had not; and I had finished 1995 in third with Mika down in seventh.

Personal politics are part and parcel of Formula 1. It is not a one-driver sport. Therefore, it is unavoidable that drivers within teams compete against each other. As each driver is assigned an engineer and a 'team', these people, by definition, become embroiled in competition, too. I was always aware of that and perfectly happy with the concept. If my team-mate drove brilliantly and took pole from me, I knew and relished the fact that (back then when qualifying was different), I had to go straight back out there and snatch pole back.

The first signs that there might be a specific favouritism

towards Mika came in that very first race for McLaren, in Melbourne 1996. I was with my race engineer talking about various issues and Mika was chatting to his engineer. The door opened and Ron walked in. I stood up to shake his hand and he ignored me. Instead, he strode over to sit next to Mika and said, 'What's the plan guys?' We all listened to Mika's plans and then Ron said, 'Okay, and what are they doing?' Here was my team principal, sitting on the other side of the table to me, next to my team-mate, talking about me as if I was a rival team. 'They' is not a word you use in a team situation, surely? At that exact moment, I think the naïvety, the innocence of my youth, shattered around me. The days of pure driving evaporated right at that table. Up until then, I don't think I had really suspected that we would be treated anything other than entirely equal. Suddenly, this whole world of paranoia and cynicism gripped me.

Over the forthcoming seasons, I gradually started to sense the tinge of favouritism was actually becoming far more tangible, until it was clear – to me – that Ron blatantly favoured Mika. That's not a subjective favouritism, as in he preferred Mika socially; I am talking about professionally, on the track, in testing, at the headquarters.

Why would I think that? Let me give you some examples.

Pole position can be everything. When you are in the best car in Formula 1, as myself and Mikka were for several of the McLaren years, the competition for pole is internal. In Monaco in 1998, there was a shocking and quite honestly disturbing display of the favouritism I suspected. I went out in qualifying and got pole. I drove back to the garage and obviously my mechanics and engineers were very pleased. Mika was still out and on a fast lap and we all sat watching the monitors, me, Ron, everyone. He crossed the line and his time flashed up, showing he had snatched pole from me by a fraction. At this, Ron Dennis, Norbert Haug and Jurgen Hubbert of Mercedes erupted in cheers, clapping, roaring with delight. Remember, they hadn't snatched pole from Ferrari or another team, but from me, a McLaren driver. And they were ecstatic about it.

I vividly remember leaning against the wall, watching all this, aghast. It was very upsetting; I have to be honest. There is always a healthy rivalry within teams, of course, I accept that as I have said, but when you see your team principle and the major players from Mercedes cheering that result, it brings anger and disbelief. And all this was set against a backdrop of people telling me there was no such favouritism and that I was whinging. I was incredulous.

You might say they were simply showing admiration for a fast lap, but it was much, much more than that. It was glee. I spoke to McLaren's Martin Whitmarsh about it and said, 'Can you imagine how this makes me feel?' McLaren had pole so they just thought I was a whinging driver. To see the men from Mercedes react like that was one thing – they have after all invested their reputations and vast amounts of their company's money in the team doing well. I trust their word absolutely and I believe they just want the best for Mercedes. But to see Ron react that way was devastating.

A seed of doubt and uncertainty had been planted that would plague many of my years at McLaren. To explain that some more, it is quite clear that if you take two humans who are very similar in all physical attributes, whose capability is equal, then the biggest difference is the mind, their ability to believe they can do certain things may differ. The reason why it is so important for a sportsman to have the right feeling from the team around him is that you can't fool your mind. You need the sensation of trust and belief of those around you. You may be able to fool other people, but you cannot fool yourself. You might be in denial, you could say you are happy, but suddenly one day the reality will hit you. So as a qualifier to those who said I was a whinger, I would point out that it is the mind that controls the body and not the other way around. Therefore for any sportsman, indeed for any person in life, the environment they are in and how that makes them feel will ultimately impact heavily on their success or failure.

Let me make one thing absolutely clear, though. At times driving for McLaren was a fantastic experience. After all, for many of those nine years, Mika and I had the best cars on the grid. The highlights came thick and fast. After that subdued opening season in 1996, the very first race of the next season brought ecstasy for the team when I came in first in Melbourne – it was a watershed for both McLaren and myself.

This was far more than just another grand prix win – McLaren had gone through a forty-nine-race winless streak for several years since Senna last won for them, also in Australia (his last ever grand prix victory), and it was Mercedes' first victory in the modern era as well as my first victory for the team, so these were all very important landmarks. We had a strong car, the MP4-12, even though Jacques Villeneuve's Williams was running very fast and, ultimately, would take him to the title.

After qualifying fourth, with Mika sixth, we were at least in with a chance. As it turned out, to the delight of my team, I beat Schumacher into second with Mika coming home third, so McLaren had two drivers on the podium ... and were back in business. I'll admit to shedding a tear in private afterwards; the emotion and ecstasy of the moment was so great and everyone was so pleased. Or maybe it was because I'd just remembered a bet I'd placed with Ron Dennis several years ago ...

Some years previously at an awards ceremony, Ron Dennis had said that if I won a grand prix for his team, he would attend the next *Autosport* award ceremony wearing a kilt. He also said if he did, then would I donate £25,000 to one of the various children's charities he supports? I agreed because I thought that – Ron being Ron – he would never do it. Plus, I figured that if he did actually go through with it, everyone at the ceremony would be rolling around laughing their heads off, so it might be worth the money. Anyway, I won that race and then, at that year's award ceremony, Ron turned up with knees exposed and sporran akimbo. Worse still, the expected waves of laughter not only didn't happen, but no one batted an eyelid. Everyone just thought it was perfectly normal. There's a photograph of myself, Ron and Iain and in that picture I am smiling happily and laughing. Perhaps I hadn't written the cheque just then!

Ron Dennis certainly knows how to throw a party, you cannot dispute that. So, given the importance of that long-awaited win, it was no surprise that there was one almighty celebration afterwards in Melbourne. We had a function at a hotel for an elite list of invitees, including the Beatle George Harrison, who insisted on providing the champagne for all the guests! He even played a CD at the party called 'Bernie Says ...' – now that is what I call throwing a bash, getting one of The Beatles to write a song! He was a big fan of Formula 1 and also a friend of Bernie Ecclestone too, which meant he was a regular in the paddock and could pretty much go where he wanted because of who he was and who he was friends with. I recall he told some great tales that night; it was fascinating sitting listening to him talk.

Formula 1 attracts celebrity like perhaps no other sport and, over the years, I've been fortunate enough to meet many famous names (although I'm not personally drawn towards celebrity circles and big-name parties). Nonetheless, I met Princess Diana in the mid-1990s at Silverstone, as well as William and Harry, and that was nice. I have also showed Sylvester Stallone around a Formula 1 car and garage, so you can't deny the job doesn't introduce me to interesting people!

After this opening high, I suffered a poor run of results, with tenth in Brazil followed by three DNFs (crash, engine and a spin), then four more races without stepping on the podium, before three more DNFs. So when the cavalcade rolled into Italy for round thirteen, my season was badly in need of a lift. So, too, was McLaren's – one win out of twelve was a very poor return. I started sixth on the grid, but leapt up to third after the first corner – all those rainy days spent hurtling down to the first turn in karts were still coming in handy! I stuck on the backs of Alesi and Frentzen and, with the help of some brilliant pit work, managed to take the victory. It was this race that Frank Williams would later describe as one of my greatest, classing me as he did in the F1 'elite'.

The remainder of the season was troubled by more reliability issues for both myself and Mika, but without doubt the most notable incident of 1997 (aside from the opening win), was what happened at the last race, the European Grand Prix in Jerez. Despite all the problems, when our cars were running true, they were blisteringly quick and the whole paddock could see that the tide was turning in our favour. There was beginning to be a sense that McLaren was on its way back to the top, so I was naturally very excited about the potential. However, two controversies in consecutive races highlighted why I had concerns about favouritism towards Mika, and became famously high-profile within F1 circles and with the wider viewing public.

There was talk that beforehand, Ron Dennis and Frank Williams had apparently made an agreement that McLaren would not get in the way of the lead Williams, whose driver Jacques Villeneuve was battling with Ferrari's Michael Schumacher for the title; in return for this 'gesture', if Williams were in a position to win the title by the end of the race without having to cross the line first, they would let a McLaren driver win. Ron has this long-standing belief that Formula 1 favours Ferrari, so he would have been happy to make this agreement.

In the race itself, the headline drama was between the two title contenders, when Michael appeared deliberately to shunt Jacques off the track. The move backfired and, after Schumacher retired, Villeneuve was left with a straight run to the chequered flag, needing only a third place to win the championship.

My race was altogether different. I began behind Mika and we were both all over the back of Jacques. I came out of the pits ahead of Mika (and still behind race leader Jacques) but then, on lap sixty-six, my radio crackled into life, and my team manager Dave Ryan started telling me to move over to let Mika go through. I just said, 'Why?' and we had a fairly heated conversation that lasted for many laps. I was initially vehement, refusing to move over. Then, he said words to the effect of, 'David, the team has given an instruction and if you don't move over you are seriously compromising your position within the team . . .' I have to be honest, to me it sounded very much like, 'You're going to get fired if you don't.'

Bear in mind, this was all happening right in the middle of a grand prix, with all the speed, danger, tactics and racing going on as normal. Eventually, I was faced with an unavoidable decision and so I let Mika pass. Then, on lap sixty-eight, Jacques moved over for myself and Mika, who went on to take the chequered flag to notch up his very first grand prix win in ninety-six attempts.

There's a photograph of Mika and me holding Jacques up on the podium, because he'd won the championship. Mika was deliriously happy because he'd won his first race, but to me that seemed a little odd. For my part, I was seething; I was very pissed off indeed. I did the press conference and said all the right things, but I also remember going to see Ron after the race. I asked him directly why he'd done that and he said, 'You don't understand, we made an agreement beforehand . . .' As a side issue, Ron also asked me to move over for Mika. I was privy to neither agreement. His justification for me moving over was that the timing of Mika's pit stops helped Williams – as he had agreed – but to the detriment of Mika as it also allowed me to pass him, so he took the decision as team principle to return Mika to the front, which he felt was more honourable. I was aware of none of this.

It seemed absurd to me. All I knew was I was racing and I was in front of my team-mate. Then I was not allowed to be in front, by my own team. Apart from the time I was asked to move over for Damon, Williams always just let their drivers get on with it. McLaren stalwart Jo Ramirez said in his book that maybe Ron felt the car had let Mika down more than me before this race and, therefore, he wanted to even out the luck; likewise he felt it was good for the team to have two recent race winners, rather than just one. That's one viewpoint.

When it became common knowledge in the media that an agreement had been made between two of the leading teams, there was considerable debate, with journalists and the public questioning whether this was racing in its pure form or a pre-arranged procession. In the off-season, the rules stating that there were to be no team orders were introduced.

In March 1998, the Formula 1 circus thundered into Melbourne for the season-opener. I had eventually finished third in the 1997 standings, three ahead of Mika, but still this undercurrent of favouritism persisted and, because of what happened at Jerez, it had become acute. In Australia, Mika qualified just ahead of me on pole, by a mere four-thousandths of a second. We were both driving the first McLaren designed by Adrian Newey – the MP4-13 – and it was giving us a sizeable advantage over the other teams. We were finally sitting in a McLaren entirely capable of winning the title. (As a brief aside, McLarens were always very quick but not as enjoyable to drive as the 1995 Williams I mentioned earlier; McLarens were certainly fast, relative to the opposition, but they were always tricky to drive: nervous on entry, often too much under-steer on mid-corners.) At the same time, the team was concerned about reliability –

149

we'd got some very fast lap times, but hadn't completed grand prix distance once during winter testing.

Ron Dennis came to us prior to the race and said words to the effect of, 'Look, we all know we have a quick car. Both of you have every chance of winning this race, provided we don't push it 100 per cent. If you do that, it will probably fail. However, given the advantage over our competitors that we appear to have, I believe you do not need to drive at 100 per cent and will still be able to win.' He then suggested a strategy to avoid his two drivers pushing the McLarens into failure through competition with each other. His suggestion was to do qualifying as normal, then whoever performed best and had the dominant position could win the race. I believe I changed that to propose whoever got to the first corner ahead would go on to win the race. Mika agreed with my alternative suggestion. I partly put that forward by way of cover for myself in case of problems in qualifying.

I was expecting to beat him from the start – although he was a very good qualifier and often beat me on the grid placing, I still relied on my starts to get in front. However, as the race was about to begin, smoke from my radiators distracted me momentarily and I made a very ordinary start, leaving Mika to lead. He led the race ahead of me, and we were miles ahead of the rest of the pack, over a minute I believe. Ron's concerns about reliability were well founded and the team were frequently on the radio telling us to be careful about over-heating, brake problems, telling us to slow down and so on. We both pitted – Mika first – and he came out still in the lead, but then Mika made a mistake. I believe his hearing was adversely affected by his big crash so whether this had something to do with his error I don't know, but he thought he heard a radio instruction to pit, so he did. When he got there, there was no crew waiting for him, so he drove straight through the pit lane and rejoined the race, obviously having given me the chance to take the lead while he was coasting through past the garage. Yes, we had our pre-race agreement about the first corner, but he'd made a mistake and, in my eyes, that was something he would have to live with – if it cost him the race, then so be it.

So you can imagine how I felt when my radio crackled into life some time before lap fifty-five and the team manager said, 'David, you have to move over for Mika.' I had team orders to move over, so I did, on the pit straight. Again. We had to revert back to what was agreed before, so Mika was returned to a race-winning position. This was in contrast to Jerez, where I knew nothing of what was agreed beforehand. At least this time I knew about the arrangement and although that did not stop me from being disappointed, at least I had prior knowledge.

There was yet more out-cry after Melbourne, with people saying they had placed bets in good faith on a result that had ultimately been manipulated. It was a slightly volatile period for all of us, but as drivers we had to toe the team line and, as a result, we all struggled a bit through that time. Although, let's be honest, I would probably have struggled less if Mika had been the one doing the moving over. At the time I did say it was not team orders, knowing full well that we had agreed before that the only way we could both finish the race was to have this agreement beforehand. However, rather than a team order during the race, it was an arrangement made beforehand, a subtle difference.

It wasn't only the journalists who heaped criticism on myself,

Mika and McLaren, the public joined in as well. This felt harsh because I was not doing anything underhand, I was being given an instruction by my team and I was adhering to that. What that whole period highlights is that Formula 1 is a team sport. It may be an individual that gets all the glory, but it's a team sport and you need to support your team. Formula 1 is often seen as driver against driver, not so much team against team, but the reality is it is all about the teams. Needless to say, after Melbourne, my fears about coming second to Mika in the team's priorities were far from eased.

elcome to the glamour of FI.
bove) Posing with new
illiams team-mate Damon
ill; (right) meeting Princess
iana and Princes William
d Harry; (below) sharing a
ke with Silvester Stallone.
A Photos)

My grand prix debut for Williams, in Spain, May 1994, was overshadowed by the fact I was stepping into the car that had been occupied by Ayrton Senna. (LAT)

Is he really happy? Damon Hill applauds as I celebrate my first ever podium finish after the Portuguese Grand Prix of 1994. It helped me secure the drive for Williams the following year, and also caught the attention of Ron Dennis of McLaren. (Getty Images)

(Above) The Williams team celebrate as I cross the line, both hands in the air, to win the Portuguese Grand Prix in 1995. (Below) A perfect podium? Me, with Michael Schumacher and Damon Hill – I'm not sure they both saw it that way. (LAT)

Enjoying one of the perks of the job: taking the helm of a nuclear submarine.

(Left) Andrea Murray, the 'grid girl' I first met in 1992; we were together for four years. (PA Photos)

(Above) Heidi Wichlinski, my next serious girl-friend. (PA Photos)

Chalk and cheese. With my new McLaren team-mate Mika Hakkinen in 1996. (PA Photos)

Despite only three cars finishing the 1996 Monaco Grand Prix, I still couldn't win the race – it was that kind of season. (LAT)

The first grand prix of the 1997 season brought me my first win for McLaren, and the team's first in forty-nine races. No wonder Ron Dennis (left) was so happy. (Getty Images/PA Photos)

Celebrating with Jurgen Hubbert and Norbert Haug of Mercedes after winning the Italian Grand Prix later that year. (LAT)

ika Hakkinen (out of shot) takes the chequered flag at the European Grand Prix at the end of the 97 season in one of the closest finishes on record, but I had been told by my team to let him rough. (PA Photos)

stand confused on the podium while Mika and Jacques Villeneuve celebrate winning the race nd the drivers' title respectively. (Getty Images)

Focusing on the grid ahead of the Australian Grand
Prix at the start of the 1998 season. Again, I had to
move over to let Mika through, so I'm not sure why
he was in tears on the podium (right). (PA Photos
/LAT)

Practising my Superman act on a
Russian cargo plane. The 'weightless'
flight was part of their space programme.
(HOCH ZWEI/Juergen Tap)

THERE GOES MY HAPPY MARRIAGE

Ironically, one of my most famous on-track incidents after the debacle of Melbourne in 1998 was a coming together with Schumacher in Spa the same year that ultimately benefited my team-mate Mika and helped in some way towards him lifting the championship that season. Mika led the title race from the start and would go on to take eight race wins and nine pole positions. I won only once, in San Marino, and stood on the podium eight other times, but finished third behind Schumacher and my team-mate. Many observers stated I had the least reliable of the two cars and, by mid-season at Silverstone, I was effectively supporting Mika's title charge.

The weather at Spa on race day was atrocious and the grand prix promised much as Ferrari were catching us, while Jordan, Williams and Benetton were all also running well. Racing in wet weather and *not* being in the lead is probably the most horrible part of being a grand prix driver. People might watch the TV and see us racing in the wet and from those camera angles it looks quite manageable. However, it can be about as easy as driving blind. Perhaps the best way I can explain it is this: if you were to turn your wipers off on your car next time you're driving on the motorway in the pouring rain, see how long it is until you can't see anything in front of you (not that I'd recommend that!). That is exactly what it is like for us in a wet grand prix – except our windscreen is the visor, so that rain is obstructing your vision only a few inches from your eyes. Also, it is incredibly hard to get the water off the visor, so you really do have to drive by memory. That works fine if everyone is driving in a predictable or expected way, but in those conditions, when someone lifts off or swerves, it can be very dangerous indeed.

You get around the track by instinct, by feeling your way around from experience and memory. In the same way you know your own house, so if there was a power cut and all the lights were off at night, you'd probably have a good idea of how far it is from the bedroom door to the light switch in the hallway, maybe how many stairs there are, where the kitchen is and so on. I think it's about seeking the *feel* of the car and, because my style is relatively smooth – I'm not someone who slides the car a lot – I think I can feel any dangerous movement quite early on. Sometimes that smooth approach can be to the detriment of how fast you can drive, but in other circumstances, like the wet, it's an invaluable approach.

Yet at the same time, wet racing creates this intense battle within yourself. You know you're on a straight and you know there's a corner coming up somewhere, but you can't actually see it. You have to drive flat out, but then you doubt yourself, and your mind tells you that you are going too fast for that corner, 'I can't see where I'm going,' so you lift off a fraction, but that approach can lead to all sorts of problems, so you press on again. You have to have trust that the other drivers are going flat out as well.

Therefore, the worst thing any driver could ever do on the race track is to drive slowly on the racing line, but especially so in wet conditions. Formula 1 cars brake so incredibly sharply, a car on the cusp of a corner can be going a 100mph slower than one just a few dozen metres back, and that huge relative difference in speed can create a massive accident, even if you're going in the same direction. On the positive side, rain is a great leveller though, because you all have the same weather, similar visors and so, apart from the leader, you are all affected equally. The ideal wet-race scenario is to get to the front and run in clean air and clean space.

The day did not start well. I spun out of La Source hairpin and a massive pile-up ensued, with twelve cars involved and the track littered with debris. The restart came just over an hour later, but the rain was still debilitating, so there was scope for further problems. And so it proved.

Mika spun out of the race after he and Michael confronted each other at the first corner – a potentially big blow for his title hopes; then I had a collision with Wurz and subsequently rejoined the race in last place. The rain was lighter by now, but visibility was still poor and the track was drenched. Schumacher was miles in the lead when he came up behind me on lap twenty-five – even though he had an unassailable lead, he was still accelerating away. I couldn't see a thing and I radioed to my team to let me know when Michael was right behind me so that I could move over. I had every intention of getting out of his way, so I moved to the right and lifted off. Unfortunately,

Michael was caught unawares, apparently, and smashed into the rear of my McLaren. My rear wing was ripped off and his Ferrari lost its nose and front right wheel. He was out of the race. Computer monitoring later showed the relative speed of the impact was 137mph.

I still had my helmet on by my parked McLaren when I saw Michael storming into our garage. He was clearly livid and was shouting, 'You tried to fucking kill me!' I couldn't really say anything back because my helmet was on, but he pretty much had to be restrained by his own race engineer. I found out later he'd even pulled away from Ferrari team members in their garage, so intent was he on confronting me.

I'm not a confrontational person, but if he had come at me, then it is human nature to fight back and it is instinctive, I think, for a racer to have some degree of inner aggression. Some people's aggression can be triggered even if you smile at them, with others it takes a bit more. It takes a lot to trigger me. I certainly wouldn't have run away, why would you have to run away from something you're not responsible for and not scared of? I was later quoted as saying that if we had actually resorted to fisticuffs, I would have won since I had my helmet on and then, 'I would have used the heed, and given him a Glasgow kiss.'

Joking aside, of course I didn't mean for Schumacher to crash into me. The impact was severe and I could have been hurt, too. I was merely trying to move out of the way. The incident was all over the TV and newspapers the following day. It went without saying that the unexpected boost this had given Mika's title push did not help my cause in the eyes of the more cynical observers.

It was an uncomfortable period for me, because the Ferrari faithful were incensed. The next race was in, of all places, Monza and the Italian fans were there in their thousands. Every time I went out of the garage into the pit lane they booed and some of them had a big sheet with the words 'Killer Coulthard' daubed on it. Some accused me of brake-testing Michael, but the read-outs showed quite clearly that I had not braked at all, just lifted off, albeit on the racing line in wet conditions. Some fans even spat at me. I bowed to them, but I was frightened when my engine failed in the actual race and I had to make my way back to the paddock. That's why I ran ...

All week the tension was hyped up another notch by the media. At the grand prix, Michael and myself shook hands in front of the cameras, then we spoke in private afterwards. I said, 'Look, we are both in the same industry. We have had various run-ins over the years but, because of our respect for each other, we can do one of two things: either (a) not talk to each other again or (b) we can just accept it as one of those things that happens and get on with it.' Michael agreed to this, but at the same time was keen to make the point that it was not he who had been wrong, but me.

I was trying to make my point, but he wasn't acknowledging me or considering that he'd done anything wrong. He thought it was completely my fault and nothing to do with him. Many years later, I can reflect and say that, as I was being lapped, I should have got well off the racing line. My team were telling me Michael was about to catch up with me and that I had to let him past; McLaren were certainly behaving entirely fairly, even knowing a win for Schumacher would leapfrog him ten points in the standings with Mika out retired and scoring zero. But there was absolutely no way I was trying to take him off the track. It was stupid accusation and our chat was starting to frustrate me.

At this point I said, 'But Michael, are you ever wrong?' and if I recall correctly he said, 'Well, not that I remember.'

Despite Melbourne, despite the various other things that happened to benefit Mika, we always had a muted relationship. He was a very quiet guy, kept himself to himself and, even with all the swirling politics, there was never any real animosity between us. We both live in Monaco, so we'd both go to the airport on a Thursday ahead of that weekend's race. He owned his own plane and he'd fly to the circuit, while I would get on a chartered plane and fly there too, usually landing within a few minutes of each other. We'd then get in our separate cars, go to the circuit, then sit in a debrief and talk about the car and then head off to separate rooms again. We were never really that open with each other. It's all slightly bizarre, really, when you compare that to, say, a football team coach or rugby training ground routine. You are polite and professional and members of the same team but, ultimately, you are competitors.

I enjoyed life in the lower formulas when you didn't have a team-mate and the whole set-up was around one driver, so it was you and your team against the rest of the world. I'm more comfortable in that environment; it fostered a real solidarity. I don't like having to second-guess if someone is onside, you know, does that engineer want me to win or does he secretly want the other guy to win? You have your own dedicated mechanics, but you also have people in your crew who are for the greater good of the team and inevitably certain people pin their colours to the team mast, not yours, which is human nature, I suppose.

The most famously volatile relationships between team-mates were probably Senna and Prost or Mansell and Piquet, but for me it's never been that volatile. I had those handbags at dawn with Damon but that blew over, and there's always a few verbal parries traded in the media, but in reality there's very little else.

The pressure from sponsors and the manufacturers not to create tension and controversy is immense, so it really wouldn't be looked upon in a positive light if two team-mates were battling verbally or otherwise all the time. Not in the modern climate, but it certainly has gone on in the past. The media would love it but the sponsors wouldn't, although I suspect teams like Red Bull probably wouldn't mind.

On the track, the moment when the tension between Mika and I reached its highest point came in Portugal in 1996, when he tried to overtake me and we touched. The impact spun me around as well as Mika. There's a great photograph of me sitting there, spun round, with my middle finger out of the cockpit gesticulating at him as he drives past me.

After the race, Ron wanted to see us both and, before Mika came in, he asked me what had happened, saying, 'I want to hear what you have to say ...' When I'd finished telling him, he said, 'I hear you, but I know what you drivers are like, I want to hear what Mika has to say, too ...' In fairness to him, he had to hear both sides of the story, but I took it personally and assumed Ron didn't trust me; I was still naïve enough to think that if you know you are being truthful, other people will know that, too.

I believe I'm an honest, straightforward person and, of course, I might see an incident from a different angle, but I'm not someone who'd lie. That was kind of hurtful. We touched at another race too, where I went to win ahead of him and he refused to shake my hand afterwards. I'd touched him at the first corner and gone on to win the race. He wasn't happy afterwards. I remember Adrian was on the podium with us and he was saying, 'Right, sort this out right now, it's unprofessional, okay, you touched, but that's racing.'

Mika's a great talent but a very complex individual. I remember having a conversation with him several years into our relationship regarding some agreement or other, and I was like, 'Well, we've done that and you know you can trust me, as I've shown in previous races ...'

'I don't trust anyone,' came back the blunt reply.

I said, 'Come on Mika, you can trust me, you only have to look at what I've done before.'

'I don't trust anyone.'

'You must trust your management?'

'No.'

'Your wife?'

'I don't trust anyone.'

That conversation summed Mika up: he was always a little bit distant. Also, to be fair, if people speak a different main language, then it's sometimes difficult for you to relate. I have to balance that by saying he's a straightforward individual who's motivated by driving and being with his family and I respect that, but we just had different ways of going about our business, and that was something I found difficult.

*

Behind the scenes, concerns in my mind about the team's position regarding myself and Mika were festering. The doubters will always say it was a level playing field and the best driver won. And no, I do not have any evidence that I was specifically given a worse car, for example. It was just a feeling, something intangible, something you can't put your finger on. You cannot take out the importance of being in a happy place and your mind being settled. I did not want advantages; I just wanted a level playing field. I would refute any claim that you can provide a level playing field in terms of Formula 1 equipment. Let me explain. Formula 1 cars are never identical. They are handmade. Therefore, every one of them is unique. On paper, two cars can be identical; in reality, they can't. There is no such thing as two identical engines and no such thing as two sets of identical tyres. Inevitably there are tolerances. Millions of pounds can be spent on gaining downforce, that's because these machines are already honed and fine-tuned to such minuscule detail that the slightest improvement can benefit. Minute variations in the slightest aspect can affect performance either way.

When a team manufactures a car for a new season, it may be apparent that one is slightly better than another; an engine may run just a few bhp higher or, conversely, a set of pistons might be transparently slightly tighter – and therefore less efficient – in one case than the other. These variations are not the stuff of mystery: the advanced telemetry available to teams means they can quantify with scientific precision how well a piece of machinery, a component or even an entire car is performing.

As my disquiet about possible favouritism grew, McLaren

appeared – on the surface at least – to be at pains to extinguish such concerns. Engines were picked at random. I should state that McLaren always emphasised that there was not a No. 1 and No. 2 driver, unlike say Ferrari, where it was always very clear that Michael was the premier driver. Largely, McLaren would allow open racing until such time they thought it was hugely beneficial to the team to do otherwise. As much as I am being critical of how I would have ideally liked the environment to be, I accept McLaren's position: you sign the contract and they, to the best of their ability, give myself and Mika equal equipment.

I think Formula 1 would be better with one-driver teams. Certainly from an individual driver's point of view, things would be a lot simpler. Two-car teams just create friction: you have two cars, but only one pit team and garage, that alone is going to create potential conflict. In theory, if you put two computers in two identical cars and – assuming both cars had matching performance and fuel loads – they would both need to pit at the same time. So how do you choose which driver gets priority?

Coming in to pit is not straightforward, either. Every 10kg less that the car weighs, you will typically drive three-tenths of a second quicker – some tracks it's four-tenths, on others it's two-and-a-half tenths. By contrast, as you are able to get faster due to a lighter fuel load, your tyres are wearing out, getting old and, depending on the track, the temperature, the compound and the degradation of the tyre varies. You might suffer a big drop-off in lap time if the deterioration is severe, as much as maybe a second a lap; or it might be minimal if the tyre has worn modestly. On tracks where tyre degradation is outpaced by the speed gained from a lighter fuel load, you can get dramatic results if you time your pit stops cleverly and fire in flying laps before the tyres finally degrade too far. So pit strategy and timing is a complicated situation.

Again McLaren were at pains to appear impartial. With regard to pitting, the system many teams use is that whoever qualifies highest gets the first choice of when to pit and, generally, the preferred choice will be to pit last. So you can assume that if you are out-qualified by your team-mate, then he will take the choice of pit stop, giving him yet another advantage over you in the race, so in many ways – and I experienced this several times – the qualifying session lost me the race. All the way down the paddock, regardless of what team it is, there's always an advantage to be had for the guy who can stop second. The problem is, if you think your car is slower, then how can you out-qualify and, therefore, win pit preference?

This sort of continual analysis was how the quandary developed. I was battling on several fronts. I was battling against the rest of the grid; I was battling against Mika; I was battling against my own team; and it became such a core preoccupation that I was eventually battling against the inner turmoil created by my suspicions.

Having the engines picked at random was one example of how McLaren took steps to alleviate my doubts, but it still ate away at me. It was almost like a family with two children, where you know the parents should really love them both equally, but in reality, they don't. I kind of felt that I was *sort of* in this family, but not quite. Mika, the person some motor-sport commentators have called 'the favourite son', most definitely was.

I think that part of this was definitely down to the fact I signed to the team after Mika crashed in 1995: he had been a family member before me and that immense trauma must have made him and the team very close. I see that.

Of course, I can only see it from my point of view. What made it more exhausting was that I kept trying to rationalise the fears, so I'd say to myself, 'No, you are just being paranoid.' But then something else would happen and the doubts would fire up again. I don't want to give the impression of me complaining every week; there were long periods when all was quiet, but the subtext to much of my time at McLaren was this niggling doubt.

Conversations with myself, my managers and close confidants went on for years; it was like a slow drip-feed of self-doubt eroding my confidence. Generally, I do not like confrontation. Don't get me wrong, I have my moments. I probably take after my mother in that respect as she can be fiery, but only at times. I tend not to talk about something that is troubling me, I don't discuss it even if the tension is building up and then ... bang! I'm also a perfectionist and it can make me very demanding of standards at work. I'm not paranoid about not being perfect, I just want to be the best I can and I accept that my beliefs and desires will be different from others and, provided I am not breaking the law and I can afford the time and/or the money to live in a way I think is acceptable, then anyone who joins my party or works with me simply has to be able to keep that way. If not, it doesn't work. I'm not saying my way is the best way, but in the absence of knowing a better way, you want to live in a manner that is comfortable to yourself. I'm very open to the idea of someone coming into my life and showing me a better way, because I'm all for efficiency. People take that in different ways – some said I moaned about a car if it wasn't just right, whereas someone like Frank Williams said, 'Give him a perfect car and he is unbeatable.' Generally, though, I am fairly easy-going for the majority of the time, but with so many examples of bias towards Mika, I wasn't thick-skinned enough to remain unaffected by that. Martin Whitmarsh, to be fair, did try to still the waters between myself and Ron, but the tide was against me.

In 1998 and 1999, Mika won back-to-back championships in the same McLaren I was driving; in the same years, I came third and fourth respectively. In 1998, Mika scored nearly double my fifty-six points. Our performances also brought McLaren their first constructors' title since their run of four straight trophies from 1988–91. In 1999, matters were much closer and my title hopes only really faded in the closing few races. The two seasons saw me win three races, fifteen podiums and three poles. 1999 was pestered with six reliability retirements, but otherwise they were a fruitful pair of seasons . . . on the surface.

I don't have many regrets from my career, but moving over for Mika in Melbourne in 1998 is one of them. It shaped people's perceptions of me, which in some cases have not changed, and it was clearly not the right thing to do for myself. I shouldn't have done it. Working for the team it was exactly the right and professional thing to do, but I shouldn't have done it.

In 1996, Damon Hill had won the world championship in a

car I had been driving the year before; in 1997, Jacques Villeneuve, also in a Williams, won the world championship. Would I have won the championship if I had stayed at Williams? Yes, easy-peasy. But there you go. You are – partly – the decisions you make. At the end of the day, Formula 1 is F1; F1 spelt backwards, as they say in the paddock, is 'if'. If my aunty had balls she'd be my uncle.

What I should have done was to have believed in my ability to deliver in the Williams in 1995 and, therefore, my ability to then get a seat the following year with Frank. While I was settling in at McLaren, Williams were bagging a brace of driver titles and five constructors' titles. I still understand why an extremely lucrative, longer-term deal with McLaren compared to a one-year contract with Williams was an enticing option, particularly for a young driver riddled with debt and keen to make his mark. However, I would have won a title had I stayed at Williams.

On the other side to that argument, Williams went into decline and McLaren went into growth and I enjoyed nine successful years at McLaren. Unfortunately, after McLaren finally overhauled Williams in the late 1990s, when they finally got with the pace, I had the situation with Mika.

I missed my window to win the title in that period, I know that.

I absolutely feel that this situation within McLaren cost me the world championship, I really do. Let me qualify that a little. McLaren did not, I believe, manipulate events so that I did not win the title, not at all. I did, at times, have what I felt was an inferior car, yes. Certain specific examples of clear preference – Jerez, Melbourne, to name but a couple – suggest this affected my title chances, too. But there was also another factor: the thoughts in my head. All this swirling paranoia meant I didn't perform to the absolute best of my ability. That was in my own hands.

SILVER AND BLACK BRILLIANCE

There were still plenty of great times with McLaren laced in among these on-going problems. As I have said, Ron Dennis knows how to throw a party and, likewise, McLaren knows how to create a PR stunt. With the backing of sponsors like West – the cigarette manufacturer and a multi-billion-dollar company – I was lucky enough to go on some pretty amazing PR jaunts. Okay, sometimes it all felt a little bit awkward presenting the company and talking to the media, but I understand the dynamics of sponsorship and how much money these businesses bring to the sport; therefore, I never really had a problem with appearing at such events. Plus, I did get to do some amazing things!

On one occasion, they put me in the ring with champion boxer, Vladimir Klitschko, a giant of a man. They gave me these huge boxing gloves and we did some training, bouncing tennis balls and a little bit of gentle sparring, all in good fun. He kindly signed a pair of gloves for me too, which was good. Another time I went to New York and drove around in a police car, complete with my own full uniform, which at times felt far more dangerous than anything I do on the track. While we were sat there, this tourist came up to the car and asked if she could take a photograph of us and the car!

Perhaps one of the best PR trips was when they sent me to Zvezdnyi Gorodok, better known as Star City, to go through various simulations they used to train astronauts. Mika had already taken part in a ground-control-to-orbital-satellite chat with the MIR space station, as sponsors West were keen on all things astronautical. This particular town was small, only about 5,000 people, and pretty quiet, even though it was just twenty miles from Moscow.

Once we got there, they let us climb inside a replica of the MIR space station; it was shockingly small and it provided a fascinating insight into how astronauts have to live. There's one window in the corner and near to that is a little curtain curling around the toilet I mentioned, which naturally is the only place they have to go and do their pee and poo – basically in the same room as everyone else. They keep this exact replica in the event of an emergency, so that they can talk the astronauts through problems more precisely.

One exercise was to simulate the G-forces created by an actual rocket on the launch-pad. To do this, they sit you in a pod on a rotating arm within this laboratory, then spin you around in circles at ever-accelerating speeds. You put your finger on a button and the idea is that when you eventually pass out, you inevitably take your finger off the button and they can assess how well you did and so on.

I think they were quite keen to get me in there and put me through the grinder, so to speak. However, in actual fact, astronauts don't pull that high G, but the launch is so dramatic, with all that thunderous noise and the smoke and flames, it looks much worse. But, to be honest, it didn't feel too bad at all. The chair wasn't overly uncomfortable and the G forces were perfectly manageable.

I'm used to pulling high G. On planet earth, I weigh 72kg, which is one gravitational force for me. Under extreme breaking, a Formula 1 driver experiences a spike of 5G, meaning at that precise moment, my body weight is five times 72kg. In hard cornering it can be as high as 4G and the stresses on the neck can be huge. Drivers, therefore, need a very strong neck to cope with those pressures, otherwise their head will literally be dangling around in the cockpit. That's why if you look at a driver's neck, it is quite often relatively out-sized compared to other parts of the body, except for the obvious, and I've never had any complaints in that department ... and if I have, you'd probably have all read about it in the tabloids.

I believe only fighter pilots are subjected to higher G than an F1 driver. Even then a fighter pilot experiences Gs longitudinally, in that the plane will be leaning in the direction of the G force. However, an F1 car is stuck to the track, so it is not leaning in the same way as the G forces and that puts a severe physical trauma on the body. Because we are strapped in, we are affected by external G, which can cause issues with blood circulation and so on. It's as hostile an environment as you can be in. By comparison, an astronaut will not actually pull that much G and if he does, it's probably because he's fucked up royally.

I'd actually been asked whether I wanted to become a space tourist. West wanted to do it as a PR stunt but I was like, 'Er, no thanks!' I like it on earth, cheers. My friend Guy Laliberté, co-founder of Cirque Du Soleil, has actually paid to be a tourist, I think it will cost him about $20 million. If that's what you fancy then that's fine, but I don't see the point.

So, instead, the people at the Yuri Gagarin Cosmonaut Training Centre kindly sent me up in this military plane – a quite shabby-looking old Ilyushin cargo aircraft – that climbs to a certain extreme height, about 6,500 metres I believe, before it intentionally nose-dives almost vertically towards the ground. In so doing, it creates weightlessness akin to what an astronaut experiences. For several seconds, you get complete weightlessness. Astronauts don't usually take their cars up with them, which is what we did with the latest West McLaren-Mercedes MP4-12. It was incredible and I've got some great footage of me flying Superman-style down the length of the plane. However, I was pleased to experience it all without the danger, the tiny toilet with a curtain around it and the powdery food.

On another occasion, West ran a European-wide competition to win a drive in a Formula 1 car, providing you had no previous experience. They staged a series of eastern European competitions where the regional winners progressed through to a final with the top two then having a shoot-out to drive the Formula 1 car. At one of the functions they had a Beatles tribute group supported by this Freddie Mercury impersonator. As I wasn't involved with the actual driving, I was having a 'couple' of drinks and I thought this guy was absolutely brilliant. I was a big Queen fan, as was my father.

His birthday was coming up and I had wanted to get him something really different, so what I did was fly this Freddie Mercury impersonator all the way down to Spain to perform at my father's party the next night. I think this eastern European

Freddie Mercury was completely bemused. I thought my dad would love it, because he had famously once seen 'Pete Loaf' sing 'Bat Out Of Hell' and would announce to anyone who would listen that he was 'categorically better than the real thing'. So I got Pete Loaf there as well and my father had had a few drinks and was already in full clapping mode by the time Freddie's turn was up.

I, however, was cold sober this time around, so when Freddie walked on, I looked at him, listened to him and thought, 'Oh my God, what the fuck have I done?' They introduced him with suitable fanfare: 'Please welcome, ladies and gentlemen, all the way from eastern Europe . . .' It was a very surreal moment. I could see my father sitting there thinking, 'Why the fuck has David flown a Freddie Mercury impersonator in to Spain from the Eastern Bloc . . .?' To be fair, the guy did play up the fact he was crap and he eventually won the crowd around. And my father does have high musical standards. Even Meat Loaf can't live up to Pete Loaf, after all.

It's fascinating, because when you go to eastern Europe, they treat you like some visiting dignitary, or a major politician coming to town. They always assign you with full security, all these massive ex-military bodyguards and limos that, looking at them, must surely be bullet-proof. They even sweep your hotel rooms for bugs, the full works.

On one trip there, we went into a bar in town. I met with a young local lady, shared a drink and some coffees and had a lovely time. She joined me in my hotel room later to do our bit for the European community and, as far as I was concerned, that was that. The security guards even escorted her out of the hotel afterwards. The next day, I was doing a phone interview on a radio station, which was also live in front of quite a few local journalists. Part of the interview was a Q&A phone-in. The first few callers were easy to answer, but then a familiar voice came on the line.

'Hello, David, how do you do, do you like the ladies?'

'Well, yes, of course!' I said, a little bemused.

'Well, do you like Kiev ladies, David?'

I replied yes again, suddenly feeling a little bit unsettled. A penny was beginning to drop as to why the voice sounded familiar. It was only the woman I had slept with the previous night calling in. I was sitting there, on a live phone-in radio interview with the massed ranks of the press ten feet away who could surely feel the heat coming off my rapidly reddening cheeks.

'Do you like Russian ladies?'

'Er, yes, er, um, yes, of course . . .'

'Do you remember me from last night, David?'

Regardless of the disputes and doubts about the priorities of the McLaren team, one aspect of my time with Ron's outfit that was undeniably a brilliant experience was their attitude to innovation – for me, one of the most enjoyable aspects of being a Formula 1 driver. Much is made of the modern era and how technology has changed the sport so much, but innovation in the garages and pits is nothing new. Way back in the 1920s they had to cut back on engine sizes because of fears for driver safety and excess speeds; in the late 1960s, manually operated wings heralded the era of aerodynamics; Tyrrell introduced their ill-fated six-wheel car in 1976; and, in the late 1980s, Ferrari revolutionised the sport with their steering-wheel-mounted shift. Technological genius is part of the lifeblood of Formula 1.

McLaren were certainly at the forefront of innovation, it is steeped in the company's psyche – way back in the early 1980s, for example, John Watson won the team's twenty-fifth race in the MP4, an all-carbon fibre chassis. Being in an environment like that is very rewarding. You are working with technically brilliant people, designers, engineers and so on, all at the top of their game. These people are constantly coming up with ideas that have never been done before, materials that have never been used before; there does not appear to be any boundaries to the scope of their thinking. In many ways, it is the sports equivalent of the space race. As the ultimate test pilot of those ideas, it can be very challenging and very rewarding. You can literally find yourself in a 200mph car with a specific system that has never been tested by a human being before. As most of these ideas filter down in some form, diluted or not, into everyday road cars, I guess that makes me a very well-paid crash test dummy for the public!

Seriously, though, there have been so many cutting-edge innovations I've come across as a driver, it really is exciting. The actual race on the television is just the end result, but behind the scenes there is a constant hub of activity, pushing and working to develop new technology and electronics. McLaren excelled at this.

As a result, being the driver, you're constantly having to adapt yourself; I liken it to being no more remarkable than adapting your footing when you are walking on a snow-covered path, or a tiled floor that has some water on it. It's human nature, or rather human reaction. You've been trained through trial and error as a child to find your footing and even if the surface you are on changes, you adapt. Sitting in a Formula 1 car with a host of new devices and systems is simply another way of changing what is under your feet. You have to relearn how to drive that car, almost instantly.

McLaren always looked to innovate. For example, they spent an awful lot of time and money on a simulator, similar to that used by the aircraft industry. My friend Kerry Spackman, a neuroscientist who I had first worked with back at PSR, was brought in to assist with that project. The results were very good, but the simulator will never replace being out on the circuit. If you can imagine walking fast on a sheet of ice. You can simulate that experience, clearly. However, if the slightest movement or sensation in your foot tells you that you may be about to slip, that cannot be simulated in the same way. Likewise, when it comes to driving a Formula 1 car at 200mph, you instinctively pick up so many little nuances and feelings and noises and vibrations that cannot be copied by a computer in a room, no matter how advanced it is. The simulator was, however, excellent for practising reaction times and aspects like that.

When I first came to McLaren, they'd been experimenting with a 'third' wing on the car. A year later, in 1997, the team developed a system they called the 'fiddle brake' (called a 'second brake pedal' by others) and that is a prime example of the way F1 pushes the boundaries all the time and the repercussions of that mentality on the practicalities for a driver. In those days you had a throttle and a brake in the tiny footwell. Current Formula 1 cars have the clutch on the steering wheel, so nowadays everyone brakes with the left-foot because it isn't needed for the clutch.

Then McLaren introduced a new pedal, the fiddle brake, bringing the total of pedals to three. The idea was this: the fiddle brake could control each rear wheel independently of the other, so in other words, if you came to a corner you could slow down one wheel but not the other with this brake. It was not dissimilar to how a tank works, in essence.

The core problem the engineers were trying to solve was the fact that as you turn a car into a corner, you lose downforce and, therefore, it steers less accurately, but you need steering to take you safely around the corner. The problem is, your wheels are now at an angle and this creates drag and lower efficiency. Consequently, you have this constant battle not to put too much steering lock into the car to get around the corner in the most efficient manner. Therefore, the engineers came up with this system to make the car more efficient in cornering, by effectively slowing the inside wheel down and helping it turn without actually creating more drag. The best part was that, although the concept was complex and involved, considering drag, downforce and a whole host of other calculations, the technology itself was actually very simple and worked extremely well. We were able to run this system for the best part of a year without anyone knowing about it. It was legal, at that time, by the way.

As a driver, this represents an entirely new way of operating a car. In some ways it could be like learning to drive again, you physically have to do something different. If you only drive automatics and then step into a manual car, it's the same situation. Actually, however, it is remarkable how quickly you adapt to such a new set-up. You couldn't just use the fiddle brake as you were lifting off the throttle, because all you'd do was lock the rear wheels and spin the car; what you had to do was increase the brake pressure on the inside wheel and increase the throttle *at the same time* to overpower the fact that you were slowing down that wheel and to accelerate the other two wheels to help turn the car. Physically, this involved balancing both your feet together as well as the fiddle brake; mentally it added a whole new element into the equation and all done at speeds of up to 200mph.

What was interesting was that Mika Hakkinen and myself, independently of each other, discovered that we could also use it to reduce wheel spin accelerating *out* of slow corners. It had been designed to reduce under-steer at high speed, as I've mentioned, but here was another use that we had both worked out separately.

If you stopped the inner wheel spinning, it naturally transmitted more of the torque into the wheel that had grip. Looking at the telemetry showing steering input, brake pressure, throttle opening, suspension movement and all of those things, I could see Mika was experimenting with this and I dare say he could see I was doing the same. However, we never talked about it with engineers. It was not something the team needed to know. It might have been an advantage for whoever was most adept at first, but after a period of time we realised we were both using it to a similar degree.

I suspect the device gained us maybe a couple of tenths, which might not sound like much, but to gain that in pure horsepower or downforce could cost hundreds of thousands of pounds, sometimes millions. Through the course of a season, teams can literally calculate a finite cost in pounds per horse-power, so you can see why innovations such as the fiddle brake can be spectacular.

Of course, once your competitor knows about it, every team runs it. Casual observers might then think we'd all be on the same level, but in this case, Mika and I had got hours of testing and racing under our belts using it and anyone else would have been playing catch up. Also, back then – and it might only be ten years ago, but that is a lifetime in F1 – there was a lot less personnel movement between teams than there is now.

The brake pedal was actually exposed by *F1 Racing* magazine. Some of their writers had noticed in pictures of our two cars that our brake pads were glowing bright red as we accelerated out of the Niki Lauda Kurve at the Austrian circuit. No other cars on the grid were doing this. Realising that the McLarens were braking here when, in conventional theory, they shouldn't be, the photographer and writer started to investigate and, by the next race, at the Nurburgring, they were fired up to get a scoop with their cameras. It just so happened that both Mika and myself did not finish the race, retiring very close to each other having led the race 1-2. The photographer in question, Darren Heath, somehow managed to get over to the cars and stuck his camera in Mika's car – he'd taken his steering wheel off in frustration; I'd remembered to replace mine to prevent anyone taking any pictures of my car. Several rolls of film later and the whole industry knew what we'd been up to. Ron Dennis was not a happy man. Ferrari eventually managed to persuade the FIA to declare this so-called 'brake-steer' illegal and it was banned before the 1998 Brazilian Grand Prix.

Of course, technology doesn't always work. Developments can sometimes feel like a huge step backwards. Famously, McLaren's 2003 car, the MP4-18, never surfaced as a race car due to multiple difficulties. Nonetheless, experiments such as the fiddle brake were one of the highlights of my time at McLaren.

The paddock is a small pond with several very big fish in it, but what goes on in those murky waters is watched by hundreds of millions of people twice a month during the season. It's a sport of contradiction. A sport of technology development that requires the secrecy of the CIA and yet is set up in such a way that such secrecy is almost impossible to achieve. Then, when we have spent millions of pounds on technology, we let cameras on to the grid and people with zoom lenses that can shoot a bumble bee at 300 yards. Of course, we use screens to hide the cars at testing and measures are taken to avoid blatant spying, but ultimately secrets do get out. When we used the fiddle pedal at McLaren, that was a rare case of the secret staying quiet for a very long time.

One reason why the technology in Formula 1 spreads like a virus is the intimate nature of the paddock. It is, after all, just twenty-two cars and drivers, eleven teams. The paddock is a strange place in many ways. There's a joke that test drivers are always looking to put banana skins in front of the race drivers, whatever it takes to get an opportunity. After all, there are only twenty-one other people in the world who do the same job as me. The paddock can make you a firm believer in conspiracy theories.

I wouldn't say I was paranoid, but having a vision of who's around and might be coming up on your heels is, in my opinion, vital. There can be a lot of smiling assassins behind the pleasantries. But that's no different to most jobs at such a high level. Certainly my years at McLaren and the concerns about favouring Mika did little to dilute such worries, it only fuelled them.

Making sure I am in the car all day testing and stuff like that is as good a way to stop someone else having influence over the development of the car and, therefore, over the team. I've survived this many years in Formula 1 by avoiding accidents on the track and swerving away from catastrophes off it. Remember, Formula 1 is effectively a private sports club, it's not governed under European law or British law or anyone else's; it's a private members' club. You get accepted and there's only eleven members/teams (I think twelve is the maximum there can be) and the other members even get a vote as to whether you are accepted into the party. The rules are decided not by what would be deemed fair and reasonable in the eyes of the public, but by those who make the rules. If they agree to a new rule, then that's it.

The chain of command in F1 is very clear: you have Bernie Ecclestone; the FIA, headed by Max Mosley (son of fascist politician Oswald); then your team owners, designers, mechanics, drivers and so on. And yet, because the minutiae of the design and technology are pored over by mechanics, overheard by trainers or people at the factory, there are so many places and ways in which that information can be overheard and, thus, events affected. Some of these guys have access to highly confidential information about developments which teams may have spent months and millions of pounds developing, so armed with that sort of power they might share that knowledge with a mate down the pub and then, suddenly, that information has somehow transferred over to another team. Then there are the not-so-secretive examples of 'spying', because there will always be a defector who jumps ship and joins another team.

The physical layout of the grid itself is bizarre too, if you think about it. All the teams are side by side, in testing, in racing, it's like having the Premiership football sides all training on one huge field right next to each other, or two boxers who are about to fight each other, sharing the same gym.

F1 is a small travelling circus of which the ringleader is Bernie Ecclestone. Very close to that ringmaster there are several star attractions, people such as Flavio Briatore, Frank Williams, Ron Dennis and Jean Todt. Just below that, and I shall continue with the circus analogy but won't publicly call any of them clowns, are the high-profile drivers. As much as the teams would want to sell their image and build their brand, ultimately the public relate to the drivers because they are seen as the modern-day gladiators, wheel-to-wheel, risking life and limb. The paddock *is* Formula 1 – within half a square kilometre you have the entire operating world of F1, all the key players, the money men, the technology brains, the business minds, the sportsmen, everything. I think there are some good people in the paddock, of course, but for sure there are groups of individuals that are not so pleasant.

Back in the late 1990s when I then left my management at IMG, I needed someone to be my manager, so I gave my friend Iain Cunningham the job – Iain being the man who'd helped me get the Williams test, if you recall – as I credited him with getting my career started in F1. Iain created that opportunity for me and that's why I reciprocated and gave him the opportunity to manage my day-to-day business affairs. I thought he deserved a pay-back, so for a period of time he took care of my business.

After about a year, I also took on the former F1 driver Martin Brundle to be my motor-sport commercial manager. He'd been the chairman of the Grand Prix Drivers' Association, known as the GPDA, and with his combination of racing experience and behind-the-scenes knowledge, he seemed an ideal ally. We bumped into one another in the paddock and I was particularly unhappy with certain aspects of my work, we got chatting and it just went from there. I actually asked him to help on a plane journey at the end of the 1997 season heading home from Suzuka. We are still working together to this day – and I think he enjoys my regular 'insider' updates from the paddock for his ITV1 commentating job! So that was an example where the intimacy of the paddock worked in a positive way.

Martin Brundle is still my motor-sport commercial manager; I worked with Iain Cunningham for a few years as my business manager; after a year or so I moved to Monaco and, with Iain being in Oxford, it eventually came to an end, something that, because we were good friends, was uncomfortable for me. We actually didn't speak for about a year, but happily we are on great terms again now. Iain knows me well because he lived through some of my changing relationships and he knows my character.

Some people display their personalities in the paddock more than others. I tend to stay in the team's motorhome – Red Bull's is called an 'Energy Station' – in my little room, because it's private and I can gather my thoughts and watch the telly and do no-brainer type things. If you sit in the public areas you are accepting that you are going to meet people, or they are going to come and talk to you, photograph you, whatever. I noticed that once a driver gets married and has kids, you tend to see them a lot less in the paddock. It's unusual to see a wife and baby out there. The only driver who really did that recently is Montoya, but to my mind in a slightly exploitative way – you know you are being photographed, you are accepting the photographers are trying to catch that theme, the girlfriend in the tight top or, in his case, the wife and kids. It's behind-the-scenes shots like these they are after. I don't get how an experienced person would do that knowingly and comfortably, without thinking of the consequences or how that's perceived; it's almost like a politician going to a school and shaking hands with little kids – they are doing it because it's part of the propaganda.

The paddock is a supremely competitive environment, so you have to expect some intense personalities, and the small physicality of the garages and pit area can sometimes make it feel like a zoo, this slither of caged animals running alongside the track. And in any zoo there are dominant individuals with strong personalities. Let's just say I don't socialise with many people from the paddock; in contrast, I have formed friendships with those I do spend time with that I think will endure for a lifetime.

SLOW DOWN

I've never been gung-ho or crazy. My brother was always quite crazy and another childhood friend, Ian Wilson, was too. We used to play in his field and, as a little boy, Ian was fucking mad! One day he launched himself into the field flat out on his motorbike and almost immediately got a speed wobble and went straight down on his face. I would never have done that, because it was just a question of when he fell off rather than if. Even as a young kid, I just wouldn't have put myself in that environment.

The first time I rode a motorbike in my father's field, I fell off and wouldn't go back on it again for a few weeks. When I did, I let the clutch out too soon and made the bike jump and, again, I didn't go back on it for a while. I eventually did, but only if I was push-started so that I didn't have to work the clutch. Similarly, the first time I went on a quad bike, I pushed the thumb throttle and it took off quicker than I expected, so I pulled up, got off and that was it, I didn't want to ride a quad bike anymore.

I did a brief boxing match with Cawthorne when I was at the

local boys' club, before I was eleven and had started kart racing. We put on these over-sized gloves and I was thinking, 'Yeah, this will be fun ...' then he whacked me and my ear started ringing, so I put my gloves down and said, 'I've had enough!' He carried on smacking me and I was shouting, 'You bastard! I don't want to play anymore.'

As I have said, I grew up being scared of the dark, with those recurring nightmares of some monster coming to get me through the whistling winds in the dark streets of Twynholm. That scared me.

I've had ex's who have hidden behind doors and gone 'BOO!!!' and I hate it, that scares me, that is fear. That sounds really squeamish, but I am just trying to be honest. I've always been the sort to dip a toe in the water, then think, 'Yup, that's all right, yeah, I can do that ...' before leaping in. That has been my approach to life.

So you can see, I'm not the daredevil.

I hate being scared.

But racing? It has never scared me.

It just isn't something that frightens me.

I wouldn't do it if I was scared; I don't like being scared, so why would I want to do that? I've never been fearful about getting into a racing car, and I can see the contradiction between that and how I view certain other things in life, but I would not get in any race car if I was scared. It's not part of my nature.

I do get nervous energy before the start of a grand prix or indeed any race, pondering if it is going to be okay. That's only natural, but I have seen grown men shaking before races. If I felt that way, I just wouldn't do it for a job. And this isn't because I've been racing for years, I just never felt scared when I was a kid, either.

It is a controlled environment and by the time you have reached Formula 1 the safety measures are staggering. Plus, safety is all relative. For a fact it is much safer to drive an F1 car now than when I started in 1994. There were two driver fatalities that year. There hasn't been one since. So, we were clearly taking a bigger risk back then, but it all moves on so quickly that I think in ten years' time we will look back at the 2006 grand prix cars and say, 'Shit, did we really used to drive around in those shit boxes?'

Now, put me on a MotoGP or Superbike and then I would be scared senseless. I wouldn't go anywhere near one of those. I can ride a motorbike, but I would never race one. Those guys can be flicked off like a rag doll and be killed at any second. You talk to them and they say they have their own rationalisation, their own logic too, explaining that they know how to fall and all that, but for me that is the meaning of the word scary. You come off a bike and get thrown across a track at 150mph and knowing how to fall isn't going to be a lot of use. Fuck that.

A good racing driver is brave, but a great one knows how to use fear to his advantage. Fear is an essential part of doing what we do, because fear defines a limit and if you are good at understanding the physics of what a car can sustain through a corner, for example, then you drive it more quickly than others. To be fearless is no use – you have no limits and so you just go flat out, exceed what the car can do and, therefore, crash. That's why so many of those boy racers get killed, their lack of fear or excess of bravado is out of proportion to the physical limits of their car and their driving ability.

So fear is an ally, but I am not scared.

I really admire sports people who do dangerous or scary jobs. I don't do that. Mountain biking is about as dangerous as I get off the track. Even then I come down the hills relatively slowly. I like to climb on quiet roads because there is less traffic; then, when I'm coming down a hill, I take it easy, because I don't need to fall off at 30mph with cycling shorts on, rip the skin off my arse and break my bloody collar bone again, not least because then I can't go racing.

If you have a big shunt, it shakes you up, but I've never found myself not wanting to get back in the car afterwards. My mother has a little phrase that says, 'What is for you, won't go by you,' so in other words if it's meant to be, it's meant to be. I like racing and, in my eyes at least, it is not a frightening thing to do. That may seem illogical to some, but to me it is extremely logical and natural.

Yet, there is a core contradiction about my saying that.

I never thought I would get past the age of thirty.

I assumed that something would happen to me before then. I believed this so firmly that I never actually planned anything that would take place after my thirtieth birthday. I just thought I enjoyed racing and, on balance, what would be, would be.

Only ten months before I turned thirty, something happened that nearly proved my premonition of a premature death correct.

Obviously my job involves a lot of travel. To give you an idea, in the 2006 season I caught nearly sixty flights and clocked up almost 100,000 air miles. Add to that all the transfers and other trips by car I need to make, and you can see I am on the move a lot. One year in Barcelona, after a particularly heavy stint of continental flights and air travel, I was actually sitting in the car itself and couldn't remember which circuit I was on. I'd been in about four different countries in as many days. I picked my head up and glanced across the garage, saw a layout of the circuit – which I recognised to be Barcelona – and then knew where I was and what was expected of me.

Travel is synonymous with being a race driver. I know that. However, I never thought it would increase my risk of having an incident, but I guess it does in a way, although the odds of being in a car accident are still reassuringly very low; the chances of being in a plane crash are almost negligible ... aren't they?

Ten days previously I'd won at Silverstone, so I was feeling very buoyant. It was the week leading up to the Spanish Grand Prix, the day was Tuesday, 2 May 2000. I'd been flying a lot between Nice and the UK and the flight I caught on that Tuesday was no different from any other. I have never owned an aircraft and I used to charter privately a lot – back then I was perhaps more well-known and in the public eye because of my success at McLaren, so jumping on an Easyjet was not necessarily an easy option. I often jump on commercial flights nowadays because I am not recognised as much and, anyway, I am far more at ease with that situation.

I booked a plane for an afternoon flight and then, relatively late in the day, I decided I wanted to go in the morning instead. Unfortunately, the company I normally used did not have a plane available for a morning flight, so they did what is called a 'sub-charter', namely they hired out a plane from another firm and dealt with it that way. This second firm was actually owned by David Murray, who was chairman of Rangers Football Club (and as an aside, he'd suffered a horrendous injury in a car crash and lost both his legs many years before).

My insistence on flying in the morning rather than simply waiting for my usual set-up in the afternoon probably would have got me to my destination maybe two hours earlier . . .

. . . had we ever arrived.

I met and introduced myself to the pilots, David Saunders and Dan Worley, as I usually did when arriving and got on board the aircraft with my American girlfriend of the time, Heidi Wichlinski, her dog Moody and my personal trainer, Andy Matthews. It was an eight-seater Learjet 45, a pretty standard aircraft for this type of use. It's one of those twin-engined planes with extra fuel tanks on the wing tips that are shaped like torpedoes.

We took off from Farnborough as normal, but about an hour into the flight I started to hear this weird noise. I'd been in aircraft so many times before and I knew what they were supposed to sound like; this was not normal. My father used to have a light aircraft when I was younger, and I have taken the controls on a few occasions; I've flown a little bit and, therefore, have a basic understanding of flight rules and all of those sorts of things. It just didn't sound right, this odd, mechanical noise. On a previous flight, the air-conditioning had failed and this sound was not dissimilar to that, so at the same time I was not duly concerned.

I didn't say anything to Heidi or Andy, but then a short while later there was a bang and a shudder. I looked ahead of me across the few feet into the cockpit and saw a particular light flashing, which I recognised to be a fire extinguisher signal, from which I deduced that an engine must have failed.

One had, on the left side.

I wasn't in any form of panic though, because this was not a single-engined plane. Had it been then we would have been sinking fast. I did not panic, there was no logical reason to be anxious; we still had another engine, so what we had to do was locate a viable landing site and use the remaining engine to land safely. That might sound strange, but I was only slightly less relaxed at this point than before the shudder had hit. I wasn't in any of kind of panic, because (a) there was no need to be and (b) I couldn't do anything about it anyway, I was not in charge of the aircraft.

There followed a small commotion in the cockpit between the pilot and co-pilot and, after about maybe ten minutes, the co-pilot came round and said, 'We've had an engine failure and we are going to do an emergency landing at the nearest airport at Lyon, but everything should be fine,' which is pretty much what I'd said to Andy and Heidi at the time. They were all a bit nervy. Heidi was a nervous flyer anyway, so this wasn't an ideal situation for her.

We made a steady descent over a period of about thirty minutes, I believe from a height of 38,000 feet. We were heading for Nice, but because of the emergency had to be diverted to Lyon-Satolas, a big airport with lengthy runways, which would help, as a single-engine landing in this situation requires a faster landing speed to accommodate one of the engines being out of operation. The worst thing you can do in an aircraft is stall, because basically a stalled aircraft is a metal can, it will just plummet, whereas an aircraft with velocity is a glider with velocity, so you need that extra speed when you come into land. My mechanical mind was ticking over these requirements quite coldly if I am honest. I really didn't think we were in a potentially life-threatening situation at this stage.

As we were coming in on the approach, the pilot was playing with the engine a bit and I thought it strange, because you just want to get it set, something they are trained to do. We began the final approach and when we got level with the height of the trees, I could see there was no wind on the windsock and it all seemed quite salvageable. I remember saying to Andy and Heidi, by way of jokingly calming them down – a bad joke as it turned out – 'Hey, we're only about fifty feet up now so even if we crash, we'll be fine.'

Within a few seconds of the words coming out of my mouth, the plane was ploughing into the ground and grinding to a halt in a mangled wreckage.

We started to land at 12.38 p.m..

Only twenty-six seconds later, we had crashed and the two pilots were dead.

Unfortunately, the pilot came in too low and too slow, which is a dangerous combination. At least too fast and too high allows you more control, but this combination proved a fatal one. Tragically, this was the last thing that either he or his co-pilot ever did, as both were killed by the impact. Although we had made it to a height of just fifty feet relatively safely, he realised we were going to miss the end of the runway and so went to full throttle – the problem with that was that only one engine was operational. The working engine went to full thrust, which slammed the aircraft sideways because only one side of the plane had power. So the lone operational engine accelerated the aircraft and, at the same time, rotated it violently.

Instead of heading down the runway to take off and have another approach, the plane's wing tip hit the ground as we swerved to the left, this rammed the nose into the ground – with the cockpit and the two pilots taking the full force of the impact – and then slid to a stop on the grass.

I don't remember any noise whatsoever. I also don't remember seeing anything during the crash itself. All I recall, immediately before the impact I was sitting in my chair belted up, trying to pull my legs and body away from the nose of the plane, just an instinctive and ultimately futile reaction to pull away from the source of danger, the impact point. You have a safety briefing on private and commercial aircraft and they always say assume the crash position, but that is moving forward towards the impact and that wasn't what my instinct told me to do. I tried to get away, even though I was belted up. I guess a simple analogy would be if someone went to hit you, you'd probably move backwards away from that strike, not forwards into it.

I have no sound or visual memory of anything after that feeling of shrinking backwards in my chair. When we stopped, my memory returns and I recall I could see that the impact had ripped off the front of the fuselage. It was like a road car with the front of the car completely gone, so it was clear to me that the pilots could not have survived. It later transpired that one of the pilots was actually found under the aircraft.

From half-joking we would be okay at fifty feet, to realising the pilots had made this mistake at the very last second, to experiencing the crash, not seeing or hearing anything and then coming to a complete stop only took a few seconds.

I looked around and Heidi was trying to open the emergency door next to her, above the wing. I could see there was a fire right outside that door, so I suggested we all go out of the front of the plane in an orderly fashion, which had a gaping hole where the nose had been severed. Andy went out first and I went out next, so I could help Heidi down. I handed Heidi's dog Moody to Andy, and he literally just threw this mutt about thirty feet across the grass, like a rugby ball. It was such a surreal moment, in among all this fire, smoke and craziness – and death as it transpired – to see this Maltese soaring off into the long grass. Andy was just so highly charged and he wanted to get the dog clear of danger.

We got Heidi out safely and ran off about fifty metres or so from the aircraft. Heidi was a little hysterical, saying, 'What about my stuff? What about my stuff?' which, of course, we'd left in the wreckage. So I got hold of both of them and said, 'Look, this is quite shocking, but today wasn't meant to be our day, let's keep it together and focus on the fact that we are okay ...' I felt really quite calm and almost a little detached at this point. I remember looking over my shoulder at the smouldering wreckage and thinking, 'Um, that was close, now, how are we going to get home?'

We started to trudge towards the airport building, as the fire engines and vehicles weren't yet at the scene. That might sound strange, but they were not expecting a crash; they were on alert that we were doing an emergency landing, but it is not uncommon for planes to lose an engine and a safe landing is the usual outcome.

So it took the emergency services a bit of time before they arrived at the scene. Meanwhile, a police van pulled up and this officer got out and walked over to us. As there was a blazing wreckage with bodies in it behind us, I presumed he'd say, 'Come over here, we've got an ambulance for you, are you okay?' that sort of thing.

Do you know what he said?

'Passeports?'

I couldn't believe what I had heard.

'They're in the fucking plane if you want them,' I said, and walked past him.

A few minutes after my exchange with the policeman, I started to collect my thoughts and realised I had to get a message to my parents and Heidi's and Andy's families. When a known name is in a crash, rumours can spread wild and fast and I could not afford for my parents to get an erroneous phone-call saying I was dead. My mobile phone was still on the aircraft, so I asked to borrow a mobile phone from a farmer who had witnessed the crash ... and do you know what he said to me?

'Is it for an international call though?'

I told him I would pay for the call and even then he was anxious while I phoned my father's office, which was one of the few numbers I could recall from memory. It turned out my parents were on holiday in La Manga, so I spoke to someone there and said, 'Please listen very carefully, please make a note – what I want you to do is the following ... Phone my parents, phone Heidi's parents, phone Andy's parents and tell them the following: we've had a plane crash, the pilots are dead but we are okay and we are going to have to go to medical facilities and then my intention is to get back to Monaco tonight. We don't have our phones or anything, but I'll contact you later today . . . but we are okay . . .' I then asked this guy in my dad's office to repeat back word-for-word what he had written down. I had to be that deliberate about it; it was such a crucial message to leave. Sure enough, in what seemed like a few minutes, the news services had picked up the incident and, had I not made it clear to our parents, who knows what rumour they might have heard.

We went to the hospital in Lyon where they didn't want Heidi to take her dog in with her, which is logical, but of course she didn't want to let go of the dog because she was very upset. I was like, 'Can't you see she's very upset? Please?' We all had full check-ups and, as it turned out, I'd broken three ribs (Heidi broke some, too), and I had some minor muscle damage. In both cases, it seemed the seat belt came up with great force into our rib cage on impact. Considering what had happened, that was perhaps the least we could have expected.

When McLaren found out, their ever-efficient office launched into action and they were absolutely first-class at dealing with such logistical issues. They contacted a lady called Petra Schleuning, an amazing woman from Mercedes Benz who organises a lot of the VIP car sales and the transport at the grands prix. Remarkably, within the hour she'd arranged for a chauffeur to come and pick us up from the hospital and drive us from Lyon to Monaco. That was brilliant.

The drive itself is several hours and, along the way, we stopped off at a roadside café to get something to eat. We were still wearing the clothes we had crashed in, which were muddy, spattered in aviation fuel and smelling of smoke. There'd been no opportunity to change and, besides, all our clothes had been left in the plane. By the time we arrived in Monaco – only a few hours after the crash itself – there were already some media outside my apartment block. We rushed into the apartment and I had Andy, my trainer, who normally stopped at a hotel, stay with us that night. I just felt it was better that we were all together for that first evening.

Finally, around midnight, I slumped into my bed and that was finally when I shivered and thought, 'Fucking hell, that could have been it . . .'

Lying in that bed was a strange feeling and in the aftermath my mind was obviously running at full speed. I did actually ask myself, 'Do I want to race at the weekend? Do I want to continue racing?' My gut reaction there and then – and remember this was the Tuesday before a grand prix weekend in Spain – was no. But then I said to myself, 'I have no choice about Spain. I am scheduled to race and yes, I do want to continue racing after that.'

With remarkable efficiency, McLaren got things organised. I'd had what I call my lucky briefcase with me in the plane sat in front of me, open. When they emptied the aircraft, all our baggage and personal items were sent to us the next day. In that box was my briefcase, covered in mud, grass and aviation fuel. I still use that very same briefcase today.

The crash was on the Tuesday and we spent that night in my apartment. The next day, Ron Dennis took us into his home in Mougins, because he knew we would get some peace and quiet up there. He also sent another medical expert to check us over again. Then, he sat me down and said it was entirely up to me whether I wanted to race that weekend in Barcelona. There was never a shred of doubt in my mind: I was paid to do a job and yes, I had a couple of broken ribs, but I felt perfectly capable of racing. Ron said if that was what I wanted then that is what would happen . . . and sent a private jet to fly me from the south of France to the Circuit de Catalunya in Barcelona.

I can honestly say I had no nerves whatsoever getting on the plane to take off to Barcelona. That is not in any kind of macho way, it just wasn't logical to me to worry that I might have another crash straight away. The chances of crashing once are very small, so the odds of crashing on two consecutive flights are statistically virtually non-existent. It was a nice flight, only an hour or so, and I didn't have a problem throughout the time in the air or on landing. This was two days after the crash. There you go, it is what it is.

Before each race there is an FIA press conference and I was called for this particular one. Four or five drivers are paraded out in front of the journalists and TV crews and questions are fired in. The media's focus on the crash had been going on all that week and I didn't want to take random Q&As about the crash, so I just requested that I make a statement and then leave it at that. I explained what had happened and paid my respects to the pilots and passed on my sincere condolences to their families. Then I said I would obviously just like to put it behind me and concentrate on the race.

There was obviously a lot of paddock speculation about whether I should or would race, with some observers saying I shouldn't out of respect to the two dead pilots. The pilot David Warley's father sent me this letter saying his son had been a passionate flyer, keen on motor-sport and would cheer for me and want me to compete that weekend. That was a very considerate letter to write, after all, I'd only met his son that morning and an hour later he was dead.

It was a very weird feeling talking about the pilots. I had no relationship with them; I shook their hand when I got on the aircraft and that was it. When the transcripts of the black box were released and the investigation had been completed, they said it had been pilot error. One point was made that the co-pilot – who was ex-military – was questioning the approach, saying it was too low and too slow but, unfortunately, he never took over the controls and they both lost their lives. The official flight investigation shows it was pilot error, the captain made some mistakes, which killed both himself and the co-pilot.

I had little time to reflect . . . I was straight into qualifying. I had injections in my side and an ice pack to ease the broken ribs, but I wasn't in particularly bad pain, only moderately uncomfortable. There is a photo of me getting out of the car looking in pain with Heidi nearby looking concerned, which was a nice thought from her. I qualified fourth and then finished second in the race behind my team-mate Mika and ahead of a very determined Michael Schumacher.

This is a result I am very proud of.

McLaren have a clause in their contracts that says they keep the trophies. After this particular race, I asked Ron if I could keep the trophy. He said, 'No, but Heidi can . . .' He couldn't bring himself to give me the trophy, presumably because it might set a precedent, but it was fairly exceptional circumstances and he'd been so helpful in the immediate aftermath of the crash, so it was something I couldn't quite understand.

I do have that trophy now and it is the only original one I possess, all the others are replicas. It is a silver steering wheel and it sits in my Monaco apartment. It is also the only trophy – real or otherwise – that I keep in my apartment, the rest are at the museum in Twynholm. As a point of interest, you might be surprised to know that the Monaco trophy is the cheapest replica, it only costs 275 euros – some replicas designed by the likes of Tiffany and so on, cost thousands.

When people are aware you've been in a life-threatening incident like that, they always ask you what the repercussions were after. I am being totally open and honest by saying that, if there were any, I don't remember them. What is there to say? People died, I didn't. The real tragedy was the death of those husbands and fathers. Tragedy is not having a couple of broken ribs. I was impatient, I wasn't prepared to wait for my own chartered aircraft, so I tried to get on an earlier flight and ended up in a plane wreck.

We should not have crashed. The aircraft was equipped to land safely with one engine, but a series of events, some mistakes and some random happenings, led to the tragedy. You cannot feel sorry for yourself. You are alive; someone else is not. I can be quite hard on people who mope or feel self-pity, because I think you have to grasp situations and get on with it, be positive. So I'm not sure I'd get a job as a counsellor. You experience something like that and, to me anyway, you have to decide what you are going to do about it. Could I change what happened? No. Should I let this affect my attitude to flying? No, and besides, as an FI driver, I have little choice in whether I fly or not, so I might as well enjoy it, or at least tolerate it. I certainly haven't been a notably worse flyer since the accident than I was before. Flying is a means to an end, so I have to get on with it. Everything in my day job is a task that requires a solution; the plane crash just left me with a few thoughts and another solution to find. You can't afford to mope about or dwell on what might have been.

What happened, happened. It is what it is.

MINCE AND TATTIES AND
A CUP O' TEA

Heidi and I had some good times, but some bizarre and rather comical ones, too. We were on holiday in Antigua with Paul Stewart and some friends one year. I said to Heidi that I was going out with a few guys for a beer – it was only a small island, so I could hardly get up to mischief in a place where you are a stone's throw from everywhere. Apparently, so I was later told, as I walked out of the door I said to her with a glint in my eye, 'Prepare yourself, I'll be back in an hour.'

Two hours later, I was still out with the boys and had sunk quite a few beers. We got in the car and headed back to the house we were staying at and, as we drove along the road, Heidi drove past at high speed in the opposite direction with a face like thunder, obviously looking for me. She eventually turned up back at the house and threw a complete fucking wobbler, which she was prone to do, shouting that 'You said you were going to be an hour! Where have you been?!' etc. It turns out she had literally 'prepared' herself for a night of good Scottish loving in the bedroom, so I can see that when I didn't actually come home on time, that would have been annoying. It had only been a throwaway comment as I walked out of the door, but it caused an almighty stink.

We were due to go out for dinner at Mick Jagger's house – the Stones singer time-shared the house with a friend of mine. Heidi had started to drink, but the problem was she was always a shit drinker, so she got pretty drunk very quickly. She was just getting her own back but, after about two hours, she was decidedly pissed. We arrived for dinner and the table was set on this elegant decking, a landscaped area on top of a beautiful fish pond. Heidi was clearly the worse for wear, but I couldn't have anticipated what happened next! As we were eating, she leant across from the table and vomited copiously in the fish pond. At this point, while we all sat there in stunned silence, there was a feeding frenzy in the pond; the fish were going nuts for these chunks of vomit, these pre-chewed pieces of gourmet food, they were in heaven.

I have been engaged to be married once, although I never actually asked Heidi to marry me. You could justifiably wonder how'd you get engaged without actually asking the woman to marry you. Well, what I actually did was I asked her 'to engage me', a deeply unromantic notion and perhaps a sign, in restrospect, that it was all wrong! 'Please engage me' sounds terrible and, indeed, it was doomed. It was the right thing to do, but not the right person to do it with.

I can't help thinking that the plane crash had something to do with me thinking it was the right time to get married. That shiver in my bed in Monaco on the evening of the crash was a life-altering moment. It changed my attitude to how I wanted to live my life and – mistakenly – I thought I should be settled down and married and having kids, all that sort of stuff. So, a short while after the crash, Heidi and I got engaged.

Looking back, it was perhaps inevitable that the engagement with Heidi would fall through. Even the way the engagement took place was evidence that I didn't want to commit; I was just doing what seemed like the right thing to do. The papers had been circling for some while before: I bought her a Cartier watch one day in London's Bond Street and while we were in there I said, casually, 'What's your style of ring?' So I also bought her a diamond ring. She liked sparkly things. There must have been a journalist or someone eavesdropping in the shop, because the next day it was all over the papers.

Heidi found a place to get married in the Bahamas, scheduled for the spring of 2001. The wedding was all paid for and arranged, but I never went. I pulled out a few months before; I just couldn't do it. I lay in bed one day thinking about the fact I was going to be thirty in a few months, a new grand prix season was coming up and I was supposed to be getting married, all within the same few weeks. I just didn't feel like I could do all three at the same time and, sadly, getting married was the first to go. Heidi spent Christmas Day in America – she didn't really like my family and they weren't that keen on her – so, in retrospect, maybe the fact we didn't share Christmas Day together said a lot. I flew out from my family Christmas in Twynholm for New Year in the States and told her that I did not want to get married.

What we agreed was that we were going to take some time to consider our position and our relationship. So I came back to the UK and readied myself for January testing. Heidi was staying at my apartment in Chelsea and I was at a Mayfair hotel, but in theory it was a kind of trial separation. When we saw each other, we would talk and it wasn't unpleasant, but it was a period of distance.

Anyway, one night I was at the bar in the hotel, met a girl and started having a chat and a few drinks. We went upstairs, more drinks were poured, a bubble bath was run and, the next day, she sold the story.

So if there had been any doubt about my relationship with Heidi being on the rocks, it was certainly over now. The tabloids ran 'the bubble bath' tale in all its glory and the angle was very much that I was in a long-term relationship with someone when the foamy incident occurred. In theory that is correct, but it was a partnership in the death throes, so to speak. I don't like to quote the over-used expression, but we were 'on a break'. Nonetheless, it was perceived that I was cheating on my partner, rightly or wrongly, which is publicity you could do without. 'Coulthard cheats on his partner again . . .' etc etc.

This exposure of your private life is a well-known downside of being in the public eye – there are so many people who want to profit out of your life. That said, the very same public watch the TV and that means you get paid enormous sums of money to do your job, so you can't really have any complaints. If I was having a niggle, I'd say that being well known was never my motivation for racing motor cars – it is a by-product of winning races from the age of eleven that I end up sharing a bubble bath with a not unpleasant-looking female and about eight million tabloid readers within twenty-four hours of the soap suds subsiding.

This might sound a little harsh, but someone said to me how would I have felt if Heidi had slept with another man during that separation. I've got to be honest, I don't think I would have flipped my chips. It was over, the difficult decision was to call the wedding off so, by then, when the bubble bath was running, I was already almost completely emotionally detached. Evidently.

After I split with Heidi, a rumour circulated in the papers that she pressed for legal custody of the dog. I have to admit, that was probably just a joke I started at the time. She'd wanted a dog and I wasn't overly keen, so I said, 'Well, if you get a dog, call her Moody, after you.' She was moody, to be fair. She still has the dog apparently. It was a cute little thing. I should have known that relationship was over a year before it actually ended, because the dog used to sleep in the bed.

Heidi later met her current husband and they have a child and are very happy by all accounts. I have never really maintained a friendship with my ex-girlfriends. I saw Heidi in Harrods with her new partner and we exchanged pleasantries, nothing more. There was certainly no animosity from me. Andrea, the Canadian girl who I lived with for four years, is probably the one I have most contact with. I have her number and occasionally I bump into her. I still think she's a lovely girl. I would always help her if she asked. I don't phone her and I don't go and have coffee with her; she's got her life and I have got mine, but I have very fond memories of that period of my life. I was a young man just starting my grand prix career, just beginning to earn good money and she was a part of that whole phase.

It's time to address the notion that I am a ladies' man. You know, the old 'Race Ace Drove Me Wild' and so on. First, the case in favour, and I will be absolutely honest in my testimony! You might think that Formula 1 is such a commercialised sport and under such immense media scrutiny that no one ever gets up to any mischief. Wrong. There are plenty of drivers who like to enjoy themselves in various ways that their sponsors – or partners – might not approve of. And myself? Well, I have never had a relationship with a young lady on a race weekend ...

... Alright, very, very rarely.

As a younger man, I cannot deny that I did play around quite a lot. I wasn't always single when I did this, which is not something I am particularly proud of. Formula 1 brings with it a lot of promotion and I would be flying around the world, doing glitzy events, then heading off to a club somewhere. Your schedules are so intense you have to grab socialising where you can, and this is where a lot of this 'extra-curricular' activity would take place. F1 attracts the attractive, so I would often end up discussing the finer points of ceramic brake technology or strategic fuel loads with a variety of splendid young women.

Yes, in my younger days I have had the knock on the hotel door and in steps a very pleasant-looking young lady who stays for an hour or so, then leaves without me actually finding out her name. I was never quite sure how these women found out my hotel room number but, to be fair, I wasn't always that bothered. Of course, I would never condone that sort of lifestyle on a Friday, Saturday or Sunday: race weekends are the days for total concentration, absolute focus and super-human dedication. But back then, when I didn't know any better ... Wednesdays or Thursdays ...?

I have to be honest and say that, despite my protestations

against being a 'ladies' man', I have clearly had dalliances with quite a few ladies over the years, including on one occasion, one from an aristocratic bloodline. I was at a stately home for a big society event and I went, as I often do for these very formal gatherings, in my kilt. One of the young daughters of a certain aristocrat was chatting away with me and we were having a great night. One thing led to another and we wandered off across a courtyard where I proceeded to show her my family tree. There was a flurry of grunts and groans and what have you, and then, as we were just finishing up, this young lady heard her mother coming across the courtyard towards the room we were in. I was all for jumping out of the window and legging it across the manicured lawns, but she said there was security and guard dogs, so that was not an option.

We waited in the shadows until we thought no one was around and made our break for freedom. Unfortunately, as we passed the family portraits and priceless silverware on our way towards this huge, ornate staircase, we spotted the mother starting to climb the stairs. We had no choice but to continue walking but as we did, by way of an alibi, I was fingering my chin and musing up at the ancient oil paintings on the walls, desperately trying to look as though I was being shown the family jewels (which in a way I had been). 'That's a very inter-esting picture isn't it?'

When we met her mother halfway down the stairs, she was looking very stern. I was a little dishevelled, but passable; the young lady, on the hand, looked somewhat more ruffled.

'What are you two up to?'

'Er, I was just giving David a tour of the house, Mummy,' said my companion.

Her mother stepped up level with us, tucked in her daughter's bra strap, which was protruding very obviously from her dress, looked me in the eye and said, 'I see you've had the full tour,' then went on her way.

So I accept there is evidence to support these lothario accusations. I have driven off the main track on occasion and I'm not stupid. I deserve those comments in some ways.

However, the case against me being a ladies' man is far more compelling. For example, when Heidi and I separated, I had a couple of months where I was single. I was going out in London all the time and I quickly realised that I wanted to be back in a relationship with someone I wanted to spend time with. It really wasn't a happy period for me. Unfulfilling one-night stands just didn't make me feel good. I like to make a connection with someone and not just in a physical sense, but be able to talk to them and communicate. I was just having shit conversations with beautiful but pretty random women for the sake of having my end away. I didn't like it, it's not me.

It seems a gross contradiction to me that I am perceived in the media as a ladies' man (although I admit my merchandise always sells best to women, maybe that's why?!). I have been variously 'linked' to numerous women, some famous, some not so well known. Given that I didn't lose my cherry until I was fifteen and, all these years later, I have had three long-term relationships, that seems odd. Furthermore, there are several specific 'incidents' which the media have 'exposed' that haven't done me any favours but which were, in fact, misleading. If you scratch under the surface of some of these 'sexposés', you will see that, actually, I was the only one not up to anything! Take the 'Coulthard's Lesbian Love Boat', for instance.

That was a headline I hadn't imagined being involved in when I was a young karter coming through the ranks. Feature articles in *Autosport* or a detailed analysis of my driving style in *F1* magazine maybe, but not my face plastered all over the tabloids with three people in the background quite blatantly having some form of sexual encounter.

In 1999, I bought a 24-metre yacht called *Highlander*. A boat like that is perhaps one of the ultimate trappings of the racing driver lifestyle – I was living in Monaco, owned the boat, had various houses and quite a decadent life really. When I look back, I have wasted millions and millions of pounds, enormous sums of money, often on things and – as I would later find out – people that were not worth it. I guess finding that out is all part of the experience, but it is a little painful to think of all the money that's been spent with nothing to show for it.

This particular tawdry headline came about when myself, Cawthorne, an ex-girlfriend of mine and my Cirque Du Soleil friend, Guy Laliberté, were on the *Highlander* around Sardinia. Guy is not particularly well known to most people, despite Cirque Du Soleil being such a huge success. He is a very wealthy, funny, charming man and one of my close friends. Guy brought two girls on board as his guests. One of them was wearing a long dress, but when she fell asleep on a sofa, this garment rode up her thighs and, let's just say, gave us all a view of Sardinia we hadn't experienced before.

Eventually, unbeknown to me, one of the women started going down on the other girl on the foredeck of the yacht who was, incidentally, smeared in strawberries and daiquiri. I was just minding my own business, drinking some tea out of a Wallace and Gromit mug on the deck. Meanwhile, a few hundred metres away, the paparazzi were snapping way like crazy – a lot of celebrities buy boats because they think it affords them some degree of privacy when they sail off miles from shore, but you have to drop anchor eventually and when you do they can snap you from miles away. The power of the long lens, eh? The next day, the photographers perfectly captured Guy and this girl entertaining each other in the background with me and my Wallace and Gromit mug in the foreground. It was in the *Daily Sport* – a frequent source of 'race ace'-type scandal stories about me – but it was such a titillating story that it went all around Europe like wildfire. It really was something out of nothing.

Guy wasn't that well known to the public, as I have said, but he did get a lot of coverage out of the lesbian love boat incident. Especially in Germany; the Germans love that sort of thing. What that incident does is to show how an image and a headline can sufficiently influence reality. The actual reality was a couple of girls kissing each other with a guy, while some friends of theirs with their girlfriends were doing nothing untoward elsewhere on the boat. That story – even though all I was doing was drinking a cup of my beloved tea – created a perception of me that was I was some sort of sex pest!

And just for the record, I'm not a lesbian, by the way.

Contrary to what you may think, having listened to all these stories, I am in fact a man driven by having a partner; my previous 'ladies' have ultimately proved the wrong partners. I have never been the 'lad's lad', owning a bachelor pad and bumping and pumping my way around the globe. I could have been: the profile, career and money could certainly have opened a lot of (hotel) doors and run a lot of bubble baths. But that has never appealed to me. I wanted to be in a long, loving relationship, and still very much do.

I don't need pink champagne in the back of a multi-million-pound yacht, because I have been there and done that. I don't think I am a ladies man, because that would give the perception that I need ladies' (plural) in my life, I don't. I want a wife. I want a partner; I want someone who I can be 100 per cent open and honest with. I don't fulfil the 'playboy' stereotype. Someone like Eddie Irvine does; he has apparently no intention of settling down and has had a string of girlfriends. It is a conscious decision that works for him, but it doesn't work for me.

Although I am adamant I am not a ladies' man, disproving the case against me has also highlighted to me perhaps one of my biggest internal contradictions: my values as a businessman and professional colleague are 100 per cent sincere and trustworthy; in the past, my values as a partner were not. I don't deny that paradox. I have struggled mentally with why I would be so honourable in business and yet so dishonourable at times in the way I live my private life. I've never had two women on the go for years, you know, these men who have long-term mistresses, that was not what it was about. It was just a case of if something happened, it happened. Even at the time that troubled me, because I thought it reflected on my character in the long term. I am beginning to realise now that this is not an affliction, something I will do all my life. It was just a reflection of the fact I hadn't found my true partner. There might have been the odd woman where you might have a repeat visit, but largely it was all one-night stands, and *always* with too much alcohol swilling around. I *never* had a sober one-night stand. But the drink is not an excuse – if you are predisposed to not having that commitment in your mind with a particular relationship, then the alcohol by-passes your guilt and off you go.

Many years ago, my father said, 'Don't get involved with women!' but I've been involved with more women than I can honestly remember. Not in a 'long-term relationship' way, as you now know, just in a 'do the business and move on' way. It wasn't important. Often, I would make a point of leaving the bed and the flat before the morning, because in my mind at that time if I didn't wake up with a girl, then I wasn't in a relationship with her. I know it sounds odd, but that made it more acceptable to me. I always had to wake up in my bed.

If the definition of a 'ladies' man' is someone who has been with women and, on occasion, with more than one woman at the same time, then yes, call me a ladies' man. I can see the argument: lurid stories about me in the press; the bubble bath; the lesbian love boat; I am a racing driver so that makes me fall neatly into the bracket of 'playboy'; I used to own a yacht; I drive a fast car for a living and fly on a lot of planes ... I can see it ticks a lot of the boxes. But I disagree. I am not a ladies' man. I am actually a country boy who eats mince and tatties and who likes a cup o' tea.

NICE TO SEE YOU

I am a professional sportsman – essentially, that means I am paid to do my hobby. The more people that watch a particular sport, the more money is generated and the more the sports-men or women are paid. So I'm lucky that F1 is generous with its wages. I earn an incredible salary for being what is effectively a high-speed billboard driver. You see these blokes driving these trucks with 'Red Bull' on the back who probably get a few hundred quid a week – I'm just doing the same job, but I get paid more because it is televised. That is undoubtedly a considerable upside and I never underestimate the benefits of earning what I do.

There are downsides to my job, but the most bothersome ones are away from the track. The obvious negative is that because you are in the public eye, by definition, so are your family. As I've said, I accept that I am in the public eye and papers will run stories about me; it is the impact of this profile on your family that is the most regrettable part of my job. They don't make the choice to be in the public eye, I do. However, I am not in control of that: the day the tabloids decide you are of interest to their readership is a day that alters your life. Pandora's Box is then opened.

Generally, before Formula 1, before the tabloids knew the Coulthard name, we were a typical family who minded our own business and kept ourselves to ourselves, so when the tabloids started to scratch around for stories after I became more well known, it was quite a shock for everyone concerned. With regard to one aunty who was serving a lengthy prison sentence, the tabloids wrote about that and contacted my family, for example. It was all very upsetting for my mother, naturally. Her parents have lived in the same house their whole life, however, so suddenly everyone in the local community was made aware of this story in the national papers … essentially as a result of me being in Formula 1. Without my public profile, it would not have been public knowledge. That is quite an odd and uncomfortable realisation for me, and to see my mum so upset – as a direct consequence of the media's interest in my life – was hard. Worse still, she worries herself about how certain stories might affect my career in some way or maybe alter people's perceptions of me and the impact that might have on my chances of certain drives and so on. Even when she is so upset, she is still thinking of me.

The tabloids can crop up in the most surprising places. There was a story running at one time about an alleged liaison I'd had with a relatively well-known woman. I was at my apartment in Chelsea when the door rang and I answered it, to be confronted by a woman who I thought at first was a friend of my girlfriend. It transpired that she was a tabloid journalist and she immediately started asking me questions about the allegations regarding this woman. I found out later that the porter had let her in, assuming she was a friend.

Another headline to cause understandable family concern was 'Race Ace Has Half-Sister'. When my mother was sixteen, she'd had a baby and put that child – now named Elaine Rowan – up for adoption. When Elaine decided to trace her parents, as many adopted children do, she first tracked down her mother's maiden name, Marshall, and that led her to my grandparents' house, which in turn linked the trail to the Coulthard name and then, logically, to the race driver. Somehow the papers found out about it in the spring of 2002 and, bang, that's your headline. Lots of people have had kids and put them up for adoption, it's not a shocking event in itself, but it is a fact that because of my career, my parents have had to live with the entire country knowing.

Bear in mind all this was a generation ago for my mother. She'd obviously told my father before they were married, but no one else knew. It was a private matter. My mother decided to tell me one time we were all in Spain in the house I'd bought for them. The way she sat me down and said, 'I have something to tell you ...' sounded so ominous, I was struck down with fear, I thought she had cancer or something hideous. Then she said, 'I have a child from when I was a teenager.' I was like, 'Thank God that's all it is!' It was such a relief.

Even aside from the immediate relief of my mother not being ill, the discovery of a half-sister was certainly not something I had any problem with at all. Mum seemed to be worried that my brother, sister and I would somehow be upset with her. Far from it. From my point of view, she had no reason to be upset or embarrassed, it is what it is. She has given the gift of life to someone else, she knows the reasons why she was unable to keep that child and if that child has grown into an adult and had kids and a happy life, then good, the journey goes on.

As it happens, the whole family have met Elaine, although I haven't and I don't feel motivated to do so. I don't go to Scotland very often and I'm not going to go there to meet someone I don't know, just because we shared the same womb – I know that sounds a bit harsh, but I just don't feel the need. On the one hand, she is my half-sister; on the other, she is a complete stranger. I like who I like, I know who I know, I know who I don't like and I'm not really looking to go beyond that. That might sound very conservative, guarded even, but I am unavoidably affected by the lifestyle of being surrounded by so many people that I don't know, new people who I am not sure of perhaps, wondering about why they want to know me and so on. I'm not saying Elaine is part of that, of course not, it just means that my instinctive reaction to a situation like that is quite reserved.

This will probably sound even harsher, but one of the great things about being an ex-pat is that I don't have to go to family functions where there is a room full of people I barely know or haven't met at all. Weddings of cousins twice-removed, that sort of thing. I don't feel obliged to go and, because of where I live, it is not expected of me. I'm kind of seen as being slightly different from the family, outside of the extended network really. As a result, I've never had to do family events. I've been away so long now that people don't even bother to invite me. I don't like feeling obliged to go to events like that. On one hand I lose contact, but it makes my life a lot simpler, because I'm not drawn into family disputes and all the various complications.

Weddings, christenings, funerals, I don't get dragged along to many of those and it gives me the clarity to get on with my life, which I probably wouldn't have if I was in London. So, from that aspect, being an ex-pat has given me a clean zone to do my job.

My dad might call me when I'm training on my mountain bike up in the hills outside Monaco, you know, 'Hi son, about Silverstone, I just want to check we are okay for passes because I want to bring a few people,' and I'll be panting away and say, 'No problem, Father.' He's always organised way ahead of time. I know what he means; he wants me to do an appearance because he'll have his family and friends and all the rest of it, a few people he'll want to entertain, so if you can bring in a token sports person who happens to be your son, then all well and good. That's about as much as the extended family crosses over with my life in Monaco.

Let me make it clear, though. I love my immediate family, my grandparents and I really like a few aunties and uncles, but I am not one for great, huge, extended families. It's just not in my nature.

Getting back to celebrity, it is a weird world and an odd concept. We clearly do have an interest in celebrities' lives. I'll buy magazines like *Hello!* and flick through; I like to see what these people's houses look like, all that. I guess we are inherently nosey by nature. But when it reaches the stage where a guy has made a mistake and it is all over the papers and this moment of madness is something he will then live to regret for ever ... it's harsh. His whole life can be undone because of a public story, whether it is true or not. My biggest disappointment with the media side of the business is the fact that, growing up, I believed everything I read in the papers, but now I realise it's individuals who write these articles and, very often, they do not tell the truth.

I have experience of talking about emotive subjects and finding myself the subject of bad press. I was once misquoted as saying that women cannot drive a car as well as a man. It was just some lady journo who perhaps didn't think the real quote was interesting. Certain elements of the press lambasted me for this apparent 'quote' and it took quite a while for that to die down. As it happens, I believe quite the opposite. I just don't understand why there haven't been more successful female racing drivers. I'm not remarkably fit so, for sure, certain women could be as strong and as fit as I am, no question. If you follow the logic that we could find women who would be equally capable of handling the car physically – which I believe you could – then you have to look at what is next, i.e. the mind, the brain. Thus, is there any mental reason why ladies should not be able to compete in my environment? No. Are there any physical reasons? No. So why are there no women in F1? Maybe there are fewer female role models, but that assumes younger women watch fewer races, which I know is not necessarily the case. As I mentioned before, my sister raced karts and she was naturally better than I was, but she wasn't as committed. Personally, I see no reason why women should not race in F1 and I endorse the need for more women in the sport at all levels.

You get used to being misquoted, but sometimes the extent of the fiction printed can be quite bizarre. Fast-forward to 2006 and I have just grabbed Red Bull's first podium in Monaco. After the race, I came across an article on the internet from some obscure newspaper in Australia that took misquoting to a whole new level. The writer had obviously stayed at The Columbus and he ran a piece with an interview with me. He said that he'd enjoyed the hotel's signature drink, a chocolate Martini, with me and that I gave him the low-down on the Schumacher controversy, my podium and all the news. He quoted me directly.

Yet I had never met him.

He had not interviewed me, either in person or on the phone. He had made it all up.

I faxed the article to Martin Brundle and said, 'Is this allowed?'

There's very little you can do really, unless the fictional quotes get you in some legal bother. Then you would have to pursue it, but I just found it alarming that the story had just been made up in its entirety.

It's not just the newspapers that might cause difficulties in your life because you are well known. People do, too. I've been lucky enough not to have too many crashes on the roads. I had an accident in a 3-series BMW when I was nineteen on one of the many early morning drives from Scotland to Milton Keynes for meetings with Jackie Stewart. In 1999, I crashed my Mercedes in a tunnel in Monaco, not long before that year's grand prix. It was wet and I lost it on the white lines and hit the wall. There were some air stewardesses I'd met and my trainer in the car at the time.

In the apartment after the crash, I felt very uneasy and wondered what might happen. It wasn't ideal for me to be seen having a crash in the tunnel the week before the grand prix. This one particular stewardess had a medical check-up at the hospital and they said she was okay. I got another doctor to check she was okay, then I chartered a plane to fly them all back to Ireland because they'd missed their flight that day.

Then one of the stewardesses made a claim against me for a very large sum of money, for an alleged back and neck injury. The claim was to go on for years and took the best part of a decade to sort out. The bottom line is that because I am a racing driver I am perceived as having money, so people sometimes come after me. I had to go to some private chambers in Monaco to discuss the claim and my position was simple: I'm not proud of the fact I had an accident and I'm not happy that I could have injured someone; if she has a genuine claim and she is genuinely injured, I will pay her exactly what she is due and then some, because if my inability to control a vehicle results in someone's injury, then I should compensate and I will. What I couldn't understand was how she could appear to be fine one minute and then supposedly injured the next. We wouldn't hear anything for a year then we'd get a new letter through from a new lawyer and on and on it went. The case was eventually dropped, but I did pay some compensation because I just wanted it over. Why was the case dropped? I hired a private investigator who discovered that a few weeks after the accident, she was an extra in a pop video in Ibiza, dancing on a rock. She wasn't wearing a neck brace in the video. So take your money and have a happy life, if that's the way you're going to be.

Situations like this, combined with stories about you in the media, do affect the way you are around people you don't know. At each grand prix, for example, Red Bull will put on a barbecue and there will be pretty young ladies there and men, obviously, chatting to them. It's part of how the brand operates and how they provide entertainment. If there happens to be a single young man there who wants to take things further with one of the girls, then so be it ... but I have to be very, very careful. Shake hands from a long distance, be very cautious with photographs, that sort of stuff. If it is a young girl or woman, I will very rarely put my arm around them for photos; a little old granny or cuddly mummy, fair enough, but not the buxom young women. Or men. I'll usually get an early night, look at some technical stuff in the motorhome, get some sleep and focus on my weekend.

The stories that have previously surfaced in the tabloids have had an undeniable affect on the way I behave now with strangers. It has made me more cynical, I can't deny that. By nature, I am a very open and accepting person and, in days gone by, I took everyone at face value and everyone was a friend till proved otherwise. Largely I'm still the same, but I know how it works today and I behave accordingly. Learning from the bubble-bath incident, when I was separated from my then-long-term partner Simone Abdelnur in 2006, I put out a press statement saying that we were no longer together, that it was amicable, blah, blah, blah. It felt a little clinical and a few journalists said it was very formal, but there was a reason for that: so that there would be no misunderstandings in the tabloids again. I just knew that if I didn't and was out and opened the old Radox again with a new acquaintance, it would be 'Coulthard cheats again!' As an aside, Simone had two dogs when she lived with me, but they returned to Brazil to be with her. I have decided not to fight for custody.

One other aspect of being a known face is that you get approached a lot by charities. Over the years, I have tended to do work for children's foundations. They tend to be very well run and well monitored; also, because of what happened to my Aunty Rose, it is something that is particularly close to home. Obviously I have experienced mental disability in my family but, tragically, Ron Dennis also lost a child, so he is heavily involved in helping to raise funds and awareness. I remember when I donated that £25,000 to Tommy's charity after my bet with Ron and, although that was a not insignificant amount on the one hand, I also thought to myself, it's not going to revolutionise our understanding of still-births or end instances of cot death. But at the same time, you have to make your gesture.

Quite often we get sick children coming round to test days and they get a picture in the car and autographs and a little tour, all that sort of stuff. I will always make myself available for that, but I have to tell you it is really difficult to get to grips with. I see these kids and I think, 'Why are they sick? What have they done to deserve this?' Then I see much older people, adults I know are bastards, and I think, 'Why are they living to a ripe old age?' I entertain these kids on that day, but when you come away it's really hard, you can't help thinking, 'They are going to leave today and continue the countdown to their death and I'm still playing racing cars.'

If I do a TV appearance, I tend to pay any fee to a charity, but there are also these events, 'celebrity' fundraisers, which can be quite strange evenings. I feel comfortable that I've done a little bit to try and help, but occasionally these events are very uncomfortable. The least enjoyable one I did, which – in my opinion – shows the bad side of charity, was at an Italian restaurant. It was full of celebrities; I think there were twenty-five or thirty main guests. I went with my cheque-book fully expecting to make a contribution, of course, you wouldn't go otherwise. They requested, as I recall, a certain amount, I think it was £10,000. But then a lady came over to me and said that as it was my first event for them, they thought it would be a good idea to 'consider' giving double the standard donation.

I felt very, very uncomfortable about all this, and obviously a little bit cornered. It was not an insignificant extra amount to ask for, and I didn't really know much about the cause at this stage. People know I earn a lot of money, so there's always someone waiting to snipe about that, plus it made it all very awkward. I was really put on the spot, so what I did – and even recounting it feels embarrassing – I said I would meet them halfway, but I wondered if they could send me loads of information about the charity, how that money would get used and so on. So I wrote the cheque, but never got any information. I've had invitations to go back to one of their events, but I won't. It's not that I don't understand the system – you go, you meet some celebs and you give some money over – but if they won't make the effort to explain to me how that money will be spent, then I'll continue to offer funds to charities helping children.

These types of events also introduce you to what I see as 'career charity people'. It is just a job for them, I appreciate that, but when I think of executives at big charities earning big money, it seems a little odd. For me, when I think of charity, I think of my grandmother and my mother baking rock cakes to take to the local bring-and-buy sales and raising £200 for the mentally handicapped. We did so much of that when we were young because of my aunty. They are giving their time and their effort for nothing, selling stuff and raising funds.

*

I don't think of myself as a celebrity in any shape or form. I race cars and it so happens this is a job that is televised and a few hundred million people watch each race and so my face has become known over the dozen or so years I've been in F1. However, I am never comfortable being around or in the 'celebrity bubble', so to speak.

Despite my time spent troubling the tabloid headline-writers, the celebrity world is alien to me. I meet a lot of celebrities, but I regularly don't recognise them. When I was on a plane to Brazil one time, there was a dark-haired man sitting across from us who I knew was famous but I couldn't place him at first. After a while, I realised it was Jimmy Page from Led Zeppelin, but even then I didn't know enough about music to know he was that band's guitarist. We chatted for quite a while and it turned out he was building houses for poverty-stricken communities in Brazil, quite a project. We'd actually met once before at a fundraiser, but I don't think he remembered me or knew who I was. He was very nice, a bit like one of my dad's mates really.

Celebrity – if I am such a thing at all – is convenient when you need a table in a fancy restaurant, but beyond that I don't need it. I don't feel better about myself because I get recognised. I don't need adulation and congratulations to feel good about myself. I am embarrassed by it, uncomfortable with it. If I give someone a present, I prefer them to open it when I'm not there; it's so awkward when they say thanks. So, you can imagine how awkward I find it when I am called a 'celebrity' or recognised. In Turkmenistan they even issued a 'David Coulthard' stamp, which was all a bit weird.

It's actually more weird when famous people know who I am. I was having lunch one time in Chelsea when Bruce Forsyth sat at the next table. It was the week preceding a race and he got up and came over to talk to me. I'd never met him before and here I was being approached by Brucie, complete with the worst-looking yellow wig I've ever seen. It was very strange but great, too. He said, 'Make sure you are just drinking water, you've got some work to do this weekend!'

I was made up, that would have been an 'ask for an autograph' moment but, as you know from my days of being around Prost, I'm not an autograph type guy. I wish I had really, because that would have been nice to give to my dad. Bruce Forsyth is one of those stars that you never imagine meeting, he is *so* famous. You don't expect to go for lunch and see Brucie sitting down, less still knowing who you are and, most bizarre of all, coming over to you, not the other way around. He doesn't seem to have aged at all and he was really very nice to me.

Although he did call me Damon ...

Only kidding.

MONACO

Monaco is a very comfortable place to live. Part of you will always look upon where you grew up as 'home' and I guess in that sense I'll still refer to 'going home' when I visit my parents. However, Monaco is my new home. It is a great place to be based in, especially with my job. The backdrop of the Alps towering over this pristine little principality is very relaxing; the weather is almost always very warm; I can ride my mountain bike through the most spectacular countryside; when I had my yacht I could cruise around the Mediterranean, and even train on jet-skis; it really is a very pleasant, albeit expensive, place to live.

I need to be close to the airports, so Monaco is well placed for that, too. Given the European bias of much of the Formula 1 schedule, it is centrally located for many of my journeys. When I am in town, my apartment overlooking the harbour is a sanctuary. I close the door, sit on the balcony and look at the sea and it feels secure and safe and very relaxing.

Monaco is a magnet for the rich and famous, that is no secret. In many ways, aside from the obvious financial benefit –

229

there is no income tax in Monaco – it is an unlikely place for me to live. I have never been one for buying flash cars, for instance. I drive a Smart car most of the time. When I got my first big cheque from racing, I didn't rush out and buy a Mk2 Escort with shiny alloys, it wasn't important to me then and it isn't now. I don't feel I am that materialistic. Yes, it's nice to have nice things, but I don't buy a new car very often, I don't need to and I don't feel the desire to.

When my mother first came down to Monaco, she said she felt so uncomfortable and scruffy among all these lavishly dressed people dripping with jewellery. I think part of that was her own self-perception, because she certainly looked lovely; she's a lovely person and a great mother, so she's got no reason to feel inferior. Part of it was that – compared to Twynholm – it is an alien environment. I forget too, you see, I've lived there a while now and I am known as a racing driver. So I tell people you can walk into any restaurant in Monaco wearing ripped jeans and a casual shirt, but maybe you can if you are a racing driver, I'm not sure. It would be interesting to see people's reactions if I was unknown to them.

Monaco has very special memories for me as a driver with my wins in 2000 and 2002. The first of my two Monaco wins was a great follow-up to victory at Silverstone back in round four, and came only two races after my plane crash. I qualified third and moved up to second behind Michael when he had a broken suspension, and other drivers retired too, so of the two I feel this win was the luckier.

My second win in Monaco came two years later and, in my eyes, is a far superior victory. It felt a much more mature win. Montoya grabbed pole in his Williams, but I blasted past him from second on the grid and took the lead at the first corner, a position I never relinquished. I knew when to push and when to back off. I had problems with graining and a transfer valve that threatened to retire me, but I held on for victory, despite the best efforts of Montoya who was all over the back of my McLaren (before an engine blow-out retired him) and Schumacher, who'd already won five of the first six races of the year. Remarkably, the transfer valve was repaired by my engineers *remotely*, after they used electronic telemetry to cure the problem without me even having to pit.

Oddly, and this is absolutely true, before the race I had put my kilt out on the bed because I was so certain I was going to win. I didn't have a premonition as such, but I just thought I was going to win the grand prix. I haven't put it out at any other race in my entire career.

Monaco is rightly seen as one of the most prestigious races on the calendar – it's the one that all the CEOs go to, all the manufacturers' board members, film stars, rock singers and so on. The people who write the enormous cheques and provide these vast sponsorships want to go because it puts real glamour into the F1 season. Girls, cars, casinos and yachts, all that stuff. Plus it's got the history – they've raced there since 1929, albeit not a grand prix. The names who've won there read like a list of the F1 greats, with multiple winners including the likes of Juan Manuel Fangio, Stirling Moss, Jackie Stewart (all twice) and six-time winner, Ayrton Senna, so I can't help but feel very proud to have notched up a brace of wins there.

Specifically, Monaco is a unique racing experience. By contrast, somewhere like Silverstone is a big open track, you do your corner then you sit and wait for the next corner for what seems like an eternity. On the straights, you can't do anything to make you stand out from your peers, you just have to wait for that next corner. If you think on a standard Silverstone lap, you are probably only in the corners for less than thirty seconds, the rest of the lap you are sitting there, waiting. I have driven around Silverstone so many times now, in all sorts of formulas and over so many years, I have actually started reading the advertising hoardings on the straights. It's something to do to while away the time before the next corner.

There's no time for reading the advertising in Monaco. There are more difficult corners and more challenges, so there is much more of an opportunity for a driver to come through and set himself apart from the rest of the grid. Monaco puts your racing senses on high alert: the sense of precision, the sense of speed, the sense of total focus and concentration. You see nothing else when you are driving around Monaco. At Silverstone, when you're on the Hanger straight, you see the bridge, you see marshals moving around, you see flags waving and it's like a Sunday drive in the country; at Monaco, you don't see anything but the track in front of you: it has your total attention – it has to, if you waver for a second, the impact can be pretty severe, and in a couple of cases, in the old days, two drivers actually ended up in the harbour!

The sports psychologists might say you were 'in the zone' and you certainly have to be to get around Monaco quickly. It is a very selfish moment in your life, driving around that circuit – what I mean by that is that you cannot think about anyone or anything else, not your loved ones, not your family, your home, other people and issues, you can only focus on that corner, that straight, and so on. I think the most rewarding

The perfect scenario for Monaco: leading the field into the first corner in 2002. I went on to win. (PA Photos)

Celebrating the win, with Prince Rainier (left). The trophy is one of the cheapest on the circuit! (LAT)

Simone Abdelnur, who was my long-term girlfriend until 2006. (PA Photos)

On the podium after winning the Australian Grand Prix in 2003. Alongside me are team mate Kimi Raikkonen and the chubby little fella. (LAT)

king to Dietrich Mateschitz, the owner of Red Bull, just after signing up for the team for the
05 season. (PA Photos)

king my debut for Red Bull at the 2005 Australian Grand Prix. (Getty Images)

My soulmate Karen Minier wishes me luck ahead of the 2006 Spanish Grand Prix. (PA Photos)

On my way to the first podium finish for Red Bull, during the 2006 Monaco Grand Prix. (Getty Images)

... started off as a really good idea . . . My overtaking manoeuvre in the 2007 Australian Grand Prix ...es horribly wrong. Fortunately Alexander Wurz and I were not injured. (PA Photos)

...ith Christian Horner (left) and Adrian Newey, two of the key men at Red Bull. (GEPA)

What fourteen years in
the top flight will do to you.
(PA Photos)

things that we do in our lives are when we are in the zone like that, professionally at least. And if you don't apply that absolute focus, the track will beat you. So Monaco enables you to be selfish without enduring the guilt of being selfish.

Spa is my favourite circuit, but Monaco is the place where I really feel like a grand prix driver. And what is a grand prix driver? Fast cars, danger, glamour, money blah de blah? No, if you think of all the clichés that could go with being a grand prix driver, for me it's about sitting in that car and hurtling around a track which has you constantly thinking, for every single second of the best part of nearly two hours, 'Christ, this is a challenge.'

Monaco is particularly physically exhausting too, because it has such a tiny margin of error, you have to be completely focused for every second you are out there. The road sides are extremely close and disaster is inches away at such huge speeds, and yet the funny thing is, I feel very comfortable with that, I feel comfortable knowing that is where the limit is. It is a finite parameter and I know I have to work within that, otherwise it is all over. I tend to struggle with not knowing where the defined limit is, because then I have to keep searching for the limit, so I think I perform in tightly controlled environments better. I think that extends to my private life too, the way I like everything neat and tidy, because that way my environment is controlled and I feel more comfortable and, by definition, more at home. I like having things organized so that I know where everything is. It works well with my type of mind. In Monaco, the track conditions tend to remain the same for the entire race, I know my limits then, whereas at other circuits someone might drag some dust or grass on the track from the gravel pits or the edges, and that makes the racing environment slightly different. I'm not so comfortable with that.

Winning Monaco is nice because I live there, it's a small principality and I'm part of the society in that I own a business there and I've lived there for eleven years, so I'm one of the local boys getting a result (my home is less than a mile from where the paddock is situated). The only way it could better for them was if I was Monégasque and winning it, as opposed to a Brit.

Monaco is special to me because it has become my home since I left Scotland. Irrespective of what people may or may not think of me as a driver, no one can take a Monaco win away from you, because you don't win that race by accident and you certainly don't win it twice by good fortune. I've been on that special podium four times now, I'm good round there, end of story and nobody could argue otherwise. I'm very proud of that fact.

As a Formula 1 driver you are well known for earning a lot of money. It is taken as a given that your wages are public know-ledge, which isn't the case for most jobs. I don't really have a problem with that although, as I have said, it can cause some awkward situations. You also get approached with a lot of business proposals unrelated to racing. Some are good, some are poor and some are just ludicrous.

Overall, my personality prefers to stick with what I know, taking a car around a track at high speed. My father never wanted to make the family transport business European; he understood the parameters of our little island, Britain, and was perfectly comfortable to stay within those boundaries. My brother worked for Curries European and served his apprenticeship as a mechanic with them. They were only thirty miles away and so essentially were direct rivals, but my father was always happy to pass on any European business to them, and keep his order book full with British work. He saw it as funding his family's lifestyle, so he stuck to what he knew.

I think I am the same. I am cut from the same cloth. I don't want to get involved in every opportunity just because it might be something great, I want to stick to something I know. In my life, history has shown that I have been successful in making money doing what I know and unsuccessful when I have tried to get involved in things I didn't know anything about (usually attracted by potentially big returns). I had a phase of trading money, betting the dollar against the euro, that sort of thing, and at first it was working and it was great but, of course, it turned and went down and down. And then it's gone. I didn't really understand what I was doing, so it's not a surprise it didn't work.

Sometimes you get mentioned in relation to business ventures that you have absolutely no idea about. I was asked by one interviewer how I came to be involved with the designer Scott Henshall, but I have never been in business with him. I remember he did a fashion show and my girlfriend at that time modelled some swimwear – which has got to be the easiest fashion accessory to make. But I didn't go to the show and I wasn't involved. He probably knows nothing about it either – but apparently I was doing a range of menswear with him and also opening some stores it seems. Or not. It was news to me. Likewise, I have never endorsed a range of 'David Coulthard' bubble bath ... although that might not be a bad idea, come to think of it.

I do have other business interests that have most definitely worked. I'm involved in a bicycle helmet company called Facesaver, making kiddies' bicycle helmets, specifically full-face helmets. It's a venture I've done with one of the designers from McLaren. I invested, he designed and now it's in Halfords and places like that. I also got involved with the Bicycle Helmet Initiative Trust as their patron for several years, because I found out from reading up on this subject that every week a child is killed from bicycle- or skateboard-related injuries, with several more suffering permanent brain damage and terrible facial injuries. And yet it's not compulsory to wear a bicycle helmet in the UK. The cost of a helmet is relatively small, but the challenge is as much about educating parents. We even went to the Houses of Parliament to try and get a bill carried to make it mandatory for children to wear helmets. What surprised me was that in the course of doing this, we came across a lobby of people who thought it was an infringement of freedom of choice to have to wear a helmet. But this is kids we are talking about – my point was this: I'm an adult and I race in a dangerous business and I assume those risks because I am aware of the consequences and I protect myself with what is required; but children don't know about these things, they don't have the choice, they don't have the understanding, of course they don't. By making it mandatory, we take that choice away from them, yes, but their safety and well-being is infinitely enhanced. You've almost got to scare the parents into it and make the kids think it's cool. The bill did not pass and I don't think it ever will, it is not a 'sexy' bill and will probably never carry.

My part-ownership of The Columbus Hotel in Monaco is probably the most obvious example of a business success I've enjoyed outside of Formula 1. I own that with Ken McCulloch, who has vast experience in the hotel trade. He is part of a business group that built up the Malmaison chain and then sold it and, as a result, he moved to Monaco to live. I already knew of Ken, because he had been involved in sponsoring a Porsche Supercup team, so I'd actually met him way back when I was driving for Jackie Stewart in 1990 at an event to drum up sponsorship.

I was becoming rather disillusioned with the stock-market style of investing the money I was earning off the track. I didn't feel in control. You put the money where these advisors told you, you were given lots of pieces of paper and in some months the paper would be worth more and in some months it would be worth considerably less. But paper wealth never appealed to me. I'm not a high-risk person in that respect.

Plus, I just wasn't 'living' the investment; I wanted something I could touch and feel. I owned my houses, but those were for me to use, they were not specific business investments. I own one square foot of a hillside in Scotland, which someone bought me for a present, which means I am actually a Laird of Glencairn! I have a certificate to prove it too, but other than that, I had not ventured into real estate.

One night I met Ken for a meal at a local restaurant and he said, 'Did you get my proposal?' and I hadn't, because he'd sent it to my manager who decided I wouldn't be interested and binned it. So Ken faxed it through to me that day – the idea was to buy a local hotel and turn it into The Columbus. I immediately liked the idea. Apart from being a tangible asset, a hotel like that was something I could use; it was something that was there for me on several levels. I trusted in Ken because he had a previous history of hotel management and operating them and so, after we discussed the idea some more, I passed it to my accountant and eventually invested. It wasn't that I was passionate about hotels, it just came at the right time when I was looking for something different.

Before we owned it, The Columbus was, in my opinion, a very run-of-the-mill, Middle Eastern-owned hotel. It was just horrible, actually: Italian styling, black marble and mirrored panels everywhere, just not nice, not stylish, not anything. We spent an absolute fortune renovating the property and immense amounts of time and attention to detail was paid to everything. Now it's a lot more modern and chic. I saw the designs, I saw it being created, I saw the show rooms. I enjoyed being involved.

There were little contributions from my side: for instance, there weren't toilet brushes in the toilets. Now, for my part, as you know, I don't like leaving any mess, but no matter how good you are at that, it's very difficult to do a skid-free dump. In some wealthier circles, there is a view that this is what the chamber maids are for; other people insist that toilet brushes are unhygienic. I am aware of those views, although I don't agree with them, but I still think it's nice to give people the choice. So I eventually got The Columbus to put toilet brushes in the rooms. My mother pointed out that the lighting wasn't very good in the toilet for ladies to put make-up on and that there was no face mirror, so there are little electrified face mirrors in there now. That all costs money and you don't really get anything back from that in the immediate term, but little details like that rather than the big elaborate design statements make all the difference.

Nonetheless, Ken made it very clear to me that we had to invest in people, too. When I was talking to him about it, I was like, 'Why will it be different to any other hotel?' and he said, 'We are going to invest in the people. A hotel,' he explained to me, 'no matter how fancy your fixtures and fittings, has no heart and soul without people and therefore I do want to make it nice and chic, but you've got to have good people.' It's a very wise approach. Many people travel and spend a lot of time away from home, they travel with very little expectation of anything being exceptional, so the idea was to make The Columbus feel like you were coming home rather then going away. I bought into that concept and largely the staff do a great job of making the place feel homely and welcoming.

When we launched The Columbus, I was quite heavily involved with the media and interviews, all that stuff. I was happy to use my profile to boost the project, of course I was. The on-going publicity it gets is encouraging, and it has become something of a destination hotel for many of the global sports personalities who visit Monaco for various tournaments, not just racing drivers.

Day to day, I am not involved in the business of the hotel, I do the racing. It's a popular place, it's well-used, it's added a bit of life and soul to the Fontveille corner of Monaco, which is through one of the tunnels and, therefore, a little away from the main Casino square.

We have also opened up The Dakota near Nottingham, and have plans to open more at various points and in different locations. The original idea was to have Monaco, London,

Lisbon and Paris at various points. My partners looked at various locations, but finding a site isn't the difficult thing – to find a site where the price is right to be able to develop the hotel there and launch with the right profit margin is extremely difficult. You want each hotel to stand alone as profitable, as opposed to one propping up another, which happens in a lot of big hotel groups. There has been a huge amount of investment – tens of millions to buy and renovate – and so you want to make sure you get it right. I want to see it continue to grow and produce a creative return on my investment. In the meantime, I enjoy the hotel – I'm in there all the time, as it is just a few hundred yards from my apartment.

I often find Brits criticising me for living in Monaco, a 'tax-haven'. Strangers come up to me and start making comments about me not contributing to the UK economy and all that. I have to be honest, it really pisses me off because although I am only in the UK for less than thirty nights each year, I still pay a substantial tax bill, which makes me think I am contributing more than most – especially as I am not taking anything out.

Overall, I really enjoy my time in Monaco. Back in my mid-teens when my father said I should live in Monaco, it seemed like another world. Now it is where I live.

My parents knew all along.

'What is for you, won't go by you.'

THERE IS NO LOVE BETWEEN
US ANYMORE

As my career in the paddock progressed, my concerns about Ron's favouritism towards Mika still troubled me greatly. My team-mate's two world titles in a row only fuelled this fear, as did the way my team principal behaved with me sometimes. In the heat of the moment, in the battle that is a Formula 1 race, you have to believe in your General. It's only sometimes with hindsight that history shows the General didn't necessarily always do the best for his troops.

Ron would go for long periods without speaking to me, busy as he was running the team. I tried to start a conversation with him many times about my concerns, but it was awkward. For a start, it seemed like every year there was speculation about who might be coming through to replace who. It seems I have spent my entire Formula 1 career being uncertain about the next season. You get used to sitting in on meetings about the next year's car, fully aware that you might not even be sitting in it. Getting into Formula 1 is difficult, staying in is very difficult and when you are out, you are forgotten about very quickly.

Eventually, the situation with Mika got quite debilitating and I had to speak to Ron directly about it. After several years of skirting around the issue with insinuation and implication, we finally sat down and I explicitly explained all my concerns. One analogy I used was that it was like him having twins, but twins that were not treated equally. I didn't want better treatment than Mika, just equal.

Finally, Ron admitted that yes, he did have a special relationship with Mika. This was how he explained it to me: Mika had very nearly died in one of his cars; the crash put him in a coma; Ron told me that when you see someone who was working for you crash and, as a result, ends up in that state, strewn across a hospital bed, it makes a big impact. The accident was the result of a deflated left rear tyre, which was later found to have a four-inch gash in it, probably from debris on the track – so it wasn't even a McLaren mistake, it was a pure racing accident. Nonetheless, Ron still felt the way he did. He acknowledged the relationship with Mika was special and said, 'That's the way it is, I'm afraid.'

It had taken him quite a few years to say that and, rather than confirm my worst fears and make me demoralised, in a way I felt it was a good development, because at least he was acknowledging that I wasn't mad and paranoid without reason. I could stop self-analysing and doubting my mind, because he had confirmed what I'd been thinking all along. Somehow, that felt like a positive step.

My relationship with Ron was always a tense, uneasy one. I have a great deal of respect for him, I think he's a very honourable man. If I called him now and said I've got a problem, he would do whatever he was physically capable of doing to help me, as indeed I believe he would for any of his employees or friends. He is a very honourable, good, family man. It's an unusual one because I have a great deal of respect for Ron as a person, but I have difficulty relating to him in business. Of course, people look at an organisation like McLaren and respect what they see as a magnificent business, rightly so in many ways, but it's not just about what you achieve, it's the way you achieve it. I think he's a much more stylish family man and friend than he is a businessman and that's a personal opinion based on his personality and my own experience of him. For example, one day he can talk to you and the next he'll ignore you – he'll rationalise that and say he's busy and that his mind is so far ahead of everyone else's that it doesn't allow him the luxury of small talk or whatever. But manners cost nothing.

At work he can be difficult, awkward, unreasonable, all of those things. During one of the many conversations we had about the internal McLaren politics, where I was airing some grievances, Ron once said to me, 'You don't have the luxury of having all of those things the way you want them to be. You're paid your salary to do the job, and it is also your job to rise above those things that you see as difficulties – if you do that you'll have a drive here and if you don't you won't.'

After Mika's pair of titles just before the Millennium, Formula 1 pretty much turned into the Michael Schumacher Show, until Renault and Fernando Alonso ended the dominance in 2005. Ferrari were exhibiting a degree of superiority that was quite awesome which, when coupled with a legendary reliability, created a status quo where for several years they were virtually unbeatable. I say virtually . . .

There is a well-known photograph of me flipping the middle finger to Michael as I tried to overtake him on a corner in the French Grand Prix. It was the 2000 season and I was angry about a manoeuvre he made, cutting across me, forcing me to lift off. If I hadn't lifted we would have crashed into each other, so I was not pleased. I thought that move was very unsporting and that fired me up even more, so I chased and quickly overtook Rubens Barrichello in the other Ferrari before turning my attention to Michael.

The anger, passion and the belief that I should win that race made me drive incredibly quickly. I was fuming. When I finally caught up with Michael, I tried to pass him on one side and he ran me wide – that's when I gave him the finger, because I knew what he was doing, he was just taking me wide to stop me from passing him. To me it was like a professional foul. I can't possibly know how it was in the car for him, maybe it was just one of those things, but I was angry and pissed off, which is why my immediate reaction was to tell him to fuck off by giving him the finger. It makes a great photo, but actually it was rather silly because he couldn't see it at the time – although I'm sure he's seen it since!

I managed to pass him on the next lap, but even then we banged wheels. That was partly me saying, 'Right, I am past you now, back off!' I went on to win the race and I feel to this day that was a great day in my career, a great win. It was full of passion, of heart, of skill and controlled aggression. I was the quickest guy on the day (Mika was nowhere near my pace) and, in my mind, I was meant to win that race, no one was going to stop me. I thought Michael had done a couple of things that were on the limit of acceptability and he had to be beaten for that. I may be wrong in my view, but that's how I felt. It also showed that when I didn't feel distracted in anyway, when I was just racing again, that's what I could achieve. That was absolutely one of my best victories.

After the race, Norbert Haug, the head of Mercedes motorsport, was interviewed and a journalist put it to him that my gesture was unsportsmanlike and set a bad example for young racing fans. Absolutely deadpan, Haug replied, 'You don't understand, in motor-racing, that is a traditional gesture used to indicate to the driver ahead that you intend to overtake him in one lap's time.'

There was still a degree of tension (and therefore distraction) at McLaren, despite the clear-the-air talk I'd had with Ron. Back at the paddock, the first half of 2000 saw me outperform Mika. After his back-to-back titles, he struggled and people again started talking about me winning the championship. Ron excused Mika PR duties after he looked weary in France in 2000, then afterwards he came back with a series of wins while I endured a poor run. Mika continued to rally for the second half of the season and appeared to have another title within his reach. When I was hit by a Jordan in Monza, Jurgen Hubbert of Mercedes even went so far as to say he expected the push to the title to be concentrated 'on one driver', namely Mika. Despite this, Schumacher still won the title; I came third with seventy-three points, with three wins and eight other podiums.

Sometimes the tension within my team was very public, such as at the next season's Spanish Grand Prix, in Barcelona, 2001. They had introduced launch control on the grid – a system in the car which was basically a button you pushed to give you the optimum balance of revs, power and wheel speed –

but we were having electrical problems with the new system. In that race, I pushed the various buttons in the correct sequence and ... the engine stopped. I consequently started from the back of the grid, but managed to haul myself up to a fifth-place finish. After the race, ITV went to Ron and asked what had happened and he said I must have had a 'brain fade'. I knew it had been a system failure so when they came to me, I said, 'I think it is fair to say that Ron has had a bit of brain fade to make that comment without talking to me or to his engineers first.' Then we went to the next grand prix in Monaco and I was in pole position. I was flying. But sadly the same thing happened again and I had to start at the back of the grid – again I'd switched correctly, but again it had cut my engine. The jokers in the pits started to call it 'McLaren's stop control' instead of launch control. It was just an electronic software issue ... but a very public disagreement. To be fair, Ron later apologised for that statement and explained that he had quali-fied the sentence at the time by pointing out he had not yet seen all the data.

This was all the more frustrating because, in that 2001 season, I'd got off to such a strong start and was initially Schumacher's main rival. In many ways, this was one of my strongest chances of winning the championship. There were even whispers that a struggling Mika should support my race for the title, something that was quickly dismissed by McLaren who stated there were no driver preferences. Unfortunately, after Monaco, my results stuttered, so much so that I won no more races and retired four times. It was disappointing, of course, because I was looking good to battle with Schumacher for the title and then those few mechanical issues scuppered the team and that was it, game over. The German won again.

I can look back and say I finished second to Michael, but so have a lot of other people, so, in my opinion, it's hardly an achievement to shout about. It's too hypothetical to argue that had Michael not been around in that period I would have won the world title – he was and he won it, it is what it is. The end of that season had me finishing runner-up to Michael, yes, but it was not a close race – his 123 points almost doubling my sixty-five. Mika came fifth and went on a 'sabbatical' in the close season. Six months later, he announced that this break had become full retirement.

My final years at McLaren brought me fifth, seventh and equal-ninth placings in the world title standings. Other than that, I really have very little recollection of specific races or events, as it was a pretty uneventful period in my career. Mika was replaced by another Finn, Kimi Räikkönen, who pretty much picked up where his countryman had left off. He was very young and had entered Formula 1 after only two years in cars. I always thought he had an amazing talent to do very little away from the race weekend but deliver on the race day itself.

Those years were dominated by Ferrari and Michael Schumacher, of course. In 2002, Michael won the title after only eleven of the seventeen races. I have to admit there came a point when that partnership's domination was so complete, so unassailable, that I said to myself, 'Fuck it, let's just enjoy this!'

I had a bit of fun at the start of the 2003 season, in a bid to challenge what I referred to as 'my perceived greyness by the British public' – I'm either a scandalous ladies' man or unexcitable 'Cool-thard', I can't win! *The Sunday Times* once called me, 'the most misunderstood racing driver of all-time'. With these misconceptions in mind, I ran a 'Tabloid Quiz' for the press pack with the prize being an all-expenses-paid weekend for two at The Columbus. The questions included such brain-teasers as, 'What was the name of the girl in the bubble bath?'; 'How many people have been photographed on the foredeck of the *Highlander* while I sat drinking a cup of tea?'; 'How many sexposés have been published about me?' (not the rumours, just the straight kiss-and-tells); and finally, 'how much do you think I have paid to outgoing girlfriends?' (answer to the closest million wins).

On the track, my final win for McLaren was a somewhat lucky one in Australia to open the 2003 season, but after that I had four retirements, one spin and only two more podiums. That was the year that single-lap qualifying was introduced and that was never something I enjoyed. The very last race for McLaren, at the 2004 Brazilian Grand Prix, was disappointing, which seemed unfortunate after so many years working together. It had started to drizzle and I was left out on slicks, and it seemed to me that we were unable to make a clear decision – I suffered and finished eleventh. However, I don't think, unlike some, that this was a pre-determined ploy to make my last race for the team a disappointment.

There is a certain inevitability about severing your ties with a Formula 1 team. I liken signing a contract with a racing team to getting married, except that on the same day you sign the register, you also prepare the divorce papers, because in Formula 1 you *will* get divorced. A grand prix driver will not spend his life driving for one grand prix team. My tenure at

McLaren was highly unusual for its longevity, even more so given the circumstances.

So you sign on and you are part of a team but, as I certainly found out, there are two driver factions within that team, and they are always fighting against each other, whether overtly or not. The marriage with your team can be fantastic, but both parties know the divorce papers are just sitting there, usually for when the team decide they no longer want the driver.

By this stage, I'd had years of the tension. At the end of that first year with Räikkönen as my team-mate, I was informed that McLaren had signed the Colombian Juan Pablo Montoya for the following season. I knew it was unlikely he was going to replace the young Finn. It seemed clear that my tenure at McLaren was entering its final weeks. Oddly, however, although I knew this privately long before any press announcement, McLaren publicly chose to announce that Montoya would be replacing me while I was on holiday . . .

. . . with Ron.

On a boat.

That was pretty strange. There aren't many places to hide on a boat, are there?

McLaren obviously thought that signing Montoya was the right thing for the team. History will show that he didn't do a better job than I did; he was actually further behind than I was, plus he only lasted a season and a half whereas I managed nine years. I believe McLaren made the wrong decision, they believe they made the right one – however, ultimately, if a guy walks away from a team in the middle of the year, it would suggest that he wasn't the right person. He didn't help his cause by making harsh remarks about me, but I've forgotten what he said, so I can honestly say it troubled me even more briefly than his time at McLaren lasted. I wouldn't stoop so low as to be that childish. I pride myself on being a consummate professional and always coolly diplomatic. I'll say this though, he's a chubby little fella.

By the end of 2004, my time at McLaren had finally come to an end. While racing for Ron Dennis, I scored twelve wins, fifty-one podiums and 412 championship points. My years at McLaren were littered with wins. Notably for British Formula 1 fans, I won two British Grands Prix at Silverstone, in 1999 and 2000. That was nice, but I am being totally honest when I say I don't really remember that much about them, just because I don't. I do know that I have the odd accolade of being the only racer to win British Grands Prix in two separate millennia! Seriously though, I tend to look forward, I don't reminisce that much. When I am asked about certain grand prix wins, it's hard to elaborate: yeah, I won it, what more is there to say? It's just a date in the diary from history. Reminiscing in sport is endemic, so maybe I am the exception, but I have always preferred to look forward. People talk fondly about winning the 1966 World Cup and yes, of course, I can see how big a day for English sport that was. But it was forty years ago: *let's move on.* Four decades ago motor-racing was basically people driving around in fast tin cans. I think part of my instinct to look forwards and not backwards is to do with the environment of racing: you are always looking to next season's car, the new contract or the next race. Having had that drilled into me from the age of eleven must have made an impact. When I was first asked to write this book, part of me was uncertain because it is essentially an exercise in looking back and I find that when I do that I can wander off and get distracted easily. Yet strangely, writing this book has made me think about myself more than I would ever normally do and so I now feel that I have a wider knowledge of myself moving forward. You see, I drifted off for a minute there ... I'm a bugger for that.

McLaren are a great organisation and I can't imagine that they will not win a championship again. They have an amazing set-up, amazing facilities and great people, but history will state that their reliability has cost them many wins and championships – if you compare them to Ferrari and Renault, that's indisputable.

That said, I always believed McLaren were an amazing group of talented people who had been assembled together who could employ some amazing strategies and produce some incredible racing cars. Despite everything that went on over the years, I had enormous faith and belief in the team.

I was at McLaren for nine years and I've raced in more grands prix for that team than any other driver in their history – those sorts of things don't happen by accident.

THE LOOKS OR THE LIFESTYLE?

Formula 1 dominates your private life. On a purely practical level, the massive amount of travelling means you get little chance to strike up new friendships because you are so rarely in one place for any length of time. I have a lot of acquaintances, but only a few true friends. In the decade or so I've lived in Monaco, I've never spent more than about ten consecutive days there – or indeed anywhere; I've never spent Christmas or New Year there either, as I always go to either Scotland or, more recently, to a chalet I bought in Switzerland. Monaco may be my home, but my job takes me away from there so often.

Holiday time is severely restricted. November is pretty much the only month you can get a really good break because you are usually not driving at all, but despite that I haven't had a full two-week vacation since I was a teenager living with my parents at home. The longest holiday I have taken since then was probably the ten days I spent in Thailand once – it wasn't until the tenth day that I woke up and didn't feel tired. Every other day I was still recovering from the rest of the year.

Such a hectic itinerary means on the one hand you crave some time in one place – it is perhaps no surprise that a racing driver sometimes wants to be going slowly – but there is a central paradox within me about this, which is that I actually mentally struggle with the idea of being in the same place for two weeks. It's a work-ethic guilt complex, I think. I can't envisage taking a three-week holiday doing nothing when I could have achieved something in that time.

I am so used to moving, at home being constantly on the road. I'm a traveller.

Yet, at the same time, I feel rootless.

I was having a conversation with a friend during the writing of this book and they asked me, 'Where do you feel most at home?' I thought about that for a while before answering, 'Nowhere.' Obviously there is a certain sense of warmth and family when I return to Scotland, but I haven't lived there as an adult, and not at all since I was eighteen. Monaco is my 'home' as such, but I am travelling so often it's almost like my life is just one long journey with Monaco as some form of base. At times it just feels like somewhere to get my laundry done, pick up some new clothes, do some training, then bugger off again to the next race or test.

When I do crash-land in Monaco, it's not like I sit at home and read a book either, or go for a stroll by the harbour. I catch up on all my e-mails, read the post, office matters that I couldn't do remotely, taking care of business and so on. Cawthorne spends a lot more time there since he moved to Monaco in 2000. He loves relaxing at home and reading books at night. I can't do that. There's some kind of internal motor that makes me feel the need to be doing something, and sitting in my home relaxing or reading a book wouldn't be the answer. Unless I am doing something, I feel restless, unsettled.

Writing this book has made me evaluate and revisit a lot of experiences and times in my life I might otherwise not have recalled. To some degree, it has made me do more soul-searching than I am used to. One of the conclusions I have come to as a result is that in many ways I have just skimmed the surface of life. Yes, on the one hand you have the Formula 1 lifestyle, the girls, the cars, the glamour, the apartments and all that jazz; but looking at it another way, I've been doing exactly the same thing since I was eleven. Now, in my mid-thirties, I am still doing the same thing.

I have travelled the world but again, looking at it from a different perspective, I'm not as worldly as most people. Why? Because I haven't stopped to take it all in. There's been no time. When I went to Melbourne for the 2006 Australian Grand Prix, I never actually left the hotel complex, other than to get in a car to drive to the circuit, do the race, go back to the hotel, get my things and fly home. Melbourne is beautiful and deeply cultural – with its beaches, its bays and its vineyards, but all of that may as well not have existed. Part of me thinks all that will still be there when I have retired and that, for now, I am there to race.

In many ways, I am a family man without a family of my own. When you look at how I have spent the last twenty years of my life, it's perhaps no surprise. Since moving to Monaco in 1995, the longest I have spent in one place is those ten consecutive nights in my home in Monaco. When you clock up all those thousands of airmiles, add to that all the transfers, sitting around in airports, attending functions, commercial commitments and so forth, it's hardly the best lifestyle to meet someone special and, for want of a better phrase, settle down. This is not just a recent inclination – I wanted to have kids and a family of my own way back when I was a teenager, long before I was twenty even. I wanted to be settled down and having kids – I think that was partly because I liked the family ideals instilled in me by my parents' wonderful marriage, but also in a more puerile and immature way, because I thought it meant I could get my end away more often. So when I got busy racing, I didn't think about it again for years.

Formula 1 has turned me into an emotional and literal nomad. Travelling is my office. I can go for weeks without a day off, travelling sometimes every single day. People think you race and then get nearly two weeks off and don't do anything in the close season. If only! I hope when I no longer race that may change, particularly when I have a family of my own. I was happy in my childhood being in one place most of the time and I never longed to travel. As I have said, I never dreamed of being a grand prix driver, everything kind of just happened and as a consequence of doing this job, travel has been my most constant companion.

There is an assumption made about well-known personalities that they crave public attention and that, when it is given, they are totally at ease. In both cases with me, this couldn't be further from the truth. This is one great attraction of living where I do. In Monaco, people tend to leave you well alone; you get the occasional autograph hunter when you are out for dinner, but they are polite and it's really no bother. In Britain I get approached a lot more and I find that if I am in a public area I can feel very self-conscious. I'm not that comfortable in crowded areas to be honest, I wish I could be.

My old team-mate Paul Stewart from PSR is friends with Simon Le Bon and he once invited me to see Duran Duran at Earls Court. Everyone was hanging out backstage afterwards and having a great time, but I found it all incredibly difficult. I was watching other people dancing away and there were so many people who were clearly really enjoying themselves. I remember thinking, 'Fuck, I wish I could lose myself like that and not be so self-conscious.'

Even writing this book makes me feel a little self-conscious. I've found myself in an unusual position. I've never actually spoken about my past in this way. I don't like to talk about myself because I find it all rather embarrassing. Being the centre of attention has never been appealing to me; racing cars has. I will always avoid a debate, because I don't really like to analyse myself or my thoughts or opinions. Cawthorne is the opposite; he loves to sit down and talk about something, almost for the sake of it. He enjoys that. I don't. He's a bright lad, he's educated and he enjoys showing that at times, whereas I don't have that much depth of knowledge. If a conversation brings up a point I know nothing about, I will just say, 'Sorry, I'm not sure to be honest.' Some people might see that as a weakness of character, but if that debate isn't going to change my life, I don't feel the need to get involved.

However, writing this book has forced me to ask an awful lot of questions of myself. I think I have the potential to be a reclusive character. I'm a loner in some respects, because I have never been the 'down the pub with people' type; if my close friends aren't there, I wouldn't just go in and chat to someone. I am very happy for people I don't know or like to just get on with their lives and keep out of my space and I'll do the same. I never got into darts night.

The biggest disappointments in my life have been people, not things, possessions, holidays, races . . . but people. It is very hard to judge people sometimes, especially when you meet so many faces every day as I do and when there is so much money washing around in my job of work. I am devastated when I find that someone I trusted shouldn't have been treated with such respect and has proved untrustworthy. It's a sad feeling. That makes me feel like having less interaction with people in general, because the less people I meet, the less frustration or disappointment I potentially have to deal with. That fuels my reclusive streak, because I just don't want the disappointment.

I can see there are arguably a lot of contradictions within my personality. Everyone likes to think they are normal, so it is a little unsettling when you realise some of your thoughts and ideas might not be consistent. At the same time, I am at ease with those contradictions, I know they are there but it doesn't really trouble me.

The only place I am completely at ease and not self-conscious in public is when I am in the car with my helmet on. Unlike celebrity functions, driving a car for me is not an alien environment. If I sit in the cockpit of an aircraft, I don't know what all the knobs and buttons do, so that would feel uncomfortable and straightaway I'd be in a defensive mode of telling myself, 'Don't touch this, don't touch that!' Getting in a grand prix car is not like that for me. In a Formula 1 car, I don't feel self-conscious, I don't feel awkward, I feel completely at ease and at home. Grand prix cars are a natural progression of what I have been doing since I was eleven years old, so it's a normal environment, and one that lets me relax and do my job. Musicians say the time on stage is their most pure experience; for me, the same can be said of the moment when all the crew and peripheral people walk away from the car on the grid and you are left alone, just you, the car, the other drivers and the race ahead. That is racing at its most pure. There is a certain emotional serenity at that moment that I love. It is a magic moment.

That said, even when I am in or around the car, there is scope to feel self-conscious. You're not going to get private time at or around a race track. One regularly awkward encounter is with people who used to race against me many years ago. I have raced against hundreds, probably thousands of people, but because I was fortunate enough to go on to Formula 1, it is my face that is known. That means former racers – from whatever level they made it to – will recall racing against me in the pissing rain twenty years ago … but I don't remember them, how can I? At test days there are often a lot of these ex-racers around and it's always excruciatingly awkward not to offend them. The honest answer would be, 'No, I don't remember you, sorry,' but you have to be nice to people and let them walk away having had a nice experience meeting you again. It's not because I am more important than them, not at all, it's just because I am in a public sport and I simply cannot recall all of those faces I haven't seen for two decades. Sometimes they say the strangest things and it really kills the conversation.

I have to be honest, I can do exactly the same in similar situations myself. In the mid-1990s I was doing some photo-shoot for a Coulthard-branded scooter and they got hold of the model Kelly Brook, who was looking very glamorous in this leather kit. At the time she was just a model and was yet to do *The Big Breakfast* and head off to LA and launch her career over there. Then, ten years later, I was on one of these huge boats at the Cannes film festival when I saw Billy Zane, who by now was dating a considerably more famous Kelly. I was trying to make conversation so I went up to Billy and said, 'Hi, I'm David Coulthard, I know your fiancée ...'

He looked at me and said, 'Oh, hi, are you the racing driver she dated?' I said, 'No, that wasn't me ...' I didn't know who that particular driver was, but it wasn't me and I was just trying to find a connection that would make him feel comfortable and, suddenly, it all became really very awkward. Within seconds of my well-intentioned ice-breaker, we were looking at our shoes with nothing to say to each other. What that teaches me is, if in doubt, say nowt. Because if I can't think of anything interesting to say or have a reason to talk to people I don't know, it's probably best not to say anything at all.

There are plenty of drivers who are much more outgoing than me, but I also know a lot that are also not comfortable in front of a crowd. One obvious exception to that rule is Jackie Stewart, who famously made public speaking in motor-sport an art-form. Even his world championship successes seem to have been surpassed by his profile off the track and his ability to talk to crowds, make speeches and so on, he is a master of the craft.

This was obviously something he was aware of many years ago and when I was at Paul Stewart Racing he, rather astutely, sent all of his drivers to an organisation called Kings Tree in London, which is where politicians and public figures can learn about speeches and public presentations. Jackie's 'Staircase of Talent' was not just about finding fast racers; it was also about producing rounded, commercially appealing drivers who understood the media and who could present themselves well – some nicknamed it 'The Jackie Stewart Charm School'. I still remember some of the lessons and tricks of the trade, but that doesn't mean I find it anymore comfortable speaking in public.

You are often asked to stand up and address the workers at the team factory, which is absolutely fair enough; these people are the backbone of the operation that puts you behind the wheel. However, even though I know I am on home territory, it is still a struggle. Other times, you would have to speak to the general pubic at certain events. On one occasion, I was talking to an audience when someone asked me about the science of tyres. They wanted to know what 'graining' was, which is the process whereby the tyre degrades as rubber is ripped off the top surface and causes a loss of grip because the rubber rolls. Once that transition is over, the grip improves – perhaps most famously this happened to me in my 2002 Monaco win, where I had to drive through the performance drop and eventually accelerate away to victory.

Now, put on the spot about a reasonably technical question like that, I had to think of a way of explaining this concept easily without patronising people at the same time. The analogy that sprang to mind was a pencil with an eraser on the end, and how, if you rub pencil marks out, you get little rolls of rubber on the paper. That seemed perfect and was indeed what I meant to say. What I actually said was, 'Do you remember at school when you used to carry around a rubber ...?'

I once tried a system of cards and bullet points, because I

had these mind-management problems where if I had to start thinking about what I am saying at that exact moment in time, I couldn't remember what I wanted to say for my next paragraph. Then I'd start to panic and forget even more. So I had these cards with bullet points neatly lined up, explaining in one-line summaries what each successive point was about. Again, there were a few hundred people there, so I was pleased to be so organised and I did feel a little more relaxed knowing I had this system in place. It all went swimmingly at first but, after about three bullet points, I looked down at the next card, read the sentence and thought, 'What the fuck does that mean?'

I realised from that experience that the only way for me to speak in public with any fluidity is to be interviewed, questions and answers if you like. One of my strengths is responding to off-the-cuff questions. I enjoy that and I can talk freely and respond quickly that way. Standing up and speaking one way is a disaster really, I just become too self-conscious and stilted. If I was filling in a form that asked me if I was confident, I would probably say I believe in myself, yes, but super-confident, no. My mother always used to say she'd love to be able to see herself as others do; I know some observers see me as a very cool and calculated customer, but I have to say, outside of racing, I still have self-doubt about whether I really do deserve to be in a certain environment or at a particular event.

In my defence, at McLaren I was known as being ideal for these sort of PR events, and compared to the rather less vocal Mika, I did a huge share of those duties. At the same time, I've noticed you only need to say the word 'poo' in a serious environment and it makes grown men giggle. I bet Sir Jackie Stewart hasn't got that in his repertoire.

WINGS AT THE SPEED OF SOUND

When it came to the end of my McLaren tenure, there were initially no obvious opportunities. I got off my arse and was prepared to go on test drives or anything to stay part of the process, not because I didn't want to let go, but because I believed I still had something to offer. I spoke with Jean Todt about a possible Ferrari test drive, for example. Some teams were very respectful about me and declined with grace, due to various circumstances. Toyota was not one of those teams. They were approached and were totally dismissive. There was pure arrogance from their management, who believed they had the best two drivers in the world, which I would suggest no one in the paddock agreed with. I'm not saying I'm the best in the world, but the combination of what I have achieved and who I am able to bring to the table, and the evidence that I can deliver on the race track, might command a little more respect than I was afforded. I was, after all, only safeguarding my career and it would have been unprofessional of me and my rep-resentatives not to have approached everyone in the paddock who might be available.

Conversations were had with various teams and advanced with Jaguar Racing. Then the energy drinks company Red Bull – owned by the billionaire Dietrich Mateschitz – bought that team outright, so it was all change again. It became apparent that the Red Bull drive might, after all, be the best option. One afternoon during this phase of looking for a new team, I sat down in my Monaco apartment with Martin Brundle. We had a notepad in front of us and we wrote down all the pros and cons of driving for Red Bull. The pros were that I believed in their commitment, they obviously wanted to succeed and I still believed in my own ability to race – that column was a couple of lines. Simple as that.

The cons were several pages long.

For example, it was a very small money deal, certainly compared to my years at McLaren. When you work out the cost of participating in Formula 1 – paying for your super licence, your insurance, your travel, which isn't always paid for in your contract and so on – that costs a lot of money before you've even competed in one race. Plus, around me were people whose own incomes would decline if I took the Red Bull drive, Cawthorne, Martin and so on. But you have to cut your cloth accordingly and, because my financial situation changed, everyone else's did, too. Also, Red Bull was effectively a new team with new management, would they deliver? Would they bring what they'd promised in regards to investment? There were a lot of reasons against taking this deal.

There comes a certain point when you have to trust people on their word and make a judgement of their character. I wanted to continue. I believed I had something to offer and I believed Red Bull had the commitment to make something possible in the future. Martin and I sat there and chewed all these thoughts over for a long time and, eventually, I took a deep breath and said, 'Let's go racing ...'

There was a transition phase between the old Jaguar management and Christian Horner coming in and heading up Red Bull and, in that period of time, Martin Brundle had a meeting with Helmut Marko, who's one of the directors of Red Bull Racing and an ex-grand prix driver – forced into retirement when he lost an eye in the 1973 season. He's an advisor to Red Bull and heads up the young driver programme. He wasn't a believer in me at that time, because he felt that new, younger drivers were the way forward.

Discussions were starting to drag on and I was getting a little bit frustrated. It was the weekend of the Race of Champions in Paris, and I spoke to Helmut again. I said, 'Look, why don't I just speak to Dietrich if he wants to do a deal – I want to do a deal, we can go forward?' Helmut was evasive, saying, 'Oh, he can be quite a difficult man to get hold of, sometimes he disappears for several days and no one can contact him ...' I was late for a function, I thought my grand prix career was potentially over and I just wanted to cut to the chase. I didn't have the patience to be fucked around. I said, 'Look, we both know that's bullshit, if you want me to do this I'm ready to do it, please get Dietrich to call me.'

An hour later the phone rang and it was indeed Dietrich. We came to an agreement on the phone and I said that, as far as I was concerned, I didn't need to see any legal paperwork. If we are on the same page then the deal is done. He agreed and said, 'That's the way I am, too. You are now my driver.' Obviously it went to a contract by necessity, but everything we had agreed on that phone-call was included in the paperwork. It was all very straightforward ... once I'd had a conversation with Dietrich.

Dietrich is certainly a big personality in the Fɪ paddock. At first, when we were having discussions, I only spoke to him on the phone. When you meet him in person, he is physically a very big man and creates quite a stir when he enters a room. You can see he has to concentrate hard on his English, but his language is good. He is a very direct personality – you know when he is enjoying things and you know when he is not happy. It is a given that he has my respect: he owns the grand prix team that enables me to race, after all, but he has also earned that respect by the way he has treated me.

Red Bull Formula ɪ is not just a whim for him – he is very knowledgeable on the sport. His brand first appeared in the paddock as a sponsor of Sauber for years, and he certainly knows his stuff. Day-to-day, of course, he cannot be involved in all the minutiae of running the team; he effectively has to be a sleeping partner/owner, but his presence is felt throughout the operation. He's got very good attention to detail for names and things like that, which is impressive when you think of the level of business he operates at. I also think he's a very honourable man, which is a dying breed. As I have discovered, if you agree on something with him, that's it, he won't go back on his word and I appreciate that.

So, finally, I signed to Red Bull. I left the decision to the last possible second. One thing I've learnt from Ron Dennis is that you should never make a decision until you absolutely have to, because only at that point do you have all the information you could possibly need. Don't decide today if you don't have to.

That's a cracking piece of advice from Ron and it's certainly one I will pass on to my children.

Although McLaren felt like a poisoned chalice at times, and the ideal place to race at others, when I left and first joined Red Bull I did so with a certain sense of trepidation. I'd been in another team for nine years and, during that time, you inevitably build up relationships with people and get familiar with your surroundings. Something as banal as going for my first seat fitting at Red Bull felt like quite a big deal; going to the first test was certainly a challenge. On a simple, personal level, you are walking into a garage where you don't know everyone, you are being introduced to people for the first time just as you step into the car to test. There were a few familiar faces at least: Red Bull had bought out Jaguar, who were previously Stewart Formula 1, which was the logical fulfilment of Jackie's 'Staircase of Talent' I had first stepped on all those years ago. So, in a sense, although Red Bull was a new era, there was also an element of me coming full circle. Of course, you soon get acclimatised to the new surroundings and environment, but I can't pretend it wasn't a little unsettling at first, it felt really quite alien to me.

People always talk about one team being much faster than another, a specific car being miles ahead of its competitors and so on. However, it is not just about the car and therefore, as a driver, it's not just about who sits in which car. If you find yourself with a team outside of the accepted front-runners – as Red Bull certainly was when I joined in 2005 – then you have different challenges to when you are sitting in one of the top cars, like at McLaren. What you then have to do is improve the resources available to you, get better people around you, work on increasing the budgets and work on yourself as a driver. I am often asked whether it feels pointless getting in a car that is widely known to be slower than several cars alongside me on the grid, knowing that if everyone drives to their ability and no one crashes, the chances are I cannot win. I have no problem with that, not at all. The challenge in that scenario then becomes what I said earlier, to try and get the best group of people around you, to try and get the best budget and so, that's the motivation; it's a technical exercise in bringing together a small army of people to go into a non-violent war on the race track. It's not just man against man; it's man-and-machine against man-and-machine.

One of the obvious benefits of a team like Red Bull is that they own the set-up outright, so decisions can be made very quickly. They have such a wealth of marketing cash available they can afford to be different; they can afford to be brave with their decisions. It's not like a team that partly relies on Mercedes or BMW money, or other teams that may rely on mobile phone sponsors or whatever. Red Bull is the sole owner and sponsor of the team and until such time it decides it would like some partners, it continues to be so, not because they can't raise sponsors, but because they choose to maximise their branding on the car and do things better their own way.

So, that is why you see Red Bull cherry-picking talent to bring to the team. There was a lot of restructuring to be done when they bought out Jaguar and the steady investment from headquarters has made that transition much easier and quicker. Red Bull wants and needs to grow to be able to compete with the bigger teams.

The initial doubts among some management about not having a younger driver on board seemed to disappear quickly. Then when I went to work there, I started a proactive campaign to recruit some of the sport's top names into the new set-up. I have been fortunate to be involved in fully funded teams with sizeable budgets in Williams, McLaren and now Red Bull. In the case of Red Bull, I have been very active in bringing key people to the team; personnel I know from the past and have identified as people who will take the team forward.

Formula 1 is one of the most politicised sports in the world, so acquiring these people for Red Bull has had to be done with the greatest tact and caution. In the first instance I ask them whether they are interested; they trust me, because we have an established relationship and they know I am being brutally honest when I say the team is limited at the moment in certain areas. The challenge is to get them motivated to believe the team will go forward with their investment and their time and then, after all of that, you finally get them in front of the person who can ultimately sign the cheques. So in the case of Adrian Newey, who is the star designer of the last decade or more, it was a very serious acquisition for Red Bull. The cars he has designed have won over a hundred grands prix, so he has had a more victorious influence in Formula 1 than even Michael Schumacher. Perhaps his most famous car was the Williams FW14B, which was devastatingly superior to its rivals and helped Nigel Mansell sweep all before him on the way to his title in 1992; perhaps the obvious car to rival this was his brilliant MP4-13, which was a lightning fast McLaren for myself and Mika to drive.

Taking a leaf out of my father's book, I initiated the first phone-call to Adrian's lovely wife, Marigold, because I know he has a very close working relationship with his wife and trusts her judgement; it transpired that he wasn't entirely happy at McLaren and so I arranged to meet with them for dinner with Christian Horner, my team principle. Once we'd got everything discussed, we arranged to take them to Salzburg to meet Dietrich. The salary on the table was very substantial, but arguably commensurate with Adrian's status as being Formula 1's premier designer and possibly the greatest of the modern era. Red Bull spend hundreds of millions of dollars a year on marketing, so Dietrich is a man with money; salaries for people like Adrian have to be very carefully considered, but I guess it is a relatively affordable investment when you are getting *the* designer. He's still such a relatively young man too, in his forties, so we are hoping his success will continue with Red Bull for many years to come.

Adrian could yet prove the guiding light for Red Bull. I am confident that since his arrival the cars will be better, because we have a man at the helm who has a proven track record. It's not just about the car he designs either – he comes with a big 'tick' next to his name, so if he asks for things from Red Bull, they are more likely to acquire them, because they believe in the fact he's won so many races. The cream rises to the top of any industry and in F1 you have the cream of the cream, so to speak. To get to that status, you have to be exceptional, which Adrian clearly is. In the team's previous incarnation as Jaguar, there were a lot of good people working with an average budget and achieving reasonable results, sometimes. The problem is, you don't get awards for doing a reasonable job. The aim is to get exceptional results regardless of the budget. With people like Adrian, that is achievable.

You have to admire Adrian's nerve. He could have stayed at McLaren earning fantastic money and with all the incredible facilities available to him there. But he wanted a new challenge and trusted in my assessment of where Red Bull was: a mid-grid team with designs to move sharply forward.

To make that move forward, you have to invest in people, people like Adrian. You get the brightest people and give them the resources to use their intelligence, to develop the machinery, then manufacture it and give the driver the best possible car. The best scenario for a team is to have such a good car that you don't need to have the best driver to win ... the utopia is to have the best car and the best driver.

Come to think of it, Adrian was at Williams when I was; then he was at McLaren when I was, too; now I've got him to join Red Bull with me ... maybe I'm stalking him?

In 2005, a lot of people mentioned I looked happier at Red Bull. I was happy, but I can honestly say I wasn't *happier*. I was happy at McLaren, not with every aspect of it as I have discussed, but I was a grand prix driver in a great team with a winning car – and I'm still a grand prix driver in a good team, except that we are not in possession of a winning car just yet.

It is funny the differences people notice. I am no longer clean-shaven, for example. I will regularly do TV or a race with stubble. That would *never* have happened, or even been contemplated at McLaren. Never. I wouldn't have dreamt of that, it was a 'must-shave' situation. McLaren has a very clean-cut image and it was a very clinical place. During my time as a driver there, I even had laser treatment on my neck to prevent the stubble growing back, because I thought, 'I'm never going to not shave again.' As you can see from pictures of that period, I sometimes had a red rash on my neck, so it didn't work!

Now I am at Red Bull I don't even think about shaving, it's just easier not to. So, yes, in that respect, the environment of my new team allows me to be more relaxed. Conversely, though, because certain things are less structured to what I'm familiar with, that's something different to get acclimatised to as well. McLaren suited the way I lived my life, which is very structured and organised and with a certain discipline. Martin Brundle finds all this talk about me being so much more relaxed as puzzling, and doesn't agree at all, he just thinks the public are seeing more of the 'real' me than before.

The situation at Red Bull is much more in favour of me than it was at McLaren. My position within Red Bull can be very rewarding. If there is a component or car that is known to be slightly better, I am certain they will give me the benefit of that part or vehicle over the other driver. To be fair, I scored more than double the points of both my team-mates put together in 2005 (twenty-four to their combined ten), so you can see why that is a logical preference – when that was happening with myself and Mika, we were both at a similar performance level. In the case of Red Bull, the team is fighting for points, so they are loading their chances of collecting some by handing me preferential treatment. I would be a liar to say it isn't a nice environment to find myself in, given my past experiences. I will always have a little paranoia, 'Is someone trying to get my drive?' and all those annual worries, but I think that's healthy, it keeps me sharp. Generally, from that point of view, the atmosphere at Red Bull is a long way from the tribulations at my previous team.

McLaren are a grand prix-winning, a world championship-winning team; Red Bull aren't . . . yet. Red Bull want to be and they will be, but they have to build an infrastructure. McLaren used to build their infrastructure in exacting detail, and that's what we need to do now.

So, yes, people say to me, 'You seem to have so much more fun at Red Bull,' to which I have to reply, 'I'm not here for a party, I'm here to get a result.'

It is interesting how people's perceptions of you change because of a few millimetres of stubble.

PROBLEMS, PODIUMS AND MUSIC FOR THE MASSES

The first two seasons at Red Bull were a mixed blessing. Initially, we proved a lot of doubters wrong in 2005. Part of the reason was that we were running Michelin tyres and that moved us up the grid a few places over competitors who were not. Also, our package was stronger than other contemporary Michelin runners, so we did well – scoring thirty-four points. By winning *F1 Racing* magazine's 'Start of the Year' award for my getaway from the grid at the Nürburgring, I also managed to defy the theory that after the age of thirty-five your ageing neuro-sensors start slowing down your reactions! The main highlight of that year came when I passed Nigel Mansell's 482 points tally, although I wasn't aware of it approaching and someone else had to tell me when I finally overhauled it with my three points for a sixth place in Malaysia, thus becoming the highest scoring British grand prix driver of all time.

Unfortunately, in my second year at Red Bull in 2006, our package was not nearly as competitive and the entire season was much harder work. We suffered from design miscalculations, then a lack of response to those mis-calculations, and subsequently a loss of weeks, rolling into months, of performance and progress.

The main problem was that we cocked up the cooling. We stripped the car down in December and there was a problem with the cooling. Then, it appeared as though the necessary steps to address that issue in the winter months hadn't been taken, because we still had the cooling issue at the very first test in January, even in the biting cold of Silverstone. You get to recognise a great car very, very quickly when you've been in the sport as long as I have. This certainly wasn't that. The first time you run a new car you try and set a lap time mainly to check systems across four or five laps. I knew straight away we had problems ahead. A quick car is difficult to drive but *quick*; a slow car is easy to drive but slow, so the irony is that you actually want it to be 'difficult' to a degree, because it will demand something of you. The car I inherited after Senna's death was exactly that – it was known for being 'twitchy'. I heard that Mansell complained the back end was unpredictable and it certainly was a difficult car: there was no power steering (the steering rack was underneath the chassis) and it was very heavy. Then, later, the McLaren I sat in for my first race for that team was much, much easier to drive – and slower. I was only thirteenth on the grid. That's the harshest example of that paradox.

To explain cooling in simple terms, if you have your window open in your car at high speeds, there's a lot of turbulence and noise and drag whereas, if you have the window closed, you have a smooth surface and a slippy car and it goes through the air quickly. The cooling vents in the side of a car suck air in to cool the radiator which is helpful, but they are working on the same principle as an open car window – they cool, but they also produce drag. The more drag they create, the slower the car goes in a straight line, simple. So the ideal solution is to create a cooling system that offers the best cooling capacity with the minimum opening and, therefore, the least amount of drag. You are trying to close that car window.

As I understand it, we had five variations of cooling packages through the year. At no point does that produce stability within the car and your performance is inevitably compromised. What frustrated me more, however, was the situation this caused within the team. Here's how I look at it: if I am driving a beautifully reliable and eminently driveable car and put it into a gravel pit through driver error, it is exactly that – driver error, my fault. Likewise, if the cooling system is fucking the car up, someone has to take responsibility. It can't be me, because I can't go into the office and redesign the cooling, because I don't have that talent, any more than the people responsible for that cooling system could climb into the car and put it on the podium. They rely on me and I rely on them. They rely on me to take responsibility for my actions and put my hand up when I make a mistake, and I rely on them to do the same. That's what a 'team' is.

However, you have to be very careful saying this to people. If you just storm in and say, 'You fucked up!' then those involved can assume a defensive – or aggressive – position. Then the tension is as debilitating as the design fault itself. But it *is* personal, because certain people are responsible. You can hide from it all you want, but if you assume control of a certain part of the design process and there is then a failure in that process, you've got to assume responsibility for that.

As a driver, I represent 400 people at the factory and hundreds of millions of pounds a year in investments. I don't try and hide from my mistakes; I don't always want to watch them and I certainly don't want to make them, but if I have made an error, I'll hold my hands up. That should apply throughout a team. When I criticised the team in Suzuka, it didn't go down too well, but I have to speak my mind and it is crucial that I do.

You can't sugar-coat it, this is a fiercely competitive business. If someone is not prepared to take the flak if they are genuinely at fault, they are in the wrong business. You don't step into a public office if you can't take public criticism and, likewise, you shouldn't be in a business like Formula 1 if you can't take some justified finger pointing.

So I thought my second year at Red Bull was quite tense, because I was frustrated by that failure and by the lack of acknowledgement from those responsible in the team; it's not that I wanted to beat up on any one individual in particular, but as adults, as men, we have to take responsibility for our actions, dwell on it for half a second and then bounce straight back, problem solved. So it was an altogether very disappointing, frustrating year. I have said that my purest, most supremely enjoyable year of driving was Williams in 1995; well, unfortunately, by contrast, 2006 was not so supremely enjoyable.

Formula 1 is a very unforgiving sport. At Red Bull – just like every other team in the paddock – there are people employed there today who will not be employed twelve months from now if we don't see an improvement in results ... and that might include me (because I might be a scapegoat or genuinely at fault), or it might be someone else in the organisation. Every individual on that team, be it the toilet cleaner or the chief designer, has to believe that they are *at least* the equal of their equivalent in any other grand prix team, because if they think they are not as good – whether it's due to resources, skills, talent or whatever – then you're beaten already. We aren't going to be the best in the world by thinking we are not quite as good as a rival; we'll only succeed by thinking we are setting the standard.

So in that troublesome second year, you can imagine how fantastic it was when I came third at the 2006 Monaco Grand Prix – of all places! – earning Red Bull their first ever podium in the process. It was magnificent and was certainly a weekend to remember, on and off the track.

One thing Red Bull are brilliant at is marketing. In Monaco in 2005, the team made quite a splash to help promote the launch of the third prequel *Revenge of the Sith*. They didn't just have any old tribute to *Star Wars* – they had none other than George Lucas turn up, with Chewbacca, Darth Vader, some Stormtroopers and other characters from the movie.

For 2006, Red Bull partnered with the new *Superman* film and among the marketing twists was the word Superman on our race costumes and new livery on the cars, with the 'S' logo and a flowing red cape painted along the length of the cars. They gave the drivers red capes, too – a part of me felt silly when we did the photo-shoot on the Saturday morning, along-side some of the stars of the film, Brandon Routh and Kevin Spacey. No one forced me to wear the cape, of course, if I had said, 'Absolutely not,' they'd have let me be, but that was the concept for how they wanted to promote the car and the movie. It was considered good for Red Bull, and that is my team, so I involved myself. It was like being a reluctant streaker and, because it was very different, it was guaranteed to get on telly.

I am surprised that when film studios spend so much money on promotion, they don't use the concept of partnering with F1 more often, because somewhere in the region of 150 million people are guaranteed to be watching every race in over 200 countries. When you think about it, I'm amazed that Hollywood and Formula 1 haven't got together so blatantly before, they seem natural bed-partners. They share the glitz and glamour, the vast sums of money and the audiences, there are lots of similarities. There's certainly a lot of very good acting in the paddock, too.

When we came third in Monaco that day, I was asked to wear the cape on the podium as well. I felt more comfortable with that because there was credibility, we'd come third, we weren't some no-hope team crawling in last and trying a cheap publicity stunt. The 'podium' in Monaco is on the side of the street; you park your cars right next to it and get out and climb up some stairs to meet Prince Albert. It is unique and I love it for that. Given that Montoya finished on the podium and it was clear fancy dress was the order of the day, I was surprised he didn't come dressed as the Michelin Man.

In the press conference afterwards, one older 'respected' journalist said I 'looked like a tit'. I reminded them that when Schumacher won the title in 2000 in Malaysia he was on the podium and in the press conference in a curly bright red wig, matched by equally lurid wigs worn by Ross Braun and his team-mate Rubens Barrichello. Deep down, when journalists say such rude things, part of you thinks, 'If you were in a bar, I'd tell you to fuck off.' But that journalist is entitled to his opinion, of course, as I'm entitled to give my response and, in my position, I have to try and give a considered and diplomatic reply. What I did was topical, we were sponsored by Superman. I don't agree with those hard-nosed, sceptical journalists. I asked Prince Albert for his permission before I did it – I'm known in Monaco because I live there and have won the grand prix twice, and I have to attend functions where Prince Albert is in attendance on occasion, so it was respectful to speak to him first. It was harmless fun. If it inspires some kiddies to see something other than just fast cars because they relate to the superhero element of it then I'm delighted. When I was growing up, I would have loved it if it had seemed like Wacky Races or Batman racing against Superman. And besides, the cape kept my neck warm.

It was slightly uncomfortable from the point of view that Édouard Michelin had just died. We didn't spray the champagne; I was going to, it just didn't register with me at that moment as something that we should not do, but thankfully Alonso mentioned it to me as we walked off the podium, so I toed the line. When I won at Monza the year Diana was killed, I instinctively knew not to spray the champagne, because I was British and she was the English rose and all that. At Monaco, I would have loved to have sprayed my engineers and mechanics, but it was indeed inappropriate. So we just accepted our trophies and walked over to the teams.

It was a super result for a little team that had suffered a terrible start to the year. Our team principle, Christian Horner, was rumoured to have said he'd jump naked into a swimming pool if we got a podium. At the celebration afterwards he did indeed jump into a pool, albeit with a Superman cape on. I really enjoyed the whole weekend. I was happy and I was really pleased to see so many people delighted for the team. It was good for the sport too, it was different from the 'normal' result.

Third place was a dream placing for the team and also for myself in many respects. Having pole at Monaco is a great feeling, but I have to say that podium for Red Bull felt good, just a great sense of achievement. The podium was the goal for the team in 2005 and we came close with a couple of fourth places, but to get that first podium in Monaco was incredible. Yes, there was a sequence of events that led to us being third, but it doesn't matter, it doesn't devalue it, history will show Red Bull came third in Monaco in 2006. As lucky as some people might call it, I'd been quick all weekend, always in the top five. I got screwed in qualifying by Fisichella, who then got penalised for holding me up, so I ended up in ninth place. I still had work to do and, regardless of how a race unfolds in front of you, a podium still has to be earned. We'd done it.

Having won there twice before and, to a degree, living there, I don't think anyone could have driven that particular car more quickly that weekend, I firmly believe that. I was in the zone, I felt good and I proved I can still perform when given the equipment to do so. It was a good reminder to me of why I do this. I do this because I really enjoy it, because I am good at it and because I can get the results. In testing we had been crap all year, but in the races I always feel I can do that little bit more – that goes for the whole of my career, not just with Red Bull.

I got a lot of texts after the podium, and I spent a lot of time reading then deleting them, so I could empty the memory and receive the next text; I was pleased by just how many texts I got and it was a nice reminder as to how people are happy for you when you do well and it was probably a nice reminder that I should be happier for myself.

A pleasant side-effect of taking points for third was a bonus clause that kicked in on my contract with Red Bull. It's strange how you don't think about the money before a race or during a race while you are hurtling around, but then at some point after, if you've done well you think, 'Oh yes, that's a thought...' Martin Brundle had cleverly negotiated a podium bonus into my contract, and we are talking substantial amounts of money, so that was nice. With that podium and also with previous good results too, we had taken what was a very small money deal in the first season and turned it – through the sheer force of my results – into a pleasantly profitable contract.

Of course, the main topic of conversation – again – was the incident with Michael Schumacher in qualifying. Although Michael was on provisional pole, Alonso was flying behind him when Michael appeared to 'park', as some people put it, right on the Rascasse corner, thus blocking his title rival's qualifying charge.

There was absolute outrage. Pundits and former racers all expressed dismay – Keke Rosberg even said Michael should be removed from the sport (although he later retracted this). Everyone gave their twopenceworth. The stewards examined the footage – to me, the in-car video made it very clear – and Schumacher was stripped of his pole and put to the back of the grid. He didn't really help himself by categorically denying any wrong-doing. Michael suffers from the fact that he's got this slightly aloof way of presenting himself to the media; this is coupled with an apparent ability to fly in the face of the consensus, even when the whole world thinks he is guilty of something. I think, deep down, he had to be disappointed and I thought he looked a bit embarrassed on the Sunday morning driver's parade. Perhaps because he felt a bit isolated.

Personally, I think a lot of people overplayed the significance of the incident, all the 'was he cheating or wasn't he?' I've come up with an analogy which I think is very simple, but for me sums it up. In soccer, how many times have we seen a guy go down in the penalty box and it looks like a penalty? He gets the penalty and scores a goal, only for TV to show the replay which reveals he wasn't even touched by the defender. What happens? One set of fans go mad, the other cheer, and the goal stands. Now you wouldn't want to teach your kid that that is acceptable behaviour, but the fact is this is accepted in modern football, they don't take the goal away. If they had video replay in soccer then there would be a lot of different results, but for now, they don't. The goal stands.

What Michael did was the equivalent. He clearly made a mistake going into the corner and realised he wasn't going to go quicker on that lap, then he automatically realised the next thing he could do was spoil anyone else's chance of a quicker lap. Okay, I can't say whether this is what he thought for a fact. I can say that, as a fellow driver watching the in-cockpit footage, I saw him lose the rear as he hit the corner (which looked a genuine mistake), but all the turning in, turning away, turning back in again just looked ham-fisted. What he did very well was to fake some urgency in apparently trying to get some marshals to push him back on line, but we all knew there was no need for any urgency because his lap was gone – if it was a race, then of course you'd want to get back on track as quickly as possible, but once you are out of qualifying, you are out. He couldn't do another lap.

It was the mind of a genius at work in ways that not everyone approved of.

I use the soccer analogy again – there must be someone who is known to be the best diver in world football ... maybe that's the equivalent of Michael? So is it cheating? Well, if you call diving in football cheating, then you'll have to call it cheating in motor-racing. It shouldn't be in our business, for sure. He tried something on and he got caught out.

Now Michael has retired, people ask the question is he the greatest of all time? Well, it's not a simple yes or no answer. He has scored the most points, the most race wins, the most fastest laps, the most pole positions and the most drivers' championships. Michael is an exceptional driver, end of story. His consistency is good and, as a result, he has rewritten the history books in every way possible. People often say he is a grafter and that is certainly true, but that shouldn't take away from his talent. It's natural talent, ability and instinctive reaction that get you to the top of F1, so yes, you need to apply yourself and have focus and commitment, but Schumacher has been better than the majority because of a God-given gift *as well as* extreme application – it's not just because he's worked hard that he's made himself quick. Schumacher is a grafter, that's why he has had such a long career and so much success – but he has talent *and* obsessive application. I'd be very surprised if Alonso or Räikkönen win as many championships as Michael.

It is tricky with Michael because I have raced against him for years. He is present day flesh and blood to me, so to put him in the same bracket as Jim Clark or Jackie Stewart seems odd. Michael could have carried on, for sure, for several more years. He wasn't not doing it for the money; he's acquired all the material things he will ever need for his life.

We've had our disagreements from time to time, but he does have my racing respect – he's an intelligent guy and a hard worker. On balance, although I have a respect for Michael, it doesn't mean I'm not able to disagree with him on certain things. Until recently, I was the chairman of the Grand Prix Drivers' Association and I didn't always agree with his position, but the worst thing in life is not to have an opinion. His career has been helped by the fact he's had the same manager and the same group of friends around him throughout his career, something many drivers – including me – don't enjoy.

I think as a family man he is a good person, too. I spent a little bit of time with him and his family once in Australia and I've been to a couple of his family BBQs in Hockenheim with his parents, wife and friends there. I see him as a good family man who is respectful of his wife and who keeps that side of his life very private. I haven't seen him in his home, but I've seen him in social environments and he's a fairly relaxed, normal individual which, given that he is a gazzillionaire and so famous and successful, is impressive. I am glad to have raced against the most successful driver in the history of our sport, partly because I know that in certain places I could, and did, beat him!

*

The end of the 2006 season was a time of big news for my old team McLaren. There were all sorts of rumours about Mika Häkkinen making a return to F1. I think by the time you read this book, that rumour will have been shown to be absolute bollocks. Only Mika knows his reasons for testing the 2006 car, but my hunch is he likes the idea of a driving income, but probably doesn't like the idea of having to compete to get it, therefore he'll be a test driver and not have to go through the strenuous process of competition. McLaren have done this before, after all, with a retired Alain Prost, when I started racing for them. That's one theory, but it may also be because Mika wanted to see if he still got a buzz from it. To me, when I saw the pictures, he looked like a fish out of water and I don't believe it will ever come to anything. Absolutely not. Not because he doesn't have the ability, but because I don't think he has the desire and commitment to do it anymore.

Since my departure from McLaren, my relationship with Ron Dennis has obviously become more distant. We had warmed to each other more in the latter years of my time there – particularly after he'd admitted his thoughts about Mika – but if you are not working with someone on a daily basis, you inevitably see less of them and the emotional distance increases. Plus, a number of McLaren staff have come to Red Bull and maybe Ron sees me as a part of that process. Would he shake my hand if he saw me in the paddock? I can't answer that. Ron's not a big hand-shaker. I can tell you that Ron once told me, 'I don't shake hands with employees,' so read into that what you will. It is what it is.

It certainly was a busy off-season for McLaren – while the

press pack were speculating about Mika's motives, the team also announced in November that the twenty-one-year-old Brit, Lewis Hamilton, would get his Formula 1 debut and partner world champion Alonso for the 2007 season.

Of course, they are looking for the next big thing. Lewis has had a much higher profile start than I did. Even as I sat in the Williams, I was relatively unknown outside of motor-sport enthusiasts. He will certainly achieve very high financial reward in a very short space of time and he'll become a wealthy man at a very young age.

He'll also be the first black Formula 1 driver – does that mean anything? Well, it shouldn't, but it does, unfortunately. Therefore, commercially, when McLaren choose to put Lewis in the car, it will open up business opportunities (although it might close some as well, because there are some guys in high-end positions who are racist and would choose not to get involved). It's always a very difficult subject to talk about, of course, but ultimately it will all boil down to what he does on the track.

I was misquoted about Lewis starting the 2007 season with McLaren, which was simply a device employed by the UK press to generate a bit of controversy as they're prone to doing when there's a lack of genuine news. I suggested that if he had the opportunity to test for a year, that might be beneficial because of the risk of going up against a double world champion, which seems entirely logical to me. I still stand by my word in that he will be a better racing driver in a year's time than he is today, however that doesn't take away at all, for me, his undoubted talent, nor the fact that he deserves the opportunity.

A couple of years ago he was asking my advice – I guess he

was asking several people – on what to do because he felt in some ways he was being held back by McLaren's insistence that he do another year in Euro Formula 3 when he wanted to move up to Formula 3000 or GP2. Therefore he was considering the pros and cons of being under the 'McLaren umbrella'. My firm advice to him was that it's a big bad world out there if you're trying to find finance yourself and deal with all the difficulties involved; he absolutely should trust in McLaren and absolutely follow their recommendations. Not based purely on my advice, but based on gut feeling, opportunities and lots of other people's opinions, he obviously took that position, took another year, won the championship, then on to GP2, won that and now he's in Formula 1. So far from being critical of Lewis as has been reported, I see myself as having been supportive of him, and the fact remains that a year from now he *will* be a better driver, no doubt about it, the following year better still and so on.

I applaud McLaren for taking that perceived risk; the reality is, of course, that Lewis has been part of the McLaren system for nine years, they have all the data to see how he is performing in testing – relative to race drivers – so in fact it should have been a very straight-forward decision based on pace and the fact that they could help him with the shortfall in his experience.

The expectations on him are now considerable. I guess that is normal, he is the new excitement in Formula 1, the first black driver, all of those things, what else can we expect? Interestingly, in the first weeks of the 2007 season, a radio station interviewed me and said, 'Is Lewis Hamilton going to be the first Formula 1 billionaire driver?' and I was like, 'Whoa! Stop!' Let's not go in Europe like they do in America. It's not about the money. Lewis is into *racing*, he's a talented racing driver, he loves to race, and a side issue of that talent and that enjoyment is that he will earn a certain amount of money, which is what people are prepared to pay, based on his perceived value in the market place. But let's try and keep the focus on the sport rather than money, money, money. He seemed pretty happy last year when he told me he didn't have much money; he will be a lot happier this year with a wee bit of money; and as time goes on he will become a very wealthy man – if he deserves it then he deserves it, however, it is not what motivates us to become Fı drivers.

With only six races completed at the time of writing, there has already been a lot of controversy about 'preferential treatment' at McLaren. When I first heard this I did smile, but then I came out and was supportive of McLaren's position at Monaco, on the basis that I thought the media were being unfairly harsh on McLaren, from what I could understand. The reality is that Fernando out-qualified Lewis, he ran in front of him for the whole race and he won the race. How can you then turn around and say that's not fair? In my situation, I was in front of Mika and I was asked to move over. That is a different scenario, different instruction. But it did make me smile because clearly I have been through a similar situation, but obviously a more extreme one.

What Lewis has done in those first six races is rewrite some of the history books, which is happening more often in modern sport as drivers get younger. After six consecutive podiums, he scored his maiden victory and I can genuinely say am happy for him and his family because I have known him as he has grown up through the sport.

This brings me to the subject of Jenson Button. In 2007, there will be four Brits on the grid, not bad out of twenty-two drivers. Of all those drivers, there is clearly renewed expectation on Jenson's shoulders after his maiden F1 victory in 2006, which was the first time a Brit had won a grand prix since my victory in Australia 2003, sixty-five races previously. One immediate example is that he has won one grand prix and by Christmas that year, he was nominated for BBC 'Sports Personality of the Year'.

The expectation on him when he first arrived, and then the mounting pressure as that elusive win remained out of reach, was a clear sign of the times to me. Through the internet and other digital forms the media has developed in a way that didn't exist when I started in Formula 1. It is all so much more intense now. Jenson debuted in a new media age, a new 'Pop Idol' atmosphere if you like, and he fitted that mould perfectly. He's a good-looking boy and he's very talented. Initially, I think it is fair to say he was over-hyped and under-delivered, but that was not because of him specifically, it was more as a result of that over-expectation looking for unrealistic results.

The new media age does not allow people time to grow, to develop, to learn, it is very unforgiving. I think Jenson was a victim of that. The super-fast media age we live in expected him to win earlier; also, his first season in 2000 was very strong, with a sixth place in only his second race in Brazil, thus becoming the youngest British driver ever to score a point in F1, and out-qualifying Schumacher in Belgium. All that raised expectations to unrealistic levels.

Jenson is a very good racing driver, but it became apparent that he just didn't seem to be able to bag the results. Both the public and the media started to get frustrated and, by 2006, they were beginning to be really quite hard on Jenson, making comments on how he'd been out-qualified by Rubens and that he was having a difficult time and so on. It was very much, 'New! Exclusive! Exciting! Jenson Button! Here he is, he looks the part, he's quick ... so when's he going to win then?'

It just isn't that simple.

Yet actually, by way of neatly contradicting myself a little, when I won my first grand prix in my twenty-first race I remember the headline in one of the motor-sport magazines was, 'At Last!' I'd been close a few times previously, so there was a sense of relief that I'd 'finally' won but, actually, twenty-one races is only just more than one season. It's also remarkably quick to win a grand prix – Barrichello took 123 races, Trulli took 117, Jenson took 112 attempts, Mansell took seventy-two races, even Mika took ninety-six before I moved over for him in 1997. So I was hardly taking my time!

People presume that all the Brits on the grid hang out together, but at first, I have to say, there was a bit of a distance between Jenson and me. We didn't know each other and his management probably saw me as direct competition, being British and all that. I worked hard to swerve those suspicions and befriend him a bit, because I liked what I saw and I felt he was a nice guy. We lived the same life; he also lives in Monaco and for a period of time we did a lot of things together, with our respective girlfriends of the time, holidays and all that. In recent years, that friendship has drifted away somewhat. We both have new partners, we are still buddies but we don't go out as much as we used to. He's maturing and he'll probably be a little bit more settled, but he's still a young man. I think of Jenson as a friend and I am genuinely happy for him that he won that first grand prix. Yes, he is my competitor and the media have at times tried to build a bit of a battle, a rift, between us, but I wouldn't allow that and neither would he, because that just spoils your own fun. An argument in the sports pages might make you a wee bit more famous and it might sell a few more T-shirts, but as far as your day-to-day life goes, what's the point? So I'm happy for Jenson and his family, they are a tight team.

He is clearly a very popular chap within the sport. I've always held a view – and it will sound a bit nationalistic – that I was never going to be Britain's favourite driver because I'm Scottish. The obvious manifestation of this is that when I win, I'm a Brit and when I lose, I'm Scottish. I am a proud Scot. I also enjoy being a British sportsman, but there seems to be a dual nationality that kicks in depending on my results. You have to be careful how you mention this, but after a second place at Estoril in Portugal in 1994, I was quoted as saying, 'I'm obviously not some hairy-arsed Highlander ...' I don't have a big Scottish chip on my shoulder and I don't like being the victim.

Jenson certainly looked pleased with his win! That famous shot of him signalling to his team, his eyes on stalks, will live with him for ever. I wonder what his face was like as he crossed the line? I've often thought that about other drivers. Michael is always so straight-faced – apart from times like when he charged into my garage in Spa, obviously! Usually, however, he is pretty placid; Kimi is even more impassive; Mika was always so sombre-looking; yet other racers show every emotion. But what do they look like when they are actually racing?

The on-board cameras are clearly right in your face as you compete in a race – imagine Beckham having a camera on his face for the entire ninety minutes of a game. However, I think they could take it one step further and find a way of putting a camera on your actual expressions ... because I find it fascinating to watch how certain sportsmen and women look when they are really in the zone.

I'll give you an example. I don't watch or know anything about cricket. Recently I saw Monty Panesar playing for England – I've been told he is an absolutely brilliant bowler. The funny thing was, when he came out to bat, his facial expression looked like he was struggling to take a dump in a dodgy European toilet. He was lining up to hit the ball and the TV did a close up of his face and I thought, 'My God, are they throwing fucking hand grenades at him?' It was so funny.

It seems a shame that all we get to see on-board is just the full-face helmet. I am calm, I breathe through my nose and my face is unmoved. I've felt like throwing a few hand grenades in my time out on the track, believe me, but I have to say I generally remain pretty expressionless. I can't help wonder what Michael Schumacher's face looks like when he is racing, or Alonso, or indeed any of my grid rivals?

Just a thought.

KEEPING THE EUPHORIA

I don't like driving. By that, I mean driving on the roads. That might sound a little strange, given my job, but it is what it is, I don't like driving. I can handle the twenty-two kilometres from my apartment in Monaco to Nice airport, but the longer trek to Geneva where my chalet is, I just think, 'Ah, shit ...' It's a chore.

A lot of people use Monaco as a base for a European tour or at least for harbour-hopping around various destinations in the south of France. They go off and discover Italy or the Riviera, Cannes, places like that. Well, I've lived there for over a decade and all I've really done is go to Cannes twice for the film festival. I once drove to St Tropez, but it was too far in the car, so I hop in the helicopter, which takes half an hour (not just because I can, but because I can't handle the drive). If some friends were in St Tropez and I couldn't fly there, I wouldn't drive to see them.

I have spent so many years of my life sitting in a car or a motorhome, clocking up mile after mile after mile. For me, travelling needs to be broken into short periods of time where

I can be thinking of other things. I'm always planning things and analysing things and if I am being driven by someone else, I can do that, but when I'm driving I can't really daydream.

People often ask me what cars I drive off the track. I have two Mercedes very kindly provided by that manufacturer and a Smart car, as well as a classic Merc too, but to be honest, I don't have the attention span to drive a road car well, because it doesn't excite me, it doesn't get my attention. One of the first things I did when I had started earning good money was to get a chauffeur in London, a guy called Billy. He started in 1995 and is full-time, even though I typically only spend about thirty nights of the year in the UK. So that's an expensive luxury, but I like being driven. I don't want to drive around and have to get involved in all that.

This dislike of driving is partly a practical aversion, but it is also symptomatic of a character trait I have. One of the peculiarities of my personality that I have become aware of, is that I very rarely feel intensely *passionate* about something. My father will react to something by saying, 'Brilliant! I can't wait to do that!' I would be like, 'Yeah, okay, that might be good.' For example, winning Monaco is nice but, to me, so is a well-prepared pizza.

I don't feel as though I experience peaks and troughs as much as most people. I don't know why that is. Maybe it is to do with having raced for so long, with the need to be calm and collected; maybe it is because driving at such extreme speeds makes you accustomed to extreme feelings and you eventually interpret them as normal; maybe it is just my nature.

There are other examples, aside from Smart cars and pizza, that to other people suggest I don't feel passionate about things, but they are not always correct. For instance, when I came second in Portugal in 1994, my first podium in only my eighth race, my manager at the time, Tim Wright of IMG, told me to look 'more happy'. I was only twenty-four, but looking at footage of the day, I can see how my expression looks very muted, defensive even. That said, I didn't agree with his notion. If you have worked hard for a result, standing on the podium is a moment for me and I should feel as happy as I want to feel – I was *very* happy, let me tell you that.

However, Tim made the point which, on reflection, I believe is a correct one, that if you want to project an image and have a job in the public eye endorsing cars, teams, even other products, then antics like the Schumacher 'jump' go down well. People love to see that because it 'shows' elation, delight. I, on the other hand, tend to just stand there and smile. I spray the champagne and smile a lot sometimes, but there's no jumping and whooping. That's just not me.

With most of the successes I've had, I've struggled with other people's perceptions of how I 'should' behave afterwards. Tim is not alone. So many times over the years, people have told me I don't look that elated after a good race. I am, I really am, but certain factors make it hard for me to run around cheering. For a start, the race itself dehydrates you enormously; I can lose up to two kilos in weight. I race around at 200mph then step out and go straight into a press conference, followed by various TV interviews and other media commitments. For example, after I'd done all the press and interviews after my 2006 podium in Monaco and finally got to the party, lots of Red Bull people were jumping into the pool, having a drink, laughing and shouting, having a great time ... and so they should. They wanted me to jump in the pool too, but I was exhausted. All I wanted to do was escape, go back to my little room, be with my girlfriend and have a cup of sweet tea and a Twix.

That to me is the celebration and it's not that I don't want to be happy for them; I want them to be happy, but I need time to be by myself and take it all in. I know some musicians go backstage after a show and keep themselves to themselves; I guess it's the same sort of thing. So I don't really live the media image of some sportsman going home and poring over every detail of his victory and hollering in the lounge about the win. I really do all the mundane stuff like be away from the noise, drink tea, eat a few energy snacks or organising myself or tidying up. I'll sometimes go home after a race and tidy the house, if it needs doing.

There was another moment at Monaco that year when I realised other people feel more passionately – or perhaps show their passion more openly – than me. My oldest buddy, David Cawthorne, came up after the race and hugged me, he was elated. I felt quite awkward, even with Cawthorne, I just thought, 'Yes, okay, right, thank you, let's go and have a cup of tea, what's happening tonight? Are we going to go out to have a nice dinner?'

I don't know how to be with people when they are happy for you. I don't know how to be with the team when they are happy. Cawthorne seemed genuinely happy and I wish I could have been as happy at that moment, because it's a nice, shared moment with an old buddy. In actual fact, my mind had already moved on, because I'm not good at keeping the euphoria, I don't hold the moment.

This is something I don't understand about myself because, on the day, I was obviously very happy and the photos of me celebrating show a real sense of happiness and joy, I don't look at all conscious of the cameras or anything. Yes, the memory of it is wonderful to me ... but do I feel elation and jump up and down when I think of that Monaco podium or indeed any other podium? No, no, I don't.

People do like to see that passion, but I can't do that and I wish I could. Some sportsmen inspire the masses because the public can see and sense what it must mean to score the goal, win the race or whatever; other sportsmen want to win just as much, but do not inspire the masses in the same way. Alan Shearer famously just lifted his hand when he scored a goal; other players get booked because their celebrations are so wild. I have often pondered on this and thought, 'How can people get excited about a person or thing that the person doesn't get excited about themselves?'

I look at other drivers and other sportsmen and I can see they get fired up so much more overtly. I look at Jenson, for example, and I imagine he will be a very inspirational example of success. That photograph of his wide-eyed look following his debut win in Hungary is the most obvious example, but when he retires from Formula 1, I have no doubt that the TV circuit will beckon: he is charismatic in a way the public and the media like. Mansell was the same, he inspired the masses.

I've never inspired that in people because I don't inspire it in myself. I've already mentioned how difficult I find it to stand up in front of a couple of hundred people at the team factory. I want to say something motivating and energising, but I don't feel as though I can. I have a problem in how I am perceived and how I project myself and I can see my insecurity. I don't think it is a childhood issue – I was never made to feel that I could not come out and perform when I was younger; we knew our place as children, but my father loved his music and we had some fantastic party nights. I also genuinely don't remember having people laugh at me or mock me at school or bully me or do anything that might trigger those intense emotions. So I think to myself, why am I that way? Some people are just natural entertainers and others aren't, I guess. I wish I could be.

This is not to say I am without passion, absolutely not. Beyond my private life, the one thing that has always fired passion in me is driving the cars. I really like how I feel when I'm in a racing car and I guess that must be *my* passion. After more than a decade of Formula 1, the thrill hasn't diminished.

Even then, I can't sincerely get out of the car, and clinically and accurately express that passion to you. In the car I can feel it, but I can't articulate it. I am not good at knowing how I am supposed to be in public, probably because I'm not doing it for the public, I'm doing for me and I used to say my perfect grand prix would be to go to a race, win, go home, sit on the sofa and reflect on it with a cup of tea . . . and then get on with the rest of my day.

I know that much of the public perceive me as very dry and strait-laced. That's why I did my tabloid quiz in 2003. I can see why people might make that assumption – I don't leap about on the podium, as I've said, and when I am talking to the world's press and effectively fronting a multi-billion-pound company investment, I don't muck about. But the more perceptive viewers will catch the side of me that my family and friends know, the odd comment I drop in to spice things up a little on the sly. I don't want to take life so seriously all the time.

One time at the Nürburgring, I was being interviewed by ITV's Louise Goodman on the grid. Now, that circuit is known as 'The Ring', and I was challenged by a friend to make some sexual reference without being spotted. Louise asked me about the circuit and I said something like, 'I'm a big fan of the Ring, as you know all drivers love to go round the Ring . . .' She knew what was going on, but couldn't say anything because we were live. I knew all my mates were watching and it was a good laugh.

Poor Louise also had the misfortune of listening to me explain about pit speed limiters during one interview by likening it to a lady's nipples. I'd got done for speeding by a couple of kilometres an hour at one race because I released the pit limiters too early and, as a result, I had a drive-through penalty and lost a position in the final placings. Louise reminded me of this and just off the cuff I said, 'Well, I'm just going to imagine that the speed limit button is like your nipple and I'm gonna keep my finger on it . . .' I know ITV got quite a few complaints about that one and it's fair to say that it's not big and it's not clever. Pretty juvenile. But it is amusing.

I've done similar jokes with Martin Brundle and you can have a certain amount of hilarity in the paddock. Not as much as in previous times, I suspect – James Hunt used to have a badge that bore the legend, 'Sex, breakfast of champions.' Imagine if I had that on my Formula 1 suit today, even for Red Bull! There's no way you could get away with it. Plus, while I've been draped in Hugo Boss or team sponsors' uniforms, Hunt was photographed at one race in patchwork-jean hot pants. Perhaps he had the legs for it.

The rigid demands of F1 mean you have to be careful, but I do like to have a good night out on occasion, to say the least. I love getting tipsy now and then. Part of that is because when I am tipsy I am less restricted by the self-conscious awkwardness I spoke about. I love being drunk just enough so that I'm not conscious of anyone watching me. Then I'll be on the dance floor listening to music, getting lost in the moment; if I'm sober you couldn't get me on the dance floor for any money in the world, I'd be too bloody awkward (well, we all have our price). I've had those moments when I'm stuttering around a dance floor, particularly at family parties, thinking, 'Christ, I wish my granny hadn't asked me to dance ...'

The sport has changed drastically, even several times during my career. Being a Formula 1 driver in the current era is a very disciplined job and there isn't an awful lot of room for outrageous behaviour. You hear a lot of talk about the paddock being bereft of so many personalities these days. Huge corporate sponsorships mean drivers have to play safe; they can't go criticising every rival or womanising in public or smoking forty-a-day. You have to toe the company line. Yes, everyone likes it when drivers sound off and speak their mind, but it can be unprofessional as well.

I hear all of these complaints and, as the oldest driver on the grid in 2006, you might expect me to agree with this view. Actually, I don't. I think we all have a tendency to look on the past with rose-coloured spectacles. Footballers probably used to go down the Kings Road and have a pint of beer before a match in the old days, but they don't do that now. It's a different world we live in. Nothing stands still.

I don't drink to excess that often, but when I do I like to enjoy myself. I recall one time that might have ruffled a few F1 feathers when I was with Jenson Button. We were on a boat on the way to Corsica to meet a bunch of people, but on the way we basically got pissed. By the time we arrived, I was well oiled, to say the least. I knew there would be some people gathering at the back of the boat to greet us, so I started to take all my clothes off. I wanted to strip off and fling open these curtains at the back of the boat, starkers in front of all these people.

'They want a picture, eh? I'll give them a picture!' I was saying, sniggering as I stripped off.

Jenson was horrified and kept saying, 'DC, no! You'll regret this tomorrow!' and I was stumbling around laughing, saying, 'Get off! I'll give them the picture they want!'

Thankfully he rugby tackled me and stopped me getting to the curtains and providing Formula 1's most revealing photograph.

One aspect of my life that I am very passionate about is my fiancée, Karen Minier. We first met on the circuit when she was covering the European races as a TF1 presenter, which is the equivalent of being a pit reporter for ITV. Motor-racing is not her passion, but this was where her career had taken her. After two years, she decided she didn't really like the environment and left. She's now co-presenter on a big TF1 programme, the most watched talk show in France.

The first night we went out together was in Paris and, at the end of the evening, no one else was around and she was about to leave in a taxi – I guess we were both curious to know if there was some sort of chemistry, so we shared a small kiss. The relationship blossomed very quickly and I started to feel that this was a very different woman to all my previous girlfriends.

We had been dating six months when I asked her to marry me in the summer of 2006. Six months might seem swift, but I didn't want to wait a year because it felt great *right then*. We've known each other for four years, so there is much more to the relationship than some whirlwind insanity. I must admit, I sometimes read articles in magazines like *Hello!* about people who declare their undying love and announce their absolute soul-mate when they've only been dating a few weeks or months and then, about two issues later, they are on the front pages describing their divorce proceedings. So I was a little wary that it might be perceived as being quick, but it felt absolutely right to me.

Just as I was getting ready to get down on bended knee, Karen said, 'I have something for you,' and she pulled out a dog-tag style chain, which had our names and the date of our first night together engraved on it (that means a great deal to me). Then I said, 'That's great because I've got something for you . . .' and I whipped out the ring and got down on my knee. I'd worried a lot that it would feel awkward, you know, like that first kiss when you are a kid and you both go to peck each other and somehow you end up kissing the girl's nose, a disaster. Thankfully, I didn't feel uncomfortable for a moment. It worked out perfectly.

I asked Karen to 'marry me' (rather than 'engage me') at L'Hotel, where we'd shared that first kiss, which was a really lovely place to pop the question. Oscar Wilde famously used to stay there and it's a very romantic place. I'd been thinking of asking her for some time – the previous New Year I'd phoned my parents to wish them all the best for 2006 and Karen was in the room so I said, 'I'm here with my future wife ...' so she must have known I had it on my mind. At the time of writing, we have not set a wedding date, but it isn't going to be years, that's for sure!

As I had planned it ahead, I'd looked at rings and settled on two different options, because I wasn't entirely sure which one Karen would like. The jeweller, Theo Fennell, was happy for me to take both rings to show Karen, which was fantastically trusting of him, but I guess I am not exactly low profile!

Refreshingly, Karen is not materialistic, unlike certain previous girlfriends she can walk past shops and generally not be interested; plus she earns her own money as well, so that atmosphere is very liberating for me. However, we'd never had the conversation about getting married, so I didn't know the style of rings she likes. I'd thought of ways of getting her to give me some idea of style, but it's impossible without letting on what you've been thinking. As it was, I got the ring out and said, ' ... if you don't like this one you ... can have ... this one!' She looked at them both and just said, 'They are both fantastic, but it's not about the ring, it's about your commitment, if that is the ring you want to give me then I'm delighted and I'll wear it with pride.'

I am actually looking forward to wearing the wedding band. I'm not a big jewellery fan, I sometimes wear the odd necklace, but when I am married I will always wear the band. My father put his wedding ring on when he was twenty-one and it's never been off his finger, he's never been in to hospital where he's had to remove it or anything, and I think that's fantastic, that's almost forty years.

When I went to get the ring resized and they asked me what size Karen was, I said, 'She's a P for perfect.' Yet when the lady returned later to check a few things she said it was 'P for Peter'. I thought to myself, 'Blimey, David, you might just be the old married romantic yet!'

I feel great about Karen and I'm very excited about the future with her. I know that when you start talking about these things people can sometimes glaze over, but I think the greatest achievement in one's life could be if you have a long, healthy and happy relationship with your partner, ideally with children if you are lucky enough to have them.

Karen has an eight-year-old daughter, Shana (she's obviously still a virgin apart from the immaculate conception of her child). So after being a family man without my own family all these years, I've kind of inherited one! One interesting coincidence is that her daughter's name – Shana – is actually Celtic in origin, based around Shannon. I know it is probably just that, a coincidence, but when you feel deeply for someone, you do find comfort in the strangest things.

Karen told me that Shana had asked, 'When are you going to get married to David?' even before we were engaged. She seems keen on the idea, which is a nice thought. I only have her mother's word for this – which, of course, I choose to believe – but, apparently, she has shown more of an interest in me and asked more questions about me than she has asked about any of her previous boyfriends. Whether that's because she has sensed her mum is happy or whether it's just because

I'm around more and friendlier, or just because she is at that age and it's a question she'd ask, I don't know, but of course I'd like to think all those things reflect nicely on me.

I'm not especially proud of a few things I have done in previous relationships. I have had three previous long-term relationships, but several have been scattered with extra-curricular activity, flings, call them what you will. I'm not particularly proud of that, but it wasn't because I wanted to live the scum-bag lifestyle, it was just kind of where I was with those people at the time and – I know now – a reflection of the relationships I had with those partners. I don't mention that proudly, but equally I'm not embarrassed by those revelations, it is what it is. I never promised anything that I didn't deliver, I just never promised anything.

It's funny how the relationship with Karen has affected me and how I notice this at the most unexpected moments. In 2006, the Williams designer Patrick Head threw a birthday party at a restaurant near the Fulham Road in London. I went and Damon Hill was also there, as well as a couple of other drivers and various F1 faces. I kicked out at midnight because I wanted to get some sleep for a busy day ahead.

I was walking back down the Kings Road and I was thinking to myself how it wouldn't have been that long ago that – regardless of whether I was with someone or not – I would have popped into Raffles for a quick beer on the way home, just to have a wee look around at what ladies were out, then I'd get chatting to someone and then join them at their table, and then before I knew it . . .

However, after I left this restaurant alone that night, I just headed straight home, got some laundry done, got a few things organised and went to bed, alone, feeling absolutely content. That was a new feeling for me and I liked it. If I was single, I could have a great time. I am lucky to have money, I am well known and that attracts certain benefits and it could be a blast. Been there, done that, not interested.

I'm not quite sure I understand the true definition of soul-mate, but maybe it is to have someone who thinks like you, acts like you, makes you want to tell them about everything and listen to everything they say, and care absolutely and totally about them. If that is what a soul-mate is, then that is what Karen is to me.

This might sound incredibly old fashioned and I certainly don't mean it to sound chauvinistic – Karen is very much her own woman and a modern woman at that – but when I was out qualifying in Monaco in 2006, she wasn't out partying with celebs or hanging out in the paddock meeting people, she was back in my apartment making me soup. That might sound like an odd thing to admire, but it was very thoughtful of her, she knows I love soup and she was making some to freeze for me later; she was thinking about what I would like. I can understand that you might not want to hear a Formula 1 driver talking about soup, and I can see the funny side in a way, but it was just a very symbolic gesture of how much time she takes out of her own very hectic life to think about me.

Making a load of money is all very well and being a successful racing driver is also something I am very proud of, but having a relationship with a wife like that, and then projecting forward and imagining how it must feel to complement that emotional achievement by having children . . . I can't imagine many things that, as a man, could be more fulfilling. You get the toys, but the toys don't talk do they? You can't have a very interesting conversation with a Ferrari.

So yes, I'm happy, very happy, with Karen, which surprises me, because I didn't think I would ever feel that way. I thought I was just doomed to have a series of fun yet ultimately unfulfilling relationships. I'm long since over the excitement of going out with the boys, getting a few beers down your neck and trying to crawl into someone's underwear. I actually want to have a straightforward, trusting relationship, that gives me a much greater sense of fulfilment. The great thing is that its success or failure lies completely in my hands, or our hands as it were, because we're two consenting adults. Much of your life is the result of the choices you make.

With Karen *everything* feels very different. For me, Karen is an amazing woman. I relish enjoying the sense of achievement if I could be a faithful, loving husband, rather than a 'race ace' with lots of women. I look at my parents and I see a blueprint for how I would like to be with Karen – they hold hands all the time, they go everywhere together, always have, and they are such a team. My father is very respectful of my mother and she is a very strong woman; she keeps him on the straight and narrow. They would be lost without each other. Their marriage is very conventional in that way, and I admire those old-fashioned values. I've grown up in that environment and it is something I aspire to. Notably, given my choice of career, it's also been something that has been extremely difficult to replicate so far, not least practically, given the amount of travelling I do.

I think marriage should be something you only do once

and you work through any rocky days ahead. I think I've waited this long because I was still looking for the person who ticks all the boxes for me. Hopefully, I have found her in Karen.

I NEVER SAW MYSELF 'TIL I
WENT AROUND THE WORLD

In the autumn of 2006, I signed an extension of my contract with Red Bull. Given that my doubters were telling me to retire after I left McLaren, I am delighted to still be racing at the top level. Time has shown that I still have a place in Formula 1 and my 2006 podium in Monaco confirmed that. I can't deny it was annoying when I left McLaren to hear people telling me to call it a day – it still is – but I think my performances at Red Bull have clearly vindicated my decision to continue.

Formula 1 is the pinnacle of motor-sport. To compete in the best and most advanced series is far more important to me than operating in a lesser formula. I'd rather not be winning in F1 than winning in a lower formula, given the choice.

Quite a lot of drivers leave F1 and head off to the United States, where there are various formulas or series that welcome drivers like us, such as Indycar. At this point, that has no appeal to me whatsoever. I like the fact that F1 is the best of the best. That's not just an arrogant statement – it's a fact that the quickest racing cars that go round a closed circuit are ours. Le

Mans cars might go quicker in a straight line and some American racers go around an oval circuit quicker, but around Monaco or Silverstone, there is nothing faster than a Formula 1 car.

Besides, driver injuries appear to be more prevalent in the States. Not that I think too much about the danger aspect as a daily part of my life, but in American races, the safety standards seem a decade or more behind F1 and, to be perfectly honest, I don't need that. As I've said, I don't feel that what I do is dangerous or inherently reckless but, of course, I'd like to imagine coming out on the other side fit and healthy.

American motor-sport has a different type of fan, too. For some reason, they typically don't know anything about F1. They are heavily into modified cars, road cars that have suddenly become these huge dragsters, so when you say, 'I drive a Mercedes,' they answer, 'Oh, yeah? Is it one of those AMGs?' You can explain it all you like, they still often repeat themselves and say, ' ... er, so, what was your car before it was converted?'

A lot of former racing drivers go into business. On the one hand, I can't imagine that I'm going to stop racing, enjoy some holiday time, have a vision then start and run a new business. However, I can see that being at the top level for so long has equipped me with various qualities or skills that will be very useful in the world both inside and outside of the paddock.

The very nature of my job is a contradiction. Being a Formula 1 driver is like enjoying a suspended childhood but with very good pocket money. At the same time, it has provided me with a fantastic education through the whole 'university of life', as they say. I didn't do my three years at university, but I have had dealings with the chairmen of huge companies that you would never get to meet otherwise. Formula 1 gives you access to some of the world's most successful business personalities – Dietrich Mateschitz of Red Bull is a great example. If I'd gone to uni and done a business degree, the chances of working with him would be pretty slim. He will take my calls and so will many other senior people at companies like Mercedes and Siemens and so on. People like that know who I am and know what I can do and that type of business experience is invaluable.

You meet some people and they seem so self-assured. I often see self-made businessmen who are so confident; they have created these businesses and are making millions and seem to know themselves so well. I often get labelled as a businessman and, yes, I do have interests in several operations outside of Formula 1. But I am not running those businesses; I have made investments in them. Likewise, yes, I have earned millions of pounds in my career, but that's by doing something I was doing as a kid.

I get to see these businessmen away from the boardroom too, and that is very interesting. It's incredible to see directors of large corporations standing nervously in the garage at a grand prix with their camera and the kids, because no matter how many millions-stroke-billions of pounds are under their control or in their bank account, at a certain point it's the passion and excitement that gets them going – they are still big kids going to racing tracks.

The clichéd thing to do when you retire is travel. Travel?! Bloody hell, I haven't done anything else for the last twenty-five years! Besides, I'm a crap tourist. I don't need to know something exists by seeing it for myself. I 'did' the pyramids and it was interesting enough but, to be perfectly honest, I thought it would be more impressive than it was. As far as travelling to all corners of the world to see a temple or some historical monument is concerned, I'm not interested. I don't need to see a rain forest to feel like I am living my life.

When I initially starting visiting Brussels to spend time with Karen, it struck me as odd that my suitcase was still on someone's floor, ready to be packed or unpacked yet again, and I'm thirty-five years old. When I visit Karen in Brussels, it is very enjoyable to spend time there, it has helped me feel less rootless. I'm always having to duck in and out of these various lives in various countries – even though my home in Monaco is close to many of my European destinations – so, no, I certainly don't anticipate doing a lot of travelling in the future.

I don't have a lot of hobbies outside of racing – I cycle a little bit and I play golf once a year, but other than that the world is my oyster, I guess. I actually get a little annoyed when people try to foist their hobbies on me, I get defensive. A friend of mine is passionate about skateboarding and surfing and that passion can actually almost become a little bit annoying, because he will sometimes say, 'You have to try skateboarding, you have to try surfing ...' That sort of thinly-veiled invite to do something that someone else loves, switches me right off. I'm the complete opposite; I'm like, 'Actually I don't want to do that, thank you very much!' and get quite objectionable.

Jacques Villeneuve loves skiing and I have been on the slopes with him a couple of times. He's significantly better than I am because he grew up with it, but he doesn't make you feel like you are holding him up. However, I just don't share his passion for the sport. He will talk about how exciting it is going down the slopes, but I'm just not interested like that. If he was to tell me about a technical aspect of skiing, like the edge could be used to shave a man's head, I'd be like, 'Oh, that's interesting!' However, imagining standing at the top of a black slope ready to go down ... whatever.

People ask me about team management and all that, but I have not thought about any of my options after I am no longer racing. Why would I? I am still passionate about racing, I have been doing it since I was eleven and I still have that fire in my belly. Naturally, given that the majority of my life has been spent in motor-sport, it seems fair to suggest that I wouldn't want to turn my back on that sport. I have found it to be very enjoyable so I can imagine an ongoing life within the sport. I have not considered any of these options yet. If you are mentally preparing to leave a job, then to me you have already left it. I am not mentally preparing to leave this job at all.

All these options are frankly irrelevant, because I have absolutely no intention of retiring. Since leaving the sport behind is not a thought in my head at present, I actually find it mildly more stimulating thinking about what I might have done if I wasn't driving racing cars.

I think I would have been in my dad's business, probably working with the customers. Remember, I didn't beg my dad to go racing. What I'm realising through this book is that I could well have ended up as the typical accountant type, the stereotypical number-cruncher, weedy, spectacles, all that. Take away racing and I would probably be the quiet guy in the corner of the office, the 'don't give him a drink otherwise he'll start singing and dancing, but ask him to do something and he'll do it for you' kind of guy. Unremarkable, not the life and soul of a party, but a chap who will get in there and make up the numbers. I was always determined without being flamboyantly passionate. I was quiet and focused without being loud and brash and I had a work ethic of try hard, try harder, try even harder. So I would have made a very good accountant, I am sure. It just so happens that my father gave me that racing licence on my eleventh birthday and a kart saved me from a lifetime of accountant jokes at my expense. Instead I became a race driver.

I accept that most people see me now as a race driver and, because I have been doing it for so long, that includes a lot of friends and family as well as mere acquaintances. It's been such an insular lifestyle in many ways that I don't feel I have a great deal to say about any other things anyway – as I've mentioned, I feel like I am skimming the surface of life rather than having serious opinions about serious things.

Clearly, motor-racing – or rather sport in general – plays its part in society, because it's an escape and people get behind sports and follow them with a passion. We all love F1 and obsess about it, watch it, debate it and all that, but if we are being brutally honest with ourselves, it's just something to do at the weekend, isn't it? It's not more important than life and death itself, to contradict Bill Shankly. It's only a sport, after all, and when you see all the death and destruction around about us, F1 can seem very superficial.

I'm curious to know who I am beyond driving, because obviously I don't enjoy much time on my own. Most of the time I spend by myself is testing alone, driving alone, travelling alone, being away from my partner, but always with something to do. There is no time for reflection. I'm there to do a job, I'm not in the frame of mind to sit back and reflect. Then, when I do get time alone, I don't like it. I need to share that time with someone else, enjoy myself in that very small window of down-time.

The thought of having more leisure time to appreciate things a little more certainly does appeal, though. I feel as though I've rushed through life with a focus on racing and it's not given me enough time to get to know every nook and cranny of my apartments, or understand the restaurants round where I live, or the best coffee shop, silly stuff as well as the big stuff. I recently realised that although I can do the evening dinners, the social events and all that jazz in my sleep, I don't 'do' coffee or a casual beer with my mates. If I have a coffee out, it is usually a business meeting – the idea of meeting a mate at 3 p.m. to order tea and just chew the fat is completely alien to me.

I'm being totally honest with you here. Life outside of racing is something I am not that familiar with: I understand going testing, I understand racing and I understand everything about my business. I don't understand everything about life. If you think back to when you were eleven and try to recall all the clear memories you have of a time *before* that – memories that you are absolutely certain of, feelings, ideas, thoughts – there's not much clarity is there? That is how far back racing began in my life. It feels as if there has virtually been no life without it. At the same time, I don't know what I don't know. A friend of mine came up with that expression – or at least it was the first time I'd heard it – it's not a remarkable expression, but I quite like it. 'You don't know what you don't know,' and it's true. People would do well to remember that, because you can put too much pressure on yourself.

I may be reading myself wrong. I'm not sure I know myself very well. Again, to be very honest with you, I can say I am slightly nervous that I've become difficult to live with on a day-to-day basis. I honestly don't know what I will be like, it will be news to myself. I think I know certain things about me, certain key character traits – like my obsession with cleanliness and my attention to detail and all that sort of thing – but there's other parts of me that I don't know, because I don't spend time discovering them. Perhaps oddly for someone who is asked questions about themselves every week, every day, there is an element of myself that doesn't *know* me.

That slight undercurrent of uncertainty makes me a little nervous about returning to 'the real world'. Although I don't consider myself to be bright academically, I am certainly not socially inept, and I feel I have a good sense of what is right and wrong. I also take great confidence in knowing that I can graft and, if the worst comes to the worst, I can organise and do stuff that takes motivation, so I don't ever think I'll be unemployed.

All these thoughts are very intriguing, but at the end of the day, it's been fantastic. Any limitations my job periodically puts on my life are far, far outweighed by the benefits. Remember that list I made about joining Red Bull? Where the 'cons' was three pages and the 'pros' was a couple of lines? Well, Formula 1 has been the opposite. I have gained so much from the sport.

My racing career has been so enjoyable. Am I talented? Clearly. However, modesty would suggest I don't judge my own talent, but I can see the results, I have made my mark. I have to accept that looking at the history of my career, drivers such as (obviously) Schumacher, Alonso and Räikkönen today represent a safer pair of hands for a team than me, not because I think they are quicker, but because they perform more *consistently*. Am I good enough to beat them? Yes. Yet history shows they have been more consistent than me. I can see reality; I am a realist. I don't accept that is a defeat and I don't see that as demotivating. That's why I can get out there and go competing, because I know I can do a good job and I know I'm an asset to the team and I know I wouldn't have been racing in Formula 1 all these years if people didn't believe that as well. I know that on my day I can beat the best drivers and, in the case of Schumacher – the ultimate benchmark – I *have* beaten him. But I also know that their day comes up more often than mine.

Why is that? I think it is because they are good all-rounders. Yes, they have great cars and teams around them, but the reality is that the guys who have usually sustained success over a period of time are good all-rounders. I think the flaw in my career has been that lack of consistency from race to race. I'm a driver who likes the car to feel a certain way and if it doesn't respond the way I like it, I readily admit I have struggled. When the car feels right for me, I have often been able to blow the doors off world champions.

Naturally, I am proud of my career statistics: at the time of writing I'm the highest scoring British driver in the history of the sport; I've amassed over 517 points from 217 grands prix – the nearest Brit behind me is Nigel Mansell on 482; I've enjoyed thirteen wins and sixty-one podiums; I've won more grands prix than drivers like Mario Andretti, Gerhard Berger, James Hunt and Rubens Barrichello; I've enjoyed an unusually long career – for example, Damon Hill's Formula 1 career was seven years from start to finish; there are only a handful of drivers who have raced in more than 200 grands prix; perhaps most significantly of all, there are only four drivers – Michael, Alain Prost, Ayrton Senna and Rubens Barrichello – who have scored more points than me in the history of Formula 1. In those terms, that makes me the fifth most successful driver of all-time.

Most people don't realise those stats and are surprised when they find out. Those are good statistics, I think anyone would agree. I never usually recite them and I'm just indulging myself here! The stats don't make me a better man or person. I don't think about it when I go to sleep or wake up, but yes, if you'd told me when I was an eleven-year-old karter, that I would win more points than Mansell and Hill, than Hunt and Stewart, then I would probably have thought you were in dreamland.

There is one statistic missing: a world title. Maybe that would have been the last piece of the jigsaw to give me absolute confidence and release me from my fear of failure. Do I have a world title in me? Yes. Do I feel unfulfilled at having not achieved that? No. It would have been nice, of course, but in the same way that it's nice to have bit of money in the bank. It's not the thing that I stand upon to feel like a man. I feel like a good man by honouring my word, by loving my partner and by making them feel good and saying something nice when it's just as easy to say something nasty and piss them off, by looking after my family and taking care of the important people in my life. Those are the things make me feel good.

I see no reason to stop. Schumacher retired at thirty-seven; Prost won a title at thirty-eight; Mansell was thirty-nine when he won in 1992. In fact, most people don't realise that the average age of Formula 1's various world champions is thirty-four, with forty of the fifty-seven champions being in their thirties or forties – only seventeen champions were in their twenties.

Stop?

Why?

Age, it seems, is on my side.

More important than any statistics, more rewarding than any podiums and more exhilarating than any amount of money are the benefits my career has brought to *my life*. Take Mum and Dad. I am glad my job as a racing driver has enabled my parents to enjoy things they would not have otherwise seen. That is a nice payback to be able to make. I know they expect nothing back, but it is nice for me to be in a position to buy them a house, fly them to races, arrange for them to meet celebs and all that stuff. I think it's been an exciting journey for them and they've got more out of their life because I have been a grand prix driver. I'm grateful for that.

I am very fortunate to have earned excellent money and, when the time comes, my new family will enjoy a very nice life. I've got more out of my life as a result of being a race driver. I believe I deserved the opportunities I've had on the basis that I've worked for them. That doesn't mean I've had a better life than anyone else, because I had a perfectly happy and healthy life before I got involved in Formula 1, but it has undoubtedly opened doors and led me to new experiences that would not have presented themselves to an accountant in Twynholm. Not least the vast array of nationalities, personalities, social classes and pretty much every strata of modern life I have met on my journey. And, of course, I've been round the world many times, it's been just fantastic.

Sometimes, I catch myself, maybe when I am on a private jet heading back to my apartment in Monaco or when I visit my chalet in the mountains of Switzerland and go walking on top of those hills ... I step back from it all momentarily and chasing cows around a field in Twynholm seems like a different life, a whole world away.

In a way, it is.

However, in another way, I look back at the path that took me from a pre-teen karter from a rural village to Britain's most successful Formula 1 driver ever and all the craziness in between, and it seems like the most natural thing in the world.

I hope you've enjoyed chasing those cows and winning those races with me.

There you go, it is what it is.

INDEX